**DO NOT REMOVE
CARDS FROM POCKET**

AMBROSIA IN
AN EARTHERN VESSEL

The Roaring Girle.

OR

Moll Cut-Purse.

As it hath lately beene Acted on the Fortune-stage by
the Prince his Players.

Written by *T. Middleton* and *T. Dekkar.*

My case is alter'd, I must worke for my liuing

Printed at London for *Thomas Archer*, and are to be sold at his
shop in Popes head-pallace, neere the Royall
Exchange. 1611.

Title page courtesy of The Folger Shakespeare Library.

AMBROSIA IN AN EARTHERN VESSEL

Three Centuries of Audience and Reader Response to the Works of Thomas Middleton

Sara Jayne Steen

AMS Press

New York

Library of Congress Cataloging-in-Publication Data

Steen, Sara Jayne, 1949-
 Ambrosia in an earthern vessel: three centuries of audience and reader
response to the works of Thomas Middleton by Sara Jayne Steen.
 (AMS studies in the Renaissance: no. 31)
 Includes bibliographical references and index.
 ISBN 0-404-62331-X
 1. Middleton, Thomas, d. 1627—Criticism and interpretation.
 2. Theater—England—Reviews. I. Title. II. Series.
 PR2717.S74 1993
 822.3—dc20

91-11029
CIP

All AMS books are printed on acid-free paper that meets the guidelines for
performance and durability of the Committee on Production Guidelines for
Book Longevity of the Council on Library Resources.

AMS PRESS
56 East 13th Street
New York, N.Y. 10003, U.S.A.

MANUFACTURED IN THE UNITED STATES OF AMERICA

Contents

Preface

Early responses to a writer's works are of enormous value. They provide a sense of what the writer's contemporaries appreciated and therefore offer access to literary and cultural values that may differ markedly from our own. They allow us to trace readers' emphases and the writer's reputation through shifts in literary taste and social standards, raising questions about the degree to which reactions are socially or individually shaped. They clarify the origins of current critical debates and ask us to examine the ideologies that underlie our personal responses to texts that others have read and applauded or denigrated for centuries. (This twentieth-century feminist female reads *Women Beware Women* in a startlingly different manner than did many nineteenth-century males, who identified with Leantio and agonized over his plight.) In short, early responses make possible an understanding of social and literary history that can be obtained in no other way. But, although Thomas Middleton's works have received a great deal of critical attention in recent decades, students and scholars have been hard-pressed to locate early commentary unless they have had access to major research collections. Even early nineteenth-century materials often cannot be loaned or copied, and many of the earlier pieces are not available in reprints or in well-edited modern texts.

Those items that most clearly indicate audience response from Middleton's own time to the beginning of the twentieth century are presented here in scholarly editions. Some have been reprinted before, such as Ben Jonson's pronouncement that Middleton was a "base" fellow (entry 6). Others are appearing in print for the first time, such as Henry Newcome's Mayor of Quinborough joke (entry 37). In each case, the guiding principle has been whether the piece would be useful to someone who wanted to understand Middleton's reception in a given era. As a result, many allusions and references, engaging in themselves, have been excluded; for example, numerous interesting references to *A Game at Chess* are omitted, but those in which the play is evaluated or its popularity indicated are included. Materials in which Middleton's works are mentioned only briefly do appear, if they show with what company Middleton was ranked.

In general, I have been more inclusive in the early periods than in the latter half of the nineteenth century, when studies became more abundant and lengthy. And because scholars often want to trace the response to an individual work, I have presented even the brief critical comments about specific works that might appear in a list that is largely bibliographical, including comments about plays now considered uncertain ascriptions, such as *Blurt, Master Constable*. To my regret, I was unable to locate texts in which women explained their responses to Middleton's works, so the study necessarily represents male reactions over the centuries. In 1747, Martha Whincop wrote a two-sentence summary of Middleton's reputation, and some of the anonymous nineteenth-century reviewers may have been female, but until more women's writings are identified and recovered, the picture remains incomplete.

Each selection is based on the earliest or best available text and is accompanied by a full bibliographical citation and a contextual introduction. Original punctuation and spelling have been retained, although I have sometimes included in brackets the modern spelling of a name that might be unfamiliar, and made no distinction between large and small capital letters. With the exception of the tittle and the per symbol, abbreviations and contractions are unexpanded. In some cases, materials are abridged, but any alterations of the text are indicated clearly.

A few of the nineteenth-century critics quoted extensive passages from the plays, and sometimes entire scenes. Quotations of fewer than fifteen lines have been retained in order to make the texts as readable as possible; however, quotations of more than fifteen lines generally have been signaled by a description or a line or two and the rest of the passage has been omitted, with act and scene numbers or the passage's full lineation according to Bullen's edition (until the Oxford appears, the last "complete works") substituted within square brackets. Nineteenth-century scholars also footnoted actively, and footnotes relevant to the issue have been retained; they are indicated by superscript letters to distinguish them from my notes, which are indicated by superscript numerals.

This research has been supported by a travel grant and a summer stipend from Montana State University. An early version of the introduction was presented at the Modern Language Association Conference session entitled "Thomas Middleton: Then and Now," chaired by Anne Lancashire, and printed in an account of that session (*RORD* 28 [1985]: 63-71). I am grateful also to Clifford Davidson and George E. Rowe, Jr., for their comments and support; to Muriel Roy, formerly Director of the Centre d'études acadiennes at the University of Moncton, for graciously extending use of the Centre's facilities and services to the spouse of a visiting scholar; to Laetitia Yeandle and the staff of the Folger Shakespeare Library for their helpfulness and warmth; to the inter-library loan personnel at Montana State University for their continued professional service; to Robert Ball, Patrizia Callahan, Pierce Mullen, and Guenter G. Schmalz for their translations; to numerous librarians at institutions in Canada, the United States, and the United Kingdom for their prompt attention to my queries; and to my students at Montana State University, whose responses to Middleton's works are ever diverse and fascinating.

INTRODUCTION

Recognition of Thomas Middleton's artistic achievements has taken a long time to arrive. Middleton was popular during his lifetime and was among the dramatists his contemporaries would have called significant, but there is not a hint in the early documents that he would ever be considered one of England's finer writers. Extant contemporary references characterize Middleton as a consistently successful playwright known for witty comedies and good entertainment — a Neil Simon supported by the public, but taking his jibes from a theater elite unimpressed by popular culture. For decades after his death, his name remained current with the London public largely for *A Game at Chess* and *The Mayor of Quinborough*, plays not generally considered among his masterworks now. Other Middleton plays were published during the interregnum and, after the Restoration, were produced and favorably received by audiences, but only until a new generation of writers could provide sufficient material for the stage. At that point, Middleton became merely another "old dramatist," a second-echelon playwright to be looked up in a theater history, his plays mined by dramatists in search of tried-and-true ideas for new plays.

The pendulum began to swing back with the Romantics, and Middleton's reputation has risen slowly ever since, with appreciation from Walter Scott, Charles Lamb, Algernon Charles Swinburne, and T. S. Eliot, whose favorite, even overused, adjective for Middleton was "great."[1] Middleton's reputation might have risen even faster had not so many influential critics feared that Middleton's open treatment of vice and human sexuality constituted an offense against public morality. His reputation now stands higher than it ever has, as critic after critic calls Middleton second only to Shakespeare (and occasionally to Jonson) and comments on the degree to which his concerns are modern, or post-modern. In 1972 Norman A. Brittin said that Middleton "speaks in such tones that one can read him very nearly as one's contemporary."[2] Given the direction of critical theory since the 1970s, it should not surprise anyone that Middleton's works are congenial to the 1990s; the issues of gender and politics that concern us form the dramatic and symbolic core of many of his plays. Gary Taylor, co-editor of the Oxford Shakespeare and currently editing Middleton's complete works for Oxford (forthcoming in 1994 or 1995), says, "It seems clear that Middleton is at least the second greatest playwright in English, and is more sympathetic to a late 20th-century sensibility than Shakespeare" because of his "urban imagery and feminist sensibilities."[3]   The extent to which Middleton is feminist has been a matter of debate,[4] but Taylor's general point about Middleton's high stature has wide consensus, and recent reviewers have commented on the "strong revival of Thomas Middleton" on the London stage.[5] Such a radical shift in reader and audience taste over the centuries deserves further examination.

To 1675: The Early Years

By most Renaissance measures, early modern English audiences loved Middleton. His plays were performed and revived; when the companies no longer staged the plays, they sold them, and the texts were printed by "good" publishers, sometimes in multiple editions.   Twentieth-century scholars regularly discuss the extent to which Brome and Shirley — or Dekker or Ford or Fletcher or others — either drew on Middleton or directly imitated him. In any age, most people would consider successful a writer who started publishing poetry in his teens, earned a living from his writing in his twenties, was the city of London's official chronologer and a prolific dramatist in his thirties, and in his forties saw one of his works become perhaps the century's most talked-about play. Middleton's plays and masques were applauded by thousands, and thousands more who never knew his name thronged London's streets to be part of his Lord Mayors' celebrations.

Public popularity, however, was not critical acclaim. The Renaissance relished its hierarchies, and Middleton rarely was singled out for special mention. The numbers and kinds of allusions that exist for Shakespeare and Jonson do not exist for Middleton; he was grouped among Webster, Heywood, Dekker, and Ford as solid, but not extraordinary. Nor, to judge from the few extant comments, did he hold an especially high position in his colleagues' estimations; comments from theater people are mixed, occasionally positive, sometimes negative, and sometimes more indicative of his success than their respect.

Middleton himself said that his works thrived in the theater. Of *The Family of Love*, he wrote that, though he had some doubts about its reception

in print, "*it past the censure of the Stage with a generall applause*" (entry 1).
Three years later he was more assured about *The Roaring Girl*: "The book
I make no question, but is fit for many of your companies, as well as the
person itselfe, and may bee allowed both Gallery roome at the play-house,
and chamber-roome at your lodging" (entry 2). Women were not only
central characters for Middleton; he knew they formed part of his audience,
too. He commented of *The Inner-Temple Masque* that he had written it for
women and achieved his aim: "*Ladies understood*" (entry 7).⁶ Even in his
dedication to *The Witch*, a play which he admitted had rested in "*Obscuritie*"
since its early performances, he suggested something other than a flaw in
stageworthiness might have been the reason: "*Witches are (ipso facto) by yᵉ
Law condemn'd, & yᵗ onely (I thinck) hath made her lie so-long, in an
imprisond-Obscuritie*" (entry 8).⁷

In 1624, a friend of Massinger's, probably William Bagnall, accused
Middleton of catering to his audiences and using cheap tricks to "*take, by
common way, the common sight*" (entry 12). Bagnall may have been jealous
that Middleton's *Spanish Gypsy* had played to even better audiences than
Massinger's *Bondman*, and modern critics would call those tricks good
theater, but Middleton does show a sharp awareness of the changeability of
audience taste. In his preface to *The Roaring Girl*, he compared the fashions
in playmaking to fashions in clothes (entry 2). In 1608, he apologized to the
readers of *The Family of Love* by saying he had not known the book was in
press in time to have overseen its printing, so faults might have escaped his
notice. He added, however, that the play would have sold better if it had
been published "*when the general voice of the people had seald it for good*,"
and went on with some resentment to compare the treatment accorded
London plays with that accorded prostitutes — both are desired only while
they are "*fresh*" (entry 1). The analogy may seem surprising, because it
allies playwriting with a trade that, although equally dependent on a paying
public, normally was considered vice and because it suggests a slightly more
sympathetic view of the prostitute's lot than usually was expressed by
Renaissance dramatists,⁸ but the comparison is the more powerful for its
unexpectedness.

In spite of audience changeability, however, Middleton consistently saw
himself as a playwright of the people, a populist pitted against elitist
opponents like Bagnall. In that prefatory note to *The Family of Love*, early
in his career, he explicitly and ironically contrasted the voice of the public
with the voice of the "*wits*" who considered themselves critical gods; the
play, he said, succeeded with the people: "*now (whether* vox populi *be* vox
dei *or no) that I leaue to be tried by the accute iudgement of the famous six
wits of the Citie.*" Surely he resented George Chapman's scornful evaluation

of him and his *Triumphs of Truth*, an early Lord Mayor's pageant that David M. Bergeron now calls Middleton's "richest."[9] In Chapman's dedicatory epistle to his translation of Homer's *Odysses*, Chapman attacked audiences who saw "*a poore Chronicler of a Lord Maior's naked* Truth" as of "*more worth*" than Homer (entry 3). It is true that the populace cheered Middleton's pageants; Horatio Busino confirms the enthusiastic crowds at *The Triumphs of Honour and Industry* (entry 5), and for many of the people Busino describes — and this is part of what Chapman deplored — any pageant would have been worthwhile if it provided a holiday. Nevertheless, city officials were impressed enough with Middleton's civic work by 1620 to appoint him Chronologer (entry 10), a position which on his death was awarded to, and accepted by, the far more classical and critically acclaimed Ben Jonson.

Middleton could be pleased that, whether or not the wits cheered, others did. When *A Mad World, My Masters* was published in 1640, not long after its Salisbury Court revival, the stationer noted that the play "hath bin sufficiently expressed, to the liking of the Spectators" (entry 28). Nat Richards, in commendatory verses to the 1657 edition of *Women Beware Women*, said that he saw the play on stage and "Never came *Tragedy* off with more applause" (entry 32). The plays also were published regularly. Humphrey Moseley printed several, and in his preface to the 1657 *More Dissemblers Besides Women* and *Women Beware Women* commented that the Middleton plays "that have already seen the Sun" sold well (entry 31). The anonymous author of an epigram to Middleton went so far in praise as to proclaim that if anyone despised Middleton "'twilbe, / Dispraise enough for him, to censure thee" (entry 29).

Two of Middleton's plays received a particularly large number of seventeenth-century references and allusions, *A Game at Chess* because of its political significance and *The Mayor of Quinborough* because Simon so amused Londoners that he took on a life of his own. With *A Game at Chess*, the appropriate word is notoriety. Whether any of the wits respected the play as a play seems irrelevant; it effectively touched a chord to which English men and women of all classes responded. Its satire was broad — probably more extravagant in the acting than we might imagine from the text — and audiences grew each night. Nearly thirty thousand people saw the play during its nine-day run, a sizeable segment of London's adult population.[10] Don Carlos Coloma, the Spanish Ambassador, reported to Spain: "All this has been so much applauded and enjoyed by the mob that here, where no play has been acted for more than one day {consecutively}, this one has already been acted on four, and each day the crowd is greater," including, he added, "all the nobility still in London" (entry 13).

The nobility did not mention the disgrace to King James, for which he chastised them (entry 15), but anyone who was anyone was talking about the play. The Florentine and Venetian ambassadors reported the insult, the Venetian ambassador adding that he had heard the play "is of no great merit . . . but it drew great crowds from curiosity at the subject" (entries 16, 18). Sir Francis Nethersole and John Chamberlain both wrote Sir Dudley Carleton, then out of the country, about the crowds and the receipts for the King's Men (entries 17, 19). Sir John Holles commented on the "extraordinary applause," although he thought the play "more wittily penned, then wysely staged" (entry 14). Thomas Salisbury, an Anglican priest, wrote his brother about it in verse (entry 20). Certainly the King's Men were happy: their profits were high, the publicity enormous, and their punishment relatively light. Only two months later, they were smiling with audiences about their "*errors*," reminding them of *A Game at Chess* in the prologue to Fletcher's *Rule a Wife and Have a Wife* (entry 21). Ben Jonson, who scorned the play, also acknowledged it had London buzzing; in *The Staple of News*, the "news" is that Gondomar has used that "poore *English-play*" for "cleansing his posterior's" (entry 22). Two editions of the play were published within the year. Richard Brome alluded to the play five years afterwards (entry 25), William Hemminge added even later that the Puritans adored Middleton for it (entry 26), and in 1663, almost forty years after the furor, D'Avenant expected his Restoration audience to remember the amazing run: "There's such a crowd at door, as if we had / A new Play of *Gundamar*" (entry 36).

For Middleton, the phenomenal crowds and ensuing scandal may have had a serious side. His son Edward answered to the Privy Council for Middleton's crime of portraying living political figures on stage, but for many years the only indication that Middleton had been penalized was an easily dismissed marginal note in an early quarto (entry 23), thought to have been written much later. In 1954, however, the discovery of Thomas Dawes's commonplace book raised new speculation. Before 1628, Dawes had recorded a poem supposedly by Middleton (entry 24), a witty plea to King James for freedom that is close to the one in the quarto, which suggests that the note is from the right years and might be authentic. Scholars believe that Middleton was active as a playwright after *A Game at Chess* — *Women Beware Women* seems a play of his maturity — and surely the King's Men would not have been amused nor Jonson so viciously cutting had Middleton been imprisoned.[11] But the only records of Middleton's professional activity between *A Game at Chess* and his death in 1627 are a civic pageant (*The Triumphs of Health and Prosperity*) and a report of his involvement with a triumphal pageant that did not take place,[12] both in 1626. He may have spent some time in prison between 1624 and 1626, if only so the King could vindicate himself to Spain. In any case, some of Middleton's public clearly thought he had been imprisoned for his audacity in saying what they thought.

No shadow touches what may have been Middleton's single most popular character, Simon, the Mayor of Quinborough. *Hengist, King of Kent; or The Mayor of Quinborough* was a tragedy and Simon only part of the comic subplot, but Simon was what people remembered. As a role, he would be hard for an actor to overplay, and his part probably acquired increasing amounts of stage business over the years the play continued in repertory, from 1616-1620 when it was first performed to at least 1641 when it was still protected by the King's Men. In 1654 Edmund Gayton alluded twice to Simon in casual, humorous ways that suggest he knew his readers would remember Simon and appreciate the allusions (entry 30). In 1655 John Cotgrave included twelve quotations from the play, which had not yet been published, in his *English Treasury of Wit and Language*, and in 1658 a brief speech from the play appeared in *Wit Restored*.[13] The corroborating evidence makes it reasonable to accept what Henry Herringman said of Simon when he published the play in 1661: *"this* Mayor *of* Quinborough *whom you have all heard of, and some of you beheld upon the Stage, now begins to walk abroad in Print; . . . I am told his drollery yields to none the* English Dramma *did ever produce"* (entry 34). The greatest confirmation of the degree to which Simon amused is that he took on a life of his own. Herringman's phraseology gives some sense of that phenomenon, as does a Mayor of Quinborough joke that an Oxford student copied into his commonplace book as late as 1670 (entry 37). In the joke, the Mayor misunderstood the statute about firing beacons and arrested someone for frying bacon, a jest which falls flat even as an undergraduate pun, but argues that the Mayor of Quinborough had entered the culture as the symbol of bungling officialdom.

Middleton's early modern contemporaries and successors celebrated him more for his humor and satire than for the characterizations in *Women Beware Women* or *The Changeling*. Those plays were valued: Richards said that *Women Beware Women* was well received (entry 32), and *The Changeling* was often revived. But early audiences emphasized the comic subplot of *The Changeling*, as they had the comic subplot of *The Mayor of Quinborough*, indicating that they more appreciated Rowley's madhouse scenes than have later readers or audiences until very recently: "Tony" entered the language as a synonym for "madman" (entry 30), and Humphrey Moseley listed *The Changeling* in the Stationers' Register as a comedy written by Rowley.[14] Moreover, Middleton's most celebrated plays, those with which the public would be most familiar, were satiric comedies. *A*

Game at Chess was the cause, Coloma said, of "such merriment, hubbub and applause that even if I had been many leagues away it would not have been possible for me not to have taken notice of it" (entry 13). Nor should it be surprising that Middleton's contemporary reputation rested on his humor when urban comedies comprised the bulk of his dramatic production over decades. The anonymous epigrammist in *Wits Recreations* extolled Middleton's humor: "Facetious *Middleton* thy witty Muse, / Hath pleased all, that books or men peruse." Anyone who disliked Middleton, he said, had an "Antipathy to wit" (entry 29).

Among those who liked to rank writers, Middleton was considered one of many good playwrights, but not the most distinguished of his colleagues. In 1615, Edmund Howes placed Middleton among Lyly, Chapman, Shakespeare, Daniel, Drayton, Marlowe, Jonson, Marston, Dekker, Fletcher, Webster, and Heywood (entry 4). In 1620, John Taylor included Middleton among those living writers of "true worth," namely Drayton, Jonson, Chapman, Marston, Rowley, Fletcher, Massinger, and Heywood (entry 9), and Thomas Heywood himself, writing in 1635 on the modern poets, by which he meant creative writers of some quality, mentioned Middleton among Greene, Marlowe, Kyd, Beaumont, Shakespeare, Jonson, Fletcher, Webster, Dekker, May, and Ford (entry 27). In 1670, Francis Kirkman placed the early writers in priority of importance (and productivity): "First, I begin with *Shakespeare*, who hath in all written forty eight. Then *Beaumont* and *Fletcher* fifty two, *Johnson* fifty, *Shirley* thirty eight, *Heywood* twenty five, *Middleton* and *Rowley* twenty seven, *Massinger* sixteen, *Chapman* seventeen, *Brome* seventeen, and *D'Avenant* fourteen."[15] Middleton is in good company, but he is listed among, not above, the others. Some observers would not have given him even that much credit. Henry Herbert, newly Master of the Revels, thought a revived *More Dissemblers Besides Women* was the worst play he had ever seen (entry 11), and in the Restoration, Pepys thought *The Mayor of Quinborough* "simple" and *The Spanish Gypsy* "very silly" (entry 33). (Pepys found *Twelfth Night* equally "silly.") John Evelyn dismissed *The Widow* as "lewd" (entry 35).

Extant contemporary references have raised questions about Middleton's relationships with his colleagues. For a professional writer who collaborated often and spent two and a half decades of his life in the theatrical milieu, Middleton was rarely referred to by his associates. As Marston Stevens Balch phrased it, with only a little exaggeration, aside from a very few mentions "we meet the unbroken silence of all the rest of Middleton's peers in an age when the meanest hack could boast a parcel of verses to his immortal credit."[16] And Middleton wrote only a few comments about others: in *The Triumphs of Truth* and *The Triumphs of Love and Antiquity* he attacked competitor Munday's pageant work, though he worked with Munday later; he commended Webster's *Duchess of Malfi*; he wrote an epitaph in praise of Burbage, and he gave tribute to Garrett Christmas and Robert Norman for their pageant artifices. Middleton was outside the group who wrote and received commendatory verses at a furious rate.

Moreover, of the negative remarks during Middleton's lifetime, the majority were made by people associated with the theater. In one respect, logic suggests that would be true; theater people would be more critical than others by virtue of their knowledge and interest. But the positive comments from theater people — Heywood's inclusion of Middleton among the important moderns (entry 27) and Richards's statement that Middleton "well deserv'd among the best / Of *Poets* in his time" (entry 32) — appeared after Middleton's death. Although that division in response could be coincidental, some critics have used the contemporary references (and the lack of them) to suggest that Middleton was, as G. C. Moore Smith put it, a "contentious" personality.[17]

The issue would be irrelevant if it did not impinge on our understanding of contemporary reactions to his plays by suggesting that some jibes by fellow professionals were addressed more at the man than at the dramas. Middleton may have been difficult, quarrelsome, or too ready to use his wit, but the evidence is simply inconclusive. Middleton attacked Munday publicly and abrasively, but he praised Webster, Burbage, and Christmas and maintained long and apparently congenial working relationships with Rowley and Dekker. R. C. Bald argues that Dekker's formal acknowledgment of Middleton in *The Magnificent Entertainment* "points to an unusual degree of friendship between the two men."[18] Scholars often have repeated Jonson's assertion that Middleton was "a base fellow" (entry 6), and no universal law decrees that good writers are never base. But there is no corroboration for Jonson's remark either. The two references that have been presumed to support Jonson come from William Hemminge's *Elegy on Randolph's Finger* (entry 26).[19]

In that elegy, likely written within a few years of Middleton's death, Hemminge used the adjective "squoblinge" to describe Middleton, and later depicted Middleton as beloved by foolish Puritans, on the surface damning commentary. When the references are re-examined in context, however, the text is less clear. The first allusion occurs in a list of the glorious processional's members, where the writing of each of the "worthyes" is praised. Other than Middleton's, the only description that could be construed as personal or as negative is to the melancholy Ford, but it too is professional praise, an allusion to his *Lover's Melancholy*. Why would Hemminge make an exception in Middleton's case and call him a squabbler?

If, on the other hand, Hemminge intended to refer to Middleton's career with a variant of "squibbing,"[20] then the line makes sense. A "squib" is a smart or satirical remark. By "squoblinge," Hemminge likely meant "squibbling," or that Middleton was famed for his wit or satire, which corresponds to other seventeenth-century references.

The exchange with the Puritans at first blush supports Margot Heinemann's thesis that Middleton was a Puritan sympathizer and thus could have been at odds with Jonson and his equally anti-Puritan followers over religion, which would explain an antagonism between Middleton and many of his theatrical colleagues.[21] The more Hemminge's text is read, however, the less the theory seems to apply to this poem. Hemminge's satire is directed not against Middleton, who tries to explain the seriousness of the tragedy of the finger, but against the Puritans, who are so anti-Catholic that they cannot sympathize with Randolph even when urged by the author of the anti-Catholic *A Game at Chess*. Hemminge's allusions illuminate Middleton's reputation as a satirist and the degree to which Puritans enjoyed *A Game at Chess*, but they do not condemn Middleton or argue him a Puritan.

The extant references, then, are inadequate to support a characterization of Middleton as quarrelsome or difficult or personable or kindly. That he and the irascible Jonson did not get along only puts Middleton in the same category with many of his peers. Another explanation of negative remarks from theater people is that popularity has its detractors, especially among competitors and competitors' friends. Chapman was translating Homer for an audience he knew would be small compared to the thousands who would love a Lord Mayor's show (entry 3). Who could blame him for resenting that? (Academic writers, too, would like to reach multitudes.) Bagnall may have disliked *The Spanish Gypsy* on literary grounds, but he also was jealous for a friend (entry 12). By the same token, Jonson probably thought *A Game at Chess* had its weaknesses, but by that point in his career he would have enjoyed seeing similar crowds at a play of his own (entry 22). Motives are often mixed, and these three references demonstrate negative response from the theatrical community at the same time that they reaffirm Middleton's public popularity.

For some years after Middleton's death in 1627, he maintained a relatively strong following. His plays were protected for repertory into the 1640s. The plays often were published during the interregnum, although not as "the collected works," which would befit a writer considered of the highest rank; nineteen Middleton plays and two masques, however, turn up in the early playlists.[22] Middleton was quoted frequently, and his were among the first plays revived after the Restoration, in performances seen by Edward Browne (*The Widow*, *A Fair Quarrel*, *The Changeling*, and *A Mad*

World, My Masters)[23] and by Samuel Pepys and John Evelyn. Eight of Middleton's plays were revived in the 1660s, and actors Betterton and Sheppy were highly praised for their interpretations of De Flores and Antonio (entry 42).

The tone of the responses, however, shifted. As one would expect, Middleton came to be seen as out of style — like Noël Coward in the 1990s, just out-of-date enough to be embarrassing. J. S., when he printed *A Mad World, My Masters* in 1640, already feared that readers would disdain the play because of "some lines that doe answer in meetre," which had been, he noted, the fashion twenty years earlier (entry 28). Nat Richards's 1657 commendatory verses to *Women Beware Women* make clear that Middleton's era was over: Middleton was among the best, Richards said, of poets "in his time" (entry 32). Pepys revealed a similar consciousness that Middleton's plays were not contemporary when he said of *The Changeling* that this was "the first time it hath been acted these 20 yeeres" and added with seeming surprise — "it takes exceedingly" (entry 33). Henry Herringman, too, in his 1661 printing of *The Mayor of Quinborough*, noted that the play was an old one, though like a good salesperson he tried to make the play's age a virtue, since wit had not been out in public during the time of "*Rebel* Oliver" Cromwell (entry 34). Soon, Restoration theater managers were able to fill their houses with plays by more modern writers, and Middleton's plays were nearly forgotten.

1675 to 1800: Decline and Signs of Reappraisal

During the later seventeenth and the early eighteenth century, Middleton's reputation declined. His plays were raided by dramatists scurrying to keep the playhouses supplied and only performed in adaptations with someone else's name on the playbill. As a result, Middleton's name was unknown to the theater-going public. If someone were sufficiently curious about Middleton, information could be found in compilations by theater historians, biographers, bibliographers, and book collectors, but the critical accounts grew shorter after Langbaine's in 1691 (entry 41). By the mid-eighteenth century, however, sufficient antiquarian interest arose that publishers reprinted a few Middleton pieces in collections of "old plays," and readers began to turn to Middleton for explanations of Shakespeare.

In the 1670s nothing could be more natural than for new dramatists to draw on the successful models from an earlier generation, and draw they and their successors did, in diverse ways and to various degrees, turning Middleton's subplots into farces, borrowing characters, incorporating scenes, and sometimes transferring speeches nearly verbatim. Such adaptations of

Middleton's works were performed in every decade from the 1670s through the 1790s. Middleton's contemporaries, too, had drawn from his works — Massinger, for example, had directly borrowed the plot of *A New Way to Pay Old Debts* from *A Trick to Catch the Old One*, and James Shirley had adapted *No Wit, No Help Like a Woman's* for the Dublin stage in 1646. What was different in the late Restoration and the eighteenth century was that plays under Middleton's name did not appear alongside the adaptations. Theater people may have known Middleton. The public did not.

The first of the Restoration adaptations was a comedy probably by Thomas Betterton, the actor Downes recalled as having been a splendid De Flores in the 1660s (entry 42). The comedy, *The Counterfeit Bridegroom* (1677), was based on *No Wit, No Help Like a Woman's*, and it was followed by John Leanard's *The Rambling Justice* (1678) with dialogue from *More Dissemblers Besides Women*; by Aphra Behn's *The City Heiress* (1682 and later revived) drawn from *A Trick to Catch the Old One* and *A Mad World, My Masters*; and by George Powell's *A Very Good Wife* (1693) drawn from *No Wit, No Help Like a Woman's*. Middleton also was echoed in many plays where the evidence for direct adaptation is less convincing, or the case has never been made. As early as 1688, Gerard Langbaine regretted that so many writers borrowed from Middleton, Marston, and Massinger without acknowledgment because they knew they could get away with it. The public, he said, did not know Middleton well enough to convict plagiarists of the thefts (entry 40). Langbaine was probably correct; even James Wright, specifically discussing the old dramatists in *Country Conversations* (1694) and *Historia Histrionica* (1699), did not mention Middleton.

The adaptations continued through generations of playwrights and changes in dramatic fashion, and in an hour-glass pattern. Early in the eighteenth century a variety of plays were drawn from Middleton; from the 1720s through the 1760s there were only revivals of earlier adaptations, though the revivals were numerous; and in the century's last three decades more dramatists borrowed directly from Middleton again. Early eighteenth-century playgoers saw *All for the Better* (1703), *The Maid the Mistress* (1708), *The Mayor of Queenborough* (1710), and *The Artful Husband* (1717). The playhouses even competed with Middleton adaptations in 1715, when Christopher Bullock's *The Slip* and Charles Johnson's *The Country Lasses*, both drawn from *A Mad World, My Masters*, contested for audiences. *The Country Lasses* proved the longer-lasting work: it was revived into the nineteenth century and was the first work to bring Middleton (albeit indirectly) to the American stage, playing Philadelphia in 1767 and New York in 1768. David Erskine Baker, who knew Johnson's comedy was based on Middleton, in 1764 described it as "ever sure to give Pleasure,"[24] and mid-century audiences applauded frequent revivals of it and *The Artful Husband*. In the late eighteenth century, dramatists again directly adapted Middleton and sometimes adapted earlier adaptations. The plays included *The Spendthrift* (1778), *The Female Chevalier* (1778), *The Ambiguous Lover* (1781) in Dublin, *l'Heureuse Erreur* (1783) in Paris, *A Match for a Widow* (1785-86), *April Fool* (1786), *The Widow's Vow* (1786), which played in New York and Philadelphia as well as London, *Marcella* (1789), and *The Bank Note* (1795), which also was performed in Philadelphia, Boston, and New York.[25]

One of these late eighteenth-century plays, William Hayley's *Marcella*, is of particular interest because its preface reveals that both Samuel Richardson and Edward Young were reading Middleton and had been impressed by the main plot, rather than the sub-plot of *The Changeling*, this at mid-century, when Middleton's reputation was low, if not at its ebb (entry 50). Young, the playwright of the two, might be expected to have had some contact with Middleton, but if Hayley's account can be trusted, it was novelist and printer Richardson who came across *The Changeling*, which had not appeared in print since 1668. Ignoring the once-popular comic sub-plot, Richardson found the morality and emotional tone of the tragic plot congenial and sent his friend Young an outline from which to write a play. According to Hayley, Young's unfinished adaptation was burned after his death in 1765, and Richardson's sketch given to Hayley, who then structured his play.

No one at the time seems to have questioned Hayley's statements. Few playwrights acknowledged their sources, and Hayley's comments may have been perceived as a sign of integrity, though the story offered the luster of two famous names to the work. But Hayley was not telling the whole truth: given the verbal parallels between the two plays, he had more than "a concise sketch of the story." Either Richardson had sent a detailed outline — right down to the she saids and he saids of Beatrice's and De Flores's exchanges in 3.4 — and Hayley coincidentally struck upon similar images of temple and basilisk, or, far more likely, Hayley worked from a copy of Middleton's tragedy.[26] Hayley did alter the play, however; he reduced it to a shadow of its source. In Hayley's hands, Middleton's sexually-intense psychological study dwindles to a safe, sentimental tragedy in which Hernandez (De Flores) is evil and Marcella (Beatrice-Joanna) is virtue betrayed, though like Lucrece and other "good" women she commits suicide from shame. Still, the adaptation provoked a playhouse competition. In November of 1789 the Drury Lane managers tried to beat Covent Garden in bringing out *Marcella*, only to have their version fail and the Covent Garden version triumph to what Hayley described as "unchequered applause" for his "dwarfish tragedy" that was "not calculated to be a popular play" (entry 51).

Marcella also stands out among the Restoration and eighteenth-century adaptations of Middleton because it is the only one based on a tragic plot. Middleton was seen by these dramatists as he was seen in his own time, as a writer of comedies. It was to the comedies, especially *A Mad World, My Masters* and *No Wit, No Help Like a Woman's*, that they went for characters, plots, witty repartee. And because taste in comedy changed less than taste in tragedy during these years, playwrights found that Middleton's humor still worked on stage. Only at the very end of the eighteenth century and in the nineteenth century were Middleton's tragedies elevated and the comedies condemned, because of a growing prudery that Charles Dibdin hinted at in 1800 when he said Middleton was sometimes "offensive" (entry 52). Even Middleton's comedies were not adapted as much in this age of adaptation and revival as were those of Shakespeare, Jonson, and Fletcher, and his reputation was not affected by the success or failure of plays that did not bear his name; but he was adapted often enough to assure us he was not completely forgotten in theater circles.

Biographers and historians also remembered Middleton in what Bonamy Dobrée has called this "grand age of scholarly and antiquarian research."[27] In the Restoration and early eighteenth century, the number of histories, biographies, collections, and lists rose markedly, perhaps the result of a need to collect and understand the past after the confusion of a national upheaval. Edward Phillips was the first to discuss Middleton, in his *Theatrum Poetarum* (1675), a collection of biographies of the "*Most Eminent*" poets of all ages (entry 38). Phillips responded to Middleton without eulogy as a writer of middling rank between the great and the contemptible. Over a decade later, William Winstanley modified Phillips's judgment in a similar set of biographies, adding that Middleton once was popular and that *Michaelmas Term* was "highly applauded both for the plot and neatness of the style" (entry 39).

It was not Phillips or Winstanley, but Gerard Langbaine, avid playgoer and collector, who was the source of most eighteenth-century commentary on Middleton, and, unfortunately, the source of durable misconceptions as well (entry 41). Langbaine was the first of the scholarly bibliographers. He worked from the texts in front of him, and accuracy mattered. His responses to Middleton were personal ones to a writer some of whose works he had read: *A Trick to Catch the Old One* is excellent, *The Triumphs of Love and Antiquity* is not a masque and has a pompous title, *A Mad World, My Masters* is "very diverting." To Langbaine, Middleton's comedies placed him in the second rank. It was Langbaine's accuracy combined with his fancy, however, which led to the misconceptions. Langbaine had seen and probably owned the 1652 *Widow*, to which Alexander Gough had added the names of Jonson and Fletcher, probably to increase sales. Langbaine faithfully recorded the attribution and from it wove a tale of mutual respect and friendship that is particularly ironic given Jonson's negative comments about Middleton (entries 6, 22). More detrimental to Middleton's reputation, Langbaine wrongly concluded that Middleton had achieved his fame by collaboration with his betters — ivy assisted by the oak. Langbaine was often consulted by later writers, so Middleton came to be seen as a playwright successful thanks to the superior talents of his friends.

The pattern of eighteenth-century commentary is similar to that of the adaptations, and for good reason: most of the biographers, critics, and theater historians who wrote about Middleton were also actors, prompters, licensers, playwrights, or at the very least friends with actor-manager-playwright David Garrick during their careers. Giles Jacob, who tried his hand at drama, and Martha Whincop, whose husband had been a playwright, reflect the diminishing interest in Middleton during the first half of the century (entries 43, 44); Middleton was deemed worthy of little space in Jacob (1719) and even less in Whincop (1747). In fact, that diminishing concern applied not only to Middleton, but to all of his contemporaries except Shakespeare. The early eighteenth century had renewed acquaintance with and admiration for Shakespeare, and by the 1730s his star eclipsed the others. When Robert Shiels was researching the Middleton biography that would appear in 1753, he found little beyond Langbaine, a deficiency which he and Theophilus Cibber attributed to Middleton's lack of genius (entry 46). Most of these books were classicizing projects, attempts to define a literary history within which to place the Renaissance writers. They were compiled by those who in many cases read only other secondary commentary and thus reflect evaluative responses very different in nature from the reactions of earlier playwrights and audiences who had directly experienced the plays on the stage or in the study.

Readers enthusiastic about Shakespeare but becoming distant from his language and conventions needed help to understand the plays they admired, and what better source than his contemporaries. The passion David Garrick and others felt for Shakespeare at mid-century slowly led to renewed appreciation for Middleton, although initially Middleton was studied solely for the light he could shed on Shakespeare. Lewis Theobald is credited with establishing the historical method as early as 1733 with an edition of Shakespeare in which he explained difficult words by reference to their use in the works of other Renaissance dramatists. Not long afterwards, in 1738,

Thomas Hayward and librarian William Oldys used the excellent library of Edward Harley to compile *The British Muse*, a commonplace book of excellent thoughts from the sixteenth- and seventeenth-century poets. They cited Middleton ninety-three times, compared to the same number for Webster and well over four hundred for Shakespeare.[28] The book was not popular, but it was valued enough to be reissued in 1740 as *The Quintessence of English Poetry* and plagiarized in 1777 in *Beauties of the English Drama*. More importantly, late in the century it may have caught the attention of Charles Lamb, whose *Specimens of English Dramatic Poets* (1808) kindled the Romantic imagination (entry 55).[29] In 1744 playwright and publisher Robert Dodsley brought out *A Select Collection of Old Plays* as a result of interest in Shakespeare's contemporaries and as a contribution to their appreciation by an expanded reading public. Dodsley included three plays usually attributed to Middleton at the time: *A Mad World, My Masters*, *The Widow*, and *The Mayor of Quinborough*.

In an attempt to imitate Dodsley's success, William Rufus Chetwood in 1750 published his own *Select Collection of Old Plays*, which included *Blurt, Master Constable*, then considered a Middleton play. Chetwood's preface to the comedy (entry 45) and his account of Middleton in *The British Theatre* are not at all reliable, but at least have the virtue of being colorful instead of repeating Langbaine. Chetwood was writing from a Dublin debtor's prison and did not have the resources he otherwise might have had, and he also enjoyed the idea that he was putting something over on people with his fabrications. In *The British Theatre*, he asserted that Middleton lived to a ripe old age, because Middleton's first play, *The Five Gallants*, was acted in 1601 and his last, *A Mad World, My Masters*, in 1665,[30] which could have been an honest error. In the preface to *Blurt, Master Constable*, however, he indulged himself in a pleasant poem of his own creation in which one of Middleton's peers, William Lower, praised the elderly Middleton's delightful "last *muse*." Later scholars responded angrily to the mention of Chetwood's name — George Steevens called him "a blockhead and a measureless and bungling liar"[31] — but the man was not without humor. And clearly few people knew much about Middleton if Chetwood's "facts" could even temporarily pass muster.

In 1764, David Erskine Baker (entry 47) allotted Middleton more space than had anyone since Langbaine, and he seems more enthusiastic than his predecessors, though he adds little beyond flowery prose. By the 1770s, however, references to Middleton became more numerous. Shakespeare editors George Steevens and Edmond Malone comfortably quoted many Middleton plays in order to explicate Shakespeare.[32] And in 1778 Steevens discovered the manuscript of *The Witch*, setting off the debate about the relationship between *Macbeth* and *The Witch* (entries 48, 52) that kept Middleton's name before scholarly audiences for decades. (The relationship between Shakespeare's and Middleton's witches is one of those disputes that seem to have independent careers; it has retained interest for scholars to our own time.) In 1779 Edward Capell compiled *The School of Shakespeare*, subtitled *Authentic Extracts from Divers English Books, That Contribute to a Due Understanding of His Writings*, which included selections from Middleton's comedies and Capell's evaluation of Middleton as "no mean comick genius" (entry 49). Even in scholarly circles, Middleton was not regaining reputation as quickly as were Jonson or Massinger or Fletcher, but being read was the first step.

Charles Dibdin, whose *Complete History of the English Stage* appeared in 1800 (entry 52), exemplifies what was occurring more widely with Middleton at the turn of the century. Though a practicing theater person, Dibdin knew little about Middleton, but he was interested enough to go beyond Langbaine or Baker and talk to people who had collected the old plays. A few of his comments were the first-hand reactions of a reader. To Dibdin, Middleton was primarily a writer of comedy, but sensibilities were changing: *A Mad World, My Masters* may be "provokingly laughable" with a "rich vein of humour," but it is not "correctly chaste." Dibdin appropriately summarized Middleton's reputation at the end of the eighteenth century: "he was a respectable writer, and made no mean stand as a dramatist, [but] had nothing in his genius that could furnish instruction to SHAKESPEAR."

The Nineteenth Century

Over the nineteenth century, Middleton was increasingly valued by a widening group of readers. The shift in his reputation occurred in two phases, the first of which might be called the Lamb-Hazlitt-Dyce era. In it the Romantics, and especially Charles Lamb and William Hazlitt, brought to Middleton a renewed appreciation that led to Alexander Dyce's edition of Middleton's complete works. In the second phase, the Swinburne-Bullen era, Algernon Charles Swinburne and others re-evaluated Middleton with such enthusiasm, and A. H. Bullen's edition of Middleton's works was so positively reviewed in England, that Middleton's stature was significantly heightened. Middleton also came to be seen as a stronger playwright in relation to his contemporaries. At the beginning of the century, he was being read primarily for what he revealed about Shakespeare, and he was a minor Jacobean writer, usually ranked below Jonson, Massinger, Beaumont, and Fletcher, and sometimes below Webster, Ford, or Dekker. By the end of the century, Middleton was considered by many the playwright closest in spirit and quality to Shakespeare. Looking at the critical history of the nineteenth century is like seeing Middleton's ghost rise, a little after others have already risen and started forward, and watching him slowly pass many of them.

The shift in assessment, however, was neither simple nor straight-forward. Two sets of values permeated nineteenth-century critical response: some critics sought the passion and fervor that, as they saw it, would elevate the soul, while others preferred a safer and more conventional morality. These interwoven strands of thought, each of which had eighteenth-century antecedents and continued into the twentieth century, sometimes mingled in the work of a critic who might praise Middleton's genius and depth, but insist his works were too frank and vice-ridden to be allowed in the schools. And sometimes writers who held different critical positions nonetheless concurred in their conclusions: Middleton's tragedies received more attention in the nineteenth century, because the critics who wanted passion found tragedy the more emotional and ennobling genre, treating lofty issues of male and female honor (the latter usually restricted to sexual purity), while critics who preferred piety regarded the comedies as too sexual and vulgar to be anything but repulsive. As a result, Middleton's reputation at the end of the nineteenth century was based at least as much on his tragedies as on his comedies, and he had achieved some standing in literary circles as a writer of high seriousness.

At the same time, nineteenth-century responses reflect a growing conflict about historicity and the role of the critic.[33] On the one hand, critics assumed they should evaluate Middleton's presentation of human truths, which they apparently believed to be enduring and unchanging. But the increase in historical understanding meant that some critics also felt an obligation to try to place Middleton in his time and to judge by Elizabethan values, which seemed to differ from their own. The question began to shift from whether Middleton was sinfully bawdy to whether he would have been considered so by his original audience. If the values of his era were different, and he accurately reflected them, perhaps his plays should not offend readers in the same way that they would if written by a playwright lucky enough to have been born in a morally enlightened later age. As criteria shift, so do literary taste and the writer's reputation. Historical critics could appreciate comedies like *A Chaste Maid in Cheapside* for their portrayal of vigorous London life in early modern England. Middleton's reputation was enhanced by the new criteria: Shakespeare might be for all time, but Middleton better captured his age.

The first notes of response to Middleton in the nineteenth century were exactly that, notes, but they illustrate that Middleton was appreciated by those few people interested in Shakespeare's contemporaries. In his 1804 edition of *Sir Tristrem*, Walter Scott explicated the text with references to *The Roaring Girl*, the much-discussed *Witch*, and *The Changeling*, in which he found "some passages horribly striking" (entry 53). Given the tenor of his own writing, Scott might be expected to enjoy Middleton — one critic calls *St. Ronan's Well* "not unlike" Middleton's tragedies[34] — but Scott was still the scholar here, writing about little-known "old" plays. The same was true of his friend William Gifford, who, while editing the plays of the more popular Massinger, briefly pointed out Middleton's "considerable powers" (entry 54).

The enhancement of Middleton's reputation in the first half of the nineteenth century can be attributed to the Romantics, whose first genuinely enthusiastic voice was Charles Lamb's. In 1808, Lamb published *Specimens of English Dramatic Poets*, in which he offered excerpts of Middleton's plays (among those of other Renaissance playwrights), accompanied by eager praise (entry 55). Stirred by the French Revolution and the accompanying turmoil of ideas, Lamb wanted from literature fewer platitudes about sensible behavior and more confrontation of the emotions. To that end, his selections were usually serious passages illustrating "moral sense," placed under subject headings like "Death" or "Mother's Forgiveness." Lamb contrasted the vapidness and "stupid infantile goodness" of plays of his own day with the refined morality of *A Fair Quarrel*. The chessboard scene in *Women Beware Women* is "an immediate transcript from life." The witches in *The Witch* are "fine creations." *The Old Law* has, he says, "an exquisiteness of moral sensibility, making one to gush out tears of delight." To Lamb, Middleton was clearly a "finer," more noble genius than the more highly regarded Massinger.

Some scholars have disputed Lamb's leadership of the Renaissance revival and suggested that he claimed too much credit for putting into print responses that others already shared.[35] Certainly Middleton was emerging from neglect when Lamb wrote, but Lamb was seen by his contemporaries and successors as having led the way — he was echoed, cited, and quoted repeatedly. After Lamb, writers contrasted Middleton's emotional power with the weakness of contemporary dramatists. After Lamb, writers emphasized Middleton's serious side and treated him as a poet.[36] After Lamb, writers described Middleton as a creator of flesh-and-blood passions, whose characters "lived" and taught admirable human truths.

Lamb's book was, on the whole, approvingly reviewed. The *Annual Review*'s anonymous reviewer, probably Lamb's schoolfriend Samuel Taylor Coleridge, chided Lamb for excess enthusiasm, but cited the passage on *The Witch* as "true and delightful" criticism.[37] Nathan Drake, too, would have moderated Lamb, but argued Middleton had a fine imagination (entry 56). Among literary figures over the next two decades, only Thomas Campbell, who in his *Specimens of the British Poets* (1819) provided excerpts with headings similar to Lamb's, wrote as though Lamb did not exist (entry 57). Campbell both harked back to eighteenth-century biographical inaccuracies and provided the first fully squeamish reaction: Middleton "cannot be rated highly for the pieces to which his name is exclusively attached," because he deals in "grossness and buffoonery" and "coarse drafts of London vice."[38]

In the same year that Campbell published his *Specimens*, William Hazlitt spoke of Middleton at the Surry Institution (entry 58). Hazlitt was only a few years younger than his friend Lamb and shared Lamb's sense that the Renaissance was an era when chains of convention had been broken. Like Lamb, he emphasized Middleton's seriousness. When Hazlitt examined Middleton's composition, he found fault — Middleton was better at creating wonderful parts than at superintending the whole, he said — but Hazlitt wrote favorably of the "manly, independent character of Leantio" in *Women Beware Women* and employed adjectives like "impressive" and "remarkable." He admired Middleton's "fine occasional insight into human nature, and cool cutting irony of expression."

Not surprisingly, other Romantics were reading Middleton as well. Thomas Medwin included Middleton among those who influenced Shelley's style in *The Cenci* (entry 59). According to Medwin, Byron also read the Elizabethans, though Byron was or pretended to be less impressed and used to do battle with Leigh Hunt about their merits. (After reading Lamb's selections and discovering how often his own works had unconsciously echoed the early dramatists, Byron was pleased to point to Shakespeare on the same count: "The invocation of the witches was, we know, a servile plagiarism from Middleton."[39]) Romantic interest was high enough that a journal, the *Retrospective Review*, was established to provide a forum for discussions of sixteenth- and seventeenth-century writers. In 1823 the *Review* published an article on Middleton and three of his plays, all "serious" plays — the tragicomedy *The Witch* and the tragedies *The Changeling* and *Women Beware Women* — commending Middleton's power and imagination and raising questions about his negative attitude toward women (entry 60).

Twice Middleton appeared in poems and plays. In 1831 John Payne Collier, who was establishing himself as a Shakespearean scholar, published a ballad purported to be from the seventeenth century, but actually composed by Collier himself, in which he imagined plays by Middleton, Dekker, and Heywood being burnt by London apprentices in a frenzy of piety (entry 61), reflecting his sense that seventeenth-century city moralists would have thought of Middleton as one of the "wandring crazyes." Not long afterwards,

Middleton appeared as a character in R. H. Horne's *The Death of Marlowe: A Tragedy* (entry 63). Horne depicted Middleton as clearly inferior to Marlowe, but bright, and perceptive enough to affirm Marlowe's greatness. Horne's tragedy, though unlikely to impress now, went through several editions, and was still read and appreciated at the end of the century.

Literary historians were less effusive than the Romantic poets and critics. In 1832 John Genest included a section on Middleton in *Some Account of the English Stage.* Genest listed Middleton's works and occasionally added a plot summary or evaluation: *The Phoenix* is a "good" comedy; *A Game at Chess* "might be very entertaining originally, but it has not much to recommend it to a modern reader"; *Michaelmas Term* has a "poor underplot" and is an "indifferent" comedy; *A Fair Quarrel* is "a good play"; and *The Witch* is "a very good play" with "a good comic character" in Firestone.[40] Genest's elevation of *A Fair Quarrel* and *The Witch* echoed Lamb's judgments, but without a jot of Romantic zeal. Genest was followed by Henry Hallam, whose *Introduction to the Literature of Europe in the Fifteenth, Sixteenth and Seventeenth Centuries* (1839) provided only a brief and mixed review (entry 64). As a whig, Hallam was biased against the Romantics and the political and literary radicalism associated with them; his analysis of Middleton reflects the eighteenth-century accounts he drew on and an "old-fashioned" preference for Middleton's comedy.

The mid-century boost to Middleton's reputation occurred in 1840 with the publication of his complete works. Although several of the plays had been included in early collections,[41] Middleton was not the Renaissance dramatist first, second, or even fifth to be reprinted. His works were first made available to the public three and a half decades after Gifford had edited Massinger and commented on Middleton's power (entry 54). Middleton was, however, lucky in his editor. Alexander Dyce had edited the works of George Peele, John Webster, and Robert Greene, and completed Gifford's edition of James Shirley; and although Dyce believed Middleton a lesser playwright than Webster or Ford, he nonetheless found Middleton of sufficient quality to spend two years editing the plays. The result was a good biography, plays very well edited by nineteenth-century standards, and a short analysis that, while it did not overvalue Middleton, gave credit to his work in both comedy and tragedy, noting that the comedies "faithfully reflect the manners and customs of the age" (entry 65). Readers without access to the British Museum or a private collection could now read the plays, and Middleton's reputation increased, though it might have been elevated even more had the drive for conventionality been less powerful. The *Gentleman's Magazine*'s review of Dyce's edition mingled enthusiasm and aversion (entry 66): Middleton is a genius, if an "inferior" one, who has energy, passion, and originality as a "Hogarth of the pen," but who is also "coarse," "indelicate," and "low," having written for a less "fastidious" Renaissance audience.

In America, James Russell Lowell was not of two minds. In 1843 the young man who would become one of the most important literary figures of nineteenth-century America, editor of the *Atlantic Monthly* and *North American Review* (and president of the Modern Language Association), was an idealistic twenty-four-year-old starting his own literary magazine. He examined Middleton's plays in his first issue (entry 67), and, eager to demonstrate life's verities in literature, ignored the comedies to focus on *The Changeling*'s emotional truths, which he proclaimed with copious quotation and all the ardor of twenty-four.

A year later, the last of that generation of English Romantics who inspired Lowell published his selection of extracts from the British poets. Leigh Hunt was nearly sixty, and his title, *Imagination and Fancy*, was expressive of his poetic values. He provided passages from thirteen Renaissance and Romantic writers, including Middleton, but his commentary was brief (entry 68). He found Middleton a little too "random," but thought Middleton had "fancy" and in De Flores had created a character that "surpasses anything I know of in the drama of domestic life."

After Hunt's comments in 1844, distaste dominated what appeared in print for two decades. George Craik, a friend of Hunt's, briefly discussed Middleton in *Sketches of the History of Literature and Learning in England* (entry 69), but he saw Middleton and Shakespeare's other "semi-barbarous" contemporaries as dead to all but antiquarian interest.[42] William Spalding, himself a Renaissance specialist, wrote in his popular schooltext (entry 70) that Shakespeare alone among the early dramatists was nearly free of "gross moral taint" and that students should read the other dramatists only in such "purified specimens" as Lamb provided.[43] Middleton, despite "striking ideas," was dismissed. And Canon Charles Kingsley explicitly linked Stuart dramatists with revolution and the decay of national moral fiber; he congratulated Victorian England on its acceptance of the Puritan code.[44]

In America, E. P. Whipple disliked reading Middleton, too, but because of Middleton's irony and cynicism (entry 71). Whipple acknowledged Middleton's power, but to him Middleton lacked the fancy Hunt praised. Middleton may have passion, Whipple argued, but neither sentiment nor pathos; Middleton is not sympathetic enough; his world is too harsh. Although Whipple's remarks have a conventional flavor, his criticism stands alone in the 1850s, because Whipple was the first to see strains of what we would call modernism in Middleton, and in doing so anticipated T. S. Eliot and many other twentieth-century commentators.

In the 1870s, the second heightening of Middleton's reputation began, even though the negative reaction was still clear. Anthony Trollope loved the early moderns and read, commented on, and sometimes raided, hundreds of plays over decades, including Middleton's, but he strongly disapproved of Middleton (entry 72). According to his autobiography, Trollope thought of himself as a preacher, writing novels that would strengthen the virtue of a shy, young, country maid.[45] His marginal notes in his copy of Dyce's edition are actively hostile to Middleton — to Middleton's construction, bawdry, poetry, morality. When Trollope finds a line he likes, he usually assures himself that Middleton did not write it. Seeming compliments are insults; *No Wit, No Help Like a Woman's* may have been "attractive on the stage" -- "to an audience devoid of all taste." But he also acknowledged with the first three acts of *Women Beware Women* that if Middleton had often written so well, he "might have excelled all the Elizabethan dramatists except Shakespeare."

At the same time, the scholarly journals saw a flurry of articles about Middleton. W. G. Clark and W. A. Wright had suggested in their edition of *Macbeth* (1869) that Middleton had revised Shakespeare's play and introduced the disputed witch materials.[46] From 1873 to 1877, seven books or articles treated that issue, including an extended debate in *Transactions of the New Shakspere Society*.[47] Historical scholars also were trying to date the plays. During the same four-year period, three additional articles appeared on *A Chaste Maid in Cheapside* and *A Game at Chess*.[48]

The mid-1870s had influential critics in William Minto and Adolphus William Ward, both of whom wrote on Middleton at length and reshaped his reputation by pointing to his comic talent and firm morality. Middleton was beginning to be sanctioned by the arbiters of high culture and to join an approved elite. To Minto, "Middleton's genius — and genius he did possess in no small measure — was essentially comical and unromantic," and though in some of the comedies "no lesson is weightily inculcated, there is less indecency than in the works of more pretentious moralists" (entry 73). To Ward, Middleton was a gentleman who alluded to university life "with the easy but not unconscious familiarity of the old University man" and wrote works with "a general flavour of good-breeding," in short, a gentleman who wrote with vivaciousness, facility, and moral intent (entry 74). Reflecting the shift to historicity in evaluative criteria, he called Middleton's comedies "perhaps the truest dramatic representation" of the age, bringing "home in a facile manner the straightforward lessons of morality and virtue which it is in the power of his comic muse to teach." Ward was the first of many to assert Middleton second only to Shakespeare: "in lightness and sureness of touch it would be difficult — with one exception — to name his superior." Soon afterwards, Minto wrote the Middleton entry for *Encyclopedia Britannica* and ranked Middleton the disciple nearest Shakespeare, this time in use of language.[49]

But the single name most closely associated with Middleton from the 1870s to the 1890s was Swinburne's. Like Lamb, whose judgment he considered "all but impeccable," Swinburne had loved the Jacobean playwrights from his teens. Long before his words saw print, his zeal was influential. Swinburne's friends, like William Minto, knew his opinions. His sonnet on Middleton (entry 75) had circulated in literary circles for years before it was published. When Bullen in 1885 brought out a new edition of Middleton's works, because, he said, "the need of a new edition has been keenly felt," he dedicated it to Swinburne, "great as scholar and critic." And Bullen shared Swinburne's enthusiasm: in Bullen's introduction (entry 77) he said he must avoid the editor's "[u]ncritical eulogy"; so he merely cited a critic who called Middleton second only to Shakespeare and then affirmed the statement as "the mature judgment of a balanced mind." To Bullen, "[i]f *The Changeling*, *Women beware Women*, *The Spanish Gipsy*, and *A Fair Quarrel* do not justify Middleton's claims to be considered a great dramatist, I know not which of Shakespeare's followers is worthy of the title."

Swinburne responded to Bullen's edition with a review in which he analyzed Middleton's weaknesses and strengths at length (entry 82). He found Middleton's construction weak, something for which Swinburne himself was criticized. He delighted in Middleton's vigorous "Hogarthian comedy," as one might expect of a poet who in his forties was still reputed a "bad boy" of Victorian letters. As Swinburne's own poetry revels in sound, so he responded more fully than many to what he termed the "noble eloquence" of *Women Beware Women* and the "flowing music and gentle grace" of *More Dissemblers Besides Women*. Swinburne described Middleton's "noble and thoughtful face, so full of gentle dignity and earnest composure" and concluded that this man was "worthy to hold his own" beside any of his age but Shakespeare.

British and American reviewers were divided in response to Bullen's edition. British reviewers found much to praise in Middleton's frankness and often mentioned how Shakespearean he seemed (entries 78, 79, 83, 84). In the United States, reactions were less positive. R. H. Stoddard evaluated Middleton as a clever entertainer whose works have so little relationship to reality that his morality is irrelevant (entry 80); while to the *Atlantic Monthly*'s reviewer, Middleton realistically portrays a vice-ridden Renaissance society, "but into such quarters and society what need to go?"

(entry 81). My favorite review, which appeared anonymously in San Francisco's *Overland Monthly*, fascinates by its very ambivalence (entry 85):

> While we should commend the plays of Middleton to the student of dramatic literature for the frequent display of great poetic genius, a lofty imagination, pictures of deepest passion, and at times passages of the highest moral dignity, we should greatly hesitate to put any volume of these works, or even any one play into the hands of youth, whose minds and hearts are easily hurt by coarseness of allusion and by indelicacy of expression. It may be that we should not decline ambrosia though offered in an earthern vessel, but we want it certain that the vessel, though roughly made, yet shall not give its earthly taste to the heavenly food. . . .

During the late 1880s and the 1890s, Middleton's reputation for excellence solidified. If some critics lacked Swinburne's zest, they nevertheless took his opinions into account and assigned to Middleton an increasingly significant place in English letters. Havelock Ellis edited two volumes of Middleton's plays for the Mermaid Series, and he described Middleton as "slow and deliberate in serious comedy, with many pauses for acute or noble reflection on life, sometimes of a Miltonic cast."[50] George Saintsbury placed Middleton among dramatists second to Shakespeare and granted that he sometimes excels Webster, Fletcher, and Massinger (entry 86). Edmund Gosse located Middleton's strengths in his romantic dramas (entry 88) and with Herford argued that Middleton is "strangely compacted of gold and clay." Felix E. Schelling said Middleton "seems to inhabit that dangerous limbo that lies between the realms of the highest genius and the ordinary levels of a work-a-day world" (entry 89).

In 1898, Middleton's *Spanish Gypsy* was produced by the Elizabethan Stage Society, the only production of a Middleton play in the nineteenth century. William Poel directed the amateur actors at St. George's Hall. Swinburne composed a prologue (entry 90) to be spoken by Gosse, in which Swinburne commended Middleton's wit, his depth, his heart. The production, however, was not particularly well received: it was noticed in *The Academy*,[51] panned in *The Athenæum* (entry 91), and attacked by William Archer (entry 92).

Middleton began to receive notice from abroad during the late 1880s and the 1890s. Most of the studies were brief surveys of his career, lists of his works, or discussions of sources or parallels. Two studies, however, are worthy of separate mention: in 1892 Otto Schulz published in German a fifty-page analysis of Middleton's rhyme and meter, treating Middleton as a serious author[52]; and from Freud's turn-of-the-century Vienna, R. Fischer employed psychology to link biography and art by tracing Middleton's "inner development" as a writer (entry 93). He argued that Middleton was a genuine artist who created masterworks of comedy.

With the application of Freud, Middleton criticism entered the twentieth century. Debates about Middleton's morality have continued, as have debates about his technique and psychology and sexual frankness. Recently scholars have debated his feminism and the nature of his urban world. The plays have been produced repeatedly, including comedies like *A Chaste Maid in Cheapside* and *A Trick to Catch the Old One* that nineteenth-century critics could not imagine a manager being brave or foolish enough to stage, but which have come in the second half of the twentieth century to be considered the masterpieces among his comedies, a shift in evaluation which in itself raises interesting cultural questions. Even in the 1920s when T. S. Eliot called Middleton "a great comic writer and a great tragic writer," as well as a "great" student of human nature and a "great" poet, and praised *The Roaring Girl* for its realization "of a free and noble womanhood,"[53] Eliot had no expectation that feminism would become one of the century's most important cultural movements, or that Moll Cutpurse in the person of Helen Mirren would stride the London stage in the 1980s to cheers,[54] or that scholars would find it difficult to keep up with the number of productions of Middleton's plays.[55] Middleton's reputation is stronger in the 1990s than at any time since the Renaissance, and, ironically, this time he has the critical acclaim he once lacked. One wonders what the populist playwright would have made of that.

Notes

1. "Thomas Middleton," 445-46.
2. *Thomas Middleton*, 149.
3. Anon., "Reader Spotlight," p. 4.
4. Recent references are literally too numerous to mention, but include Cristina Malcolmson, "'As Tame as the Ladies': Politics and Gender in *The Changeling*"; Mary Beth Rose, *The Expense of Spirit*; Simon Shepherd, *Amazons and Warrior Women*; and Linda Woodbridge, *Women and the English Renaissance*.
5. Susan Core and George Core, "London Theater-Going," p. 609.
6. I was unable to locate materials by women to confirm or refute Middleton's claim.

7. On reasons for the play's "obscurity," see Anne Lancashire, *The Witch*: Stage Flop or Political Mistake?"

8. Gary Taylor draws on *The Roaring Girl* to comment on Middleton's sympathy for prostitutes (*Reinventing Shakespeare*, 391).

9. "Middleton's Moral Landscape: *A Chaste Maid in Cheapside* and *The Triumphs of Truth*," 133.

10. Thomas Cogswell, "Thomas Middleton and the Court, 1624: *A Game at Chess* in Context," 273.

11. Paul Yachnin argues that James's response was mild because Middleton's clever satire could be interpreted by royalists as a defense of the English king and prince ("*A Game at Chess*: Thomas Middleton's 'Praise of Folly'"); on this point, see also Cogswell, "Thomas Middleton and the Court, 1624." Philip J. Finkelpearl says that "not one prominent poet or playwright was punished for libel" during James's reign ("'The Comedians' Liberty': Censorship of the Jacobean Stage Reconsidered," 124), although Jerzy Limon notes that at least one peer, the Earl of Oxford, was imprisoned in the 1620s for speaking against James's Spanish policy (*Dangerous Matter*, 9-10).

12. Gerald Eades Bentley, *Jacobean and Caroline Stage*, 4: 896, 911.

13. Bentley, *Jacobean and Caroline Stage*, 4: 887.

14. Bentley, *Jacobean and Caroline Stage*, 4: 862-64.

15. Walter Wilson Greg, *A List of Masques, Pageants, &c. Supplementary to A List of English Plays*, xlv.

16. "The Dramatic Legacy of Thomas Middleton: A Study of the Uses of His Plays from 1627 to 1800," x.

17. Notes to *William Hemminge's* Elegy on Randolph's Finger, 24.

18. "Middleton's Civic Employments," 65.

19. I initially agreed with that position in a paper that appeared in *RORD* 28 (1985).

20. Suggested by Joseph Woodfall Ebsworth in his edition of *Choyce Drollery* (Boston and Lincolnshire: R. Roberts, 1876), as cited, for refutation, in Hemminge, 24. Ebsworth thought the word implied ineffectiveness.

21. *Puritanism and Theatre*, 171. She points out that Nat Richards, who praised Middleton, was also a Parliamentary Puritan. Although Heinemann suggests that Middleton's Puritan sympathies may explain the dearth of references from colleagues, she argues that many writers had similar sympathies. Why did they not exchange verses with Middleton?

22. Greg, *A List of Masques*, l-cxx. *Blurt, Master Constable*, which most scholars no longer consider a Middleton play, is excluded.

23. G[reg], "Theatrical Repertories of 1662," 70-72.

24. *The Companion to the Play-House*, 1: E5^r.

25. For discussions of the genealogy of these plays, see Balch, "The Dramatic Legacy of Thomas Middleton: A Study of the Uses of His Plays from 1627 to 1800," sections of which were published in the 1980s by Salzburg Studies in English Literature; and Allardyce Nicoll, *A History of Restoration Drama, 1660-1700*; *A History of Early Eighteenth Century Drama, 1700-1750*; and *A History*

of Late Eighteenth Century Drama, 1750-1800, later editions of which appeared as vols. 1-3 of *A History of English Drama, 1660-1900*.

26. Balch was not the first to suggest Hayley's deception, but he explored it at some length in the 1920s ("The Dramatic Legacy of Thomas Middleton: A Study of the Uses of His Plays from 1627 to 1800," chapter 9).

27. *English Literature in the Early Eighteenth Century, 1700-1740*, 377.

28. *The British Muse*, passim.

29. Robert D. Williams, "Antiquarian Interest in Elizabethan Drama Before Lamb," 438.

30. p. 32.

31. See the Chetwood entry in the *DNB*.

32. See Steevens's notes to his edition of *The Plays of William Shakespeare* and Malone's notes in *Supplement to the Edition of Shakespeare's Plays Published in 1778 by Samuel Johnson and George Steevens*, prepared in the late 1770s.

33. George E. Rowe, Jr., first brought this issue to my attention.

34. Edgar Johnson, *Sir Walter Scott: The Great Unknown*, 2: 916.

35. Earl Reeves Wasserman, "The Scholarly Origin of the Elizabethan Revival"; Herbert Weisinger, "The Seventeenth-Century Reputation of the Elizabethans."

36. Despite Lamb's intention to use entire scenes as often as possible, his titled excerpts made the passages seem poems, and the self-contained nature of many of the "moral" passages reinforced the sense of poetry isolated from dramatic context. Lamb also may not have appreciated the dramatic aspects of the plays; his *John Woodvil* failed on the stage in part because of its lack of form.

37. p. 569.

38. Campbell's choices from Middleton's plays are psychologically revealing. All but one of the passages that he selected as excellent, like "Leantio's Agony for the Desertion of His Wife," deal with the pain of a man in his roles as husband, father, or lover. Campbell was successful as a poet, but Walter Scott wrote Washington Irving that Campbell was "afraid of the shadow that his own fame casts before him" (*DNB*). The choice of excerpts supports Scott's sense of Campbell's insecurities.

39. Medwin, *Journal of the Conversations of Lord Byron*, 90, 139-40.

40. 10: 10-16; 6: 72-73.

41. In Robert Dodsley's *Select Collections of Old Plays* (1744 and 1780); Walter Scott's *Ancient British Drama* (1810), C. W. Dilke's *Old English Plays* (1814-1815), John Payne Collier's *Select Collection of Old Plays* (1825-1827), *The Old English Drama* (1830), and editions of works of Middleton's collaborators. For more specific information on early nineteenth-century editions, see Steen, *Thomas Middleton: A Reference Guide*.

42. p. 187.

43. p. 262.

44. "Plays and Puritans."

45. p. 146.

46. pp. viii-xii.

47. F[rederick] G[ard] Fleay, "On *Macbeth*" and "On Two Plays of Shakspere's"; Horace Howard Furness, "*The Witch*"; [Frederick James] Furnivall and [J. W.] Hales, "Discussion on Mr. Fleay's *Macbeth* and *Julius Caesar* Paper"; Hales, "On the Porter in *Macbeth*"; Thomas Alfred Spalding, "On the Witch-Scenes in *Macbeth*"; Thomas Taylor, F. J. Furnivall, and [?] Marshall, "Discussion on Fifth Paper." For summaries, see Steen, *Middleton*, items 1345-46, 1350-51, 1357, 1389, and 1396.

48. Brinsley Nicholson, "On the Dates of *A Chaste Maid in Cheapside, Northward Ho,* and *The Northern Lass*"; Anon., "Middleton's *Game at Chess*"; H. A. K., "Middleton's *Game at Chess*." For summaries, see Steen, *Middleton*, items 744a, 844, and 871.

49. The article was published anonymously, but much of the same wording appears in the 2nd edition of Minto's *Characteristics of English Poets from Chaucer to Shirley* (entry 76).

50. "Preface," *Thomas Middleton*, 2: x.

51. "Notes and News," 397-98.

52. *Über den Blankvers in den Dramen Thomas Middletons.*

53. "Thomas Middleton," 446.

54. In the 1983 Royal Shakespeare Company production, directed by Barry Kyle.

55. Marilyn Roberts's "A Preliminary Check-List of Productions of Thomas Middleton's Plays" includes seventeen productions of *The Changeling* in Australia, Canada, England, and the United States between 1980 and 1984; four of *A Chaste Maid in Cheapside*; and five of *Women Beware Women*.

COMMENTARY

1. 1608 Middleton on *The Family of Love*

In this prefatory note to *The Family of Love*, Middleton confirms that the play had been successful on the stage in 1602, but wonders whether it is too "old" six years later to attract many readers.

Too soone and too late, this work is published. Too soone, in that it was in the Presse, before I had notice of it, by which meanes some faults may escape in the Printing. Too late, for that it was not published when the general voice of the people had seald it for good, and the newnesse of it made it much more desired, then at this time: For Plaies in this Citie are like wenches new falne to the trade, onelie desired of your neatest gallants, whiles the' are fresh: when they grow stale they must be vented by Termers and Cuntrie chapmen. I know not how this labor will please, Sure J am it past the censure of the Stage with a generall applause, now (whether vox populi *be* vox dei *or no) that I leaue to be tried by the accute iudgement of the famous six wits of the Citie: Farewell.*

"To the Reader," *The Famelie of Love. Acted by the Children of His Maiesties Reuells.* London: for Iohn Helmes, 1608, sig. A1ᵛ.

2. 1611 Middleton on *The Roaring Girl*

In this prefatory note to *The Roaring Girl*, Middleton seems more certain of his play's reception, less defensive, and less bitter that dramatic fashions and audience expectations change with the season. His imagery suggests that he imagines a male readership for this play about a cross-dressed, independent woman.

The fashion of play-making, I can properly compare to nothing, so naturally, as the alteration in apparell: For in the time of the Great-crop-doublet, your huge bombasted plaies, quilted with mighty words to leane purpose was onely then in fashion. And as the doublet fell, neater inuentions beganne to set vp. Now in the time of sprucenes, our plaies followe the nicenes of our Garments, single plots, quaint conceits, letcherous iests, drest vp in hanging sleeues, and those are fit for the Times, and the Tearmers: Such a kind of light-colour Summer stuffe, mingled with diuerse colours, you shall finde this published Comedy, good to keepe you in an afternoone from dice, at home in your chambers; and for venery you shall finde enough, for sixepence, but well couch and you marke it. For *Venus* being a woman passes through the play in doublet and breeches, a braue disguise and a safe one, if the Statute vnty not her cod-peece point. The book I make no question, but is fit for many of your companies, as well as the person itselfe, and may bee allowed both Gallery roome at the play-house, and chamber-roome at your lodging: worse things I must needs confesse the world ha's taxt her for, then has beene written of her; but 'tis the excellency of a Writer, to leaue things better then he finds 'em; though some obscœne fellow (that cares not what he writes against others, yet keepes a mysticall baudy-house himselfe, and entertaines drunkards, to make vse of their pockets, and vent his priuate bottle-ale at mid-night) though such a one would haue ript vp the most nasty vice, that euer hell belcht forth, and presented it to a modest Assembly; yet we rather wish in such discoueries, where reputation lies bleeding, a slacknesse of truth, then fulnesse of slander.

"To the Comicke, Play-readers, Venery, *and Laughter,*" *The Roaring Girle. Or Moll Cut-Purse. As It Hath Lately Beene Acted on the Fortune-Stage by the Prince His Players.* London: for Thomas Archer, 1611, sig. A3r-A3v.

3. 1615 George Chapman: The First Critical Commentary

Middleton's *Triumphs of Truth*, a Lord Mayoral spectacular with five Indian islands, a ship of Moors, a flaming chariot, and a seemingly naked allegorical figure of Truth, must have been stunning and memorable. Two years later, in the dedicatory epistle to his translation of Homer, George Chapman revealed his assumptions about the timeless qualities of "good" literature as he registered his disgust that Londoners valued Middleton's transitory pageant more than Homer's "*eternall Fiction.*"

Or why should a poore Chronicler of a Lord Maior's naked Truth, *(that*

*peraduenture will last his yeare) include more worth with our moderne
wizerds, then* Homer *for his naked* Vlysses, *clad in eternall Fiction?*

Dedicatory Epistle to his translation of *Homer's* Odysses. London: by Rich. Field for
Nathaniell Butter, c. 1615, sig. A4ᵛ.

4. 1615 The Poets According to the *Annales*

Edmund Howes's continuation of John Stow's famous *Annales, or
Generall Chronicle of England* includes this loosely chronological listing of
the "excellent" contemporary writers, a list that differs surprisingly little
from many a canonical syllabus for a course in late Elizabethan and early
Jacobean literature.

Our moderne, and present excellent Poets which worthely florish in their
owne workes, and all of them in my owne knowledge lived togeather in this
Queenes raigne, according to their priorities as neere as I could, I haue
orderly set downe (viz) *George Gascoigne* Esquire, *Thomas Church-yard*
Esquire, sir *Edward Dyer* Knight, *Edmond Spencer* Esquire, sir *Philip Sidney*
Knight, Sir *Iohn Harrington* Knight. Sir *Thomas Challoner* Knight, Sir
Frauncis Bacon Knight, & Sir *Iohn Dauie* Knight, Master *Iohn Lillie*
gentleman, Maister *George Chapman* gentleman, M. *W. Warner* gentleman,
M. *Willi. Shakespeare* gentleman, *Samuell Daniell* Esquire, *Michaell
Draiton* Esquire, of the bath, M. *Christopher Marlo* gen. M. *Beniamine
Iohnson* geleman, *Iohn Marston* Esquier, M. *Abraham Frauncis* gen. master
Frauncis Meers gentle. master *Iosua Siluester* gentle. master *Thomas
Deckers* gentleman, M. *Iohn Flecher* gentle. M. *Iohn Webster* gentleman, M.
Thomas Heywood gentleman, M. *Thomas Middelton* gentleman, M. *George
Withers.*

Edmund Howes, *The Annales, or Generall Chronicle of England, Begun First by
Maister Iohn Stow, and After Him Continued and Augmented with Matters Forreyne,
and Domestique, Anncient and Moderne, vnto the Ende of This Present Yeere, 1614.*
London: Thomas Adams, 1615, p. 811.

5. 1617 A Venetian's Response to a Middleton Pageant

Horatio (Orazio) Busino served with the Venetian ambassador to
England and wrote home a vivid account of a strange ceremony, the
installation of a Lord Mayor of London. The pageant that perplexed him was

The Triumphs of Honour and Industry. Although part of his report treats the very idea of such a ritual, the section quoted here deals most directly with Busino's responses and the size and behavior of Middleton's audience on the occasion. The anti-Spanish Busino was careful to record that spectators were delighted by satire against the Spanish, satire that Middleton had extended within the decade to the vigorous denunciations in *A Game at Chess.*

His Excellency received a private invitation to view the first part of the pageant, which consists of ships, galleys, brigantines, foists and barges coming up the Thames, starting from the Lord Mayor's own house and proceeding towards the palace or royal court, where he takes the oath of allegiance. On the present occasion the magistrate [George Bowles] arranged his installation with the greatest pomp, but always with allusion to his trade of a grocer. The cost he incurred exceeded the means of a petty or medium duke.

At a very early hour his Excellency went to the mansion of a nobleman commanding a fine view of a bridge over the Thames. This runs through the city like our Grand Canal, but as wide as the Giudecca Canal. Scarcely had we arrived when a dense fleet of vessels hove in sight, accompanied by swarms of small boats to see the show like the gondolas about the Bucintoro. The ships were beautifully decorated with balustrades and various paintings. They carried immense banners and countless pennons. Salutes were fired, and a number of persons bravely attired played on trumpets, fifes and other instruments. The oarsmen rowed rapidly with the flood tide, while the discharges of the salutes were incessant. We also saw highly ornamented stages with various devices, which subsequently served for the land pageant, for triumphal cars, when passing through the principal street. When the gay squadron had reached a certain point it received a salute from the sakers, which made a great echo. The compliment was repeated even more loudly when my Lord Mayor landed at the water stairs near the court of Parliament, on his way to take the oath before the appointed judges.

Bewildered by what we had seen, we proceeded to the Row (*corso*), which is the finest part of the city, to the windows assigned to us in the house of a respectable goldsmith. Whilst the pageant was being marshalled, we gazed about. The houses have many stories and all the fronts are glazed so that the windows fill the entire space. On this occasion they were all crowded with the sweetest faces, looking like so many pretty pictures, with varied head-tire and rich dresses of every possible colour and texture, including cloth of gold and silver. This charming view was spoilt by two objects, namely two ugly Spanish women (as I may conscientiously call them, apart from our national prejudice), ill dressed, lean and livid and with

deep set eye balls, perfect hobgoblins, though we could not resist looking at
them occasionally for the sake of comparing them with the English ladies
nearest to them, whose beauty thus became more manifest. On looking into
the street we saw a surging mass of people, moving in search of some resting
place which a fresh mass of sightseers grouped higgledy piggledy rendered
impossible. It was a fine medley: there were old men in their dotage;
insolent youths and boys, especially the apprentices alluded to; painted
wenches and women of the lower classes carrying their children, all anxious
to see the show. We noticed but few coaches and still fewer horsemen; only
a few gentlewomen coming in their carriages for a view at some house in the
Row belonging to their friends or relations, for the insolence of the mob is
extreme. They cling behind the coaches and should the coachman use his
whip, they jump down and pelt him with mud. In this way we saw them
bedaub the smart livery of one coachman, who was obliged to put up with
it. In these great uproars no sword is ever unsheathed, everything ends in
kicks, fisty cuffs and muddy faces.

From the windows an incessant shower of squibs and crackers[56] were
thrown into the mass beneath, for which the boys scrambled when they were
cold. On surveying the windows along the street, as far as the eye could
reach, we perceived sundry gallants in attendance on fine ladies. In our
simplicity we imagined that for each lady there would have been a brother
or a husband, but we were assured that the gallants were the servants of these
ladies, which in plain language means their lovers, being much favoured by
them and enjoying great liberty and familiarity. . . .

Foreigners are ill regarded not to say detested in London, so sensible
people dress in the English fashion, or in that of France, which is adopted by
nearly the whole court, and thus mishaps are avoided or passed over in
silence. The Spaniards alone maintain the prerogative of wearing their own
costume, so they are easily recognised and most mortally hated. Some of our
party saw a wicked woman in a rage with an individual supposed to belong
to the Spanish embassy. She urged the crowd to mob him, setting the
example by belabouring him herself with a cabbage stalk and calling him a
Spanish rogue, and although in very brave array his garments were foully
smeared with a sort of soft and very stinking mud, which abounds here at all
seasons, so that the place better deserves to be called *Lorda* (filth) than
Londra (London). Had not the don saved himself in a shop they would

56. Squibs and crackers were fireworks, as were the fireballs and wheels mentioned later as
having been used for crowd control.

assuredly have torn his eyes out, so hateful are the airs assumed here by the Spanish, whom the people of England consider harpies, which makes me think that they are less well known elsewhere.

The companies of gownsmen now began to appear, for the mere purpose of lining the streets. They carried their maces and there were officers to protect them from the crowd. Their gowns resemble those of a Doctor of Laws or the Doge, the sleeves being very wide in the shoulder and trimmed with various materials, such as plush, velvet, martens' fur, foynes and a very beautiful kind of astrachan, while some wear sables. These gownsmen belonged exclusively to the Grocers' Company, to which the present Lord Mayor belongs, and they number more than a thousand. Over the left shoulder they wore a sort of satchel, one half of red cloth and the other black, fastened to a narrow stole. There were other gownsmen in long cloth gowns with satchels of red damask. These were younger men than the others, and their duty is to wait at table during the banquet. Others again wore another kind of appendage, also red, on the shoulder, and a fourth set had small stoles about the throat.

To clear the way, the City Marshal on horseback, with a gold collar round his neck, and two footmen in livery, kept parading up and down; he was so smooth and sleek that we unhesitatingly pronounced him to be of the swinish race of jolly Bacchus. The way was also kept by a number of lusty youths and men armed with long fencing swords, which they manipulated very dexterously, but no sooner had a passage been forced in one place than the crowd closed in at another. There were also men masked as wild giants who by means of fireballs and wheels hurled sparks in the faces of the mob and over their persons, but all proved unavailing to make a free and ample thoroughfare.

The first stages which made their appearance were harnessed to griffins ridden by lads in silk liveries. Others followed drawn by lions and camels and other large animals, laden with bales from which the lads took sundry confections, sugar, nutmegs, dates and ginger, throwing them among the populace. The animals which drew these cars were all yoked with silken cords. The first pageant represented a lovely forest with fruit on the top of its trees and peopled with children in Indian costume, with the black tress falling from the back of the head, their faces stained, imitating nudity, with the little apron fringed with red feathers and others of various hues. Then came a pastoral couple with fifes, one dressed entirely in red feathers, while the other represented a tiger, being wrapped in the animal's skin. This couple played the part of man and wife, performing on their instruments in the Indian fashion, the children danced all the while with much grace and great variety of gesture, moving the whole body, head, hands and feet, keeping excellent time and performing figures, first round one tree and then another, changing their positions, so as really to surprise everybody.

Other large and handsome stages followed, one of which, I was told, represented the religion of the Indians; the sun shining aloft in the midst of other figures. On another stage was a fine castle; while a third bore a beautiful ship, supposed to be just returned from the Indies with its crew and cargo. Other stages bore symbols of commerce, or the nations which trade with India. Among the figures represented was a Spaniard, wonderfully true to life, who imitated the gestures of that nation perfectly. He wore small black moustachios and a hat and cape in the Spanish fashion with a ruff round his neck and others about his wrists, nine inches deep. He kept kissing his hands, right and left, but especially to the Spanish Ambassador, who was a short distance from us, in such wise as to elicit roars of laughter from the multitude.

[Here Busino describes the rest of the parade of religious leaders, nobility, and guildsmen with banners that "made a fine show," followed by the Lord Mayor himself, the city aldermen and sheriffs, and the "vagrant hangers on, who all lay claim to the very sumptuous banquet, which begins to-day and will be served, with open doors, for a whole year."]

"Relation of Horatio Busino," *Calendar of State Papers and Manuscripts, Relating to English Affairs, Existing in the Archives and Collections of Venice. And in the Other Libraries of Northern Italy.* Vol. 15, *1617-1619.* Ed. Allen B. Hinds. London: for His Majesty's Stationery Office, by Anthony Brothers, 1909, no. 103A, pp. 58-63.

6. 1618-19 Ben Jonson's Opinion of the Person

According to William Drummond's report of his and Jonson's conversations, Jonson disliked Middleton, as he disliked many other writers of his day. Jonson was sensitive about having been a bricklayer, and since Middleton joins those who occasionally jibe at bricklayers — despite his father's having been one — he may have been among Jonson's literary enemies. (See also entry 22.)

that Markham (who added his English Arcadia) was not of the
number of the Faithfull .j. Poets and but a base fellow
that such were Day and Midleton.

Conversations with William Drummond of Hawthornden. In *Ben Jonson.* Vol. 1. Ed. C. H. Herford and Percy Simpson. Oxford: Clarendon, 1925: 137.

7. 1619 Middleton on *The Inner-Temple Masque*

In the preliminary verse to *The Inner-Temple Masque*, Middleton notes
that this satiric and romantic masque amused its audience. That Middleton
used professional actors as well as the "Gentlemen of the House" may have
made for a more impressive performance.

> *This, nothing owes to any Tale, or Storie,*
> *With which some* Writer *pieces up a Glorie;*
> *I onely made the Time, they sat to see,*
> *Serve for the Mirth it selfe; which was found free,*
> *And herein fortunate, (that's counted good)*
> *Being made for Ladies, Ladies understood.*

The Inner-Temple Masque. Or Masque of Heroes. Presented (as an Entertainement
for Many Worthy Ladies:) By Gentlemen of the Same Ancient, and Noble House.
London: for John Browne, 1619, sig. A2ʳ.

8. c. 1619-27 Middleton and *The Witch*

Middleton's tragicomedy *The Witch* probably first played in 1613. No
revivals or early printings are known. Sometime between 1619 and 1627, at
the request of Thomas Holmes, Middleton obtained what likely was the old
playhouse manuscript and had it copied for Holmes. In his dedication,
Middleton calls the play "*ill-fated*," perhaps because it failed on the stage,
perhaps because its political allusions to witchcraft and the Essex divorce
case had touched the court too closely.[57]

> *Noble Sir./*
> *As a true Testemonie, of my readie Inclination to your Seruice, I haue*
> *(meerely uppon a tast of yoʳ. desire) recouered into my hands (though not*
> *without much difficultie) This (ignorantly-ill-fated) Labour of mine. Witches*
> *are (ipso facto) by yᵉ Law condemn'd, & yᵗ onely (I thinck) hath made her*
> *lie so-long, in an imprisond-Obscuritie: For yoʳ sake alone, She hath thus*
> *far Coniur'd her-self abroad; and beares noe-other Charmes about Her, but*
> *what may tend to yoʳ Recreation; nor no-other Spell, but to posses you wᵗʰ*
> *a beleif, That as She, So He that first taught her to Enchant, will alwaies be/*
> > *your deuoted*
> > *Tho: Middleton./*

57. Anne Lancashire, "*The Witch*: Stage Flop or Political Mistake?"

Dedication to *The Witch*. Ed. W. W. Greg and F. P. Wilson. The Malone Society Reprints. N. pl.: Oxford University Press, 1948 (1950), x.

9. 1620 The Water Poet Comments

John Taylor, Thames waterman and self-styled "water poet," shows vigorous wit and humor in poems like *The Praise of Hemp-Seed*, in which he defends hemp-seed as an appropriate subject for poetry. The relevant passage deals with hemp's virtue as a source of paper and discloses Taylor's judgments of the poets of "true worth." (Elsewhere in the volume, Taylor describes sailing to Quinborough in a brown paper boat and supping with the Mayor, likely an allusion to Middleton's *The Mayor of Quinborough*.)

> In paper, many a Poet now suruiues
> Or else their lines had perish'd with their liues.
> Old *Chaucer*, *Gower*, and Sir *Thomas More*,
> Sir *Philip Sidney*, who the Lawrell wore,
> *Spenser*, and *Shakespeare* did in Art excell,
> Sir *Edward Dyer*, *Greene*, *Nash*, *Daniell*.
> *Siluester*, *Beamont*, Sir *Iohn Harrington*,
> Forgetfulnesse their workes would ouertun,
> But that in paper they immortally
> Do liue in spight of death, and cannot die.
>   And many there are liuing at this day
> VVhich do in paper their true worth display:
> As *Dauis*, *Drayton*, and the learned *Dun*,
> *Ionson*, and *Chapman*, *Marston*, *Middleton*,
> VVith *Rowlye*, *Fletcher*, *Withers*, *Messenger*,
> *Heywood*, and all the rest where e're they are,
> Must say their lines but for the paper sheete
> Had scarcely ground, whereon to set their feete.

The Praise of Hemp-Seed: With the Voyage of Mr. Roger Bird and the Writer Hereof, in a Boat of Brown-Paper, from London to Quinborough in Kent. London: for H. Gosson, 1620, sigs. E3v-E4r, F2v-F3r.

10. 1620 The City's Recognition of Middleton

On September 6th, Middleton was officially appointed City Chronologer as a result of his work with the Lord Mayor's pageants. Before the end of

November, his yearly salary had been increased to ten pounds, and he received additional monies in 1621, 1622, and 1623. The City also granted a small amount, twenty nobles, to his widow in 1627. Middleton's records of any "memorable acts," however, have been lost.

Item, this day was read in Court (of Aldermen), a petition of Thomas Middleton, Gent., and upon consideration thereof taken, and upon the sufficient testimony this Court hath received of his services performed to this City, this Court is well pleased to entertain and admit the said Thomas Middleton to collect and set down all memorable acts of this City and occurrences thereof, and for such other employments as this Court shall have occasion to use him in; but the said Thomas Middleton is not to put any of the same acts so by him to be collected into print without the allowance and approbation of this Court, and for the readiness of his service to the City in the same employments this Court does order that he shall receive from henceforth, out of the Chamber of London, a yearly fee of 6*l*. 13*s*. 4*d*.

Analytical Index to the Series of Records Known as the Remembrancia. Preserved Among the Archives of the City of London. A. D. 1579-1664. London: E. J. Francis, 1878, p. 305.

11. 1624 A Judgment from the Master of the Revels

Of the Middleton items in Henry Herbert's record book, only one includes a value judgment. Herbert had been Master of the Revels for six months when the King's Company performed a revived *More Dissemblers Besides Women* at Whitehall. According to Edmond Malone, who worked with Herbert's manuscript before it disappeared, Herbert had added to his official entry this short marginal note. We can only guess whether Herbert meant it to refer to the script or the performance.

The worst play that ere I saw.

The Dramatic Records of Sir Henry Herbert, Master of the Revels, 1623-1673. Ed. Joseph Quincy Adams. New Haven: Yale University Press, 1917, p. 51.

12. 1624 A Sneer from the Friend of a Fellow Playwright

Philip Massinger's *Bondman* was performed soon after Middleton and Rowley's *Spanish Gypsy* had played with great success in the same theater.

Massinger's play did well — it was one of his most successful — but apparently did not receive the same response as had Middleton's hit. In commendatory verses to *The Bondman*, Massinger's friend scornfully alludes to *The Spanish Gypsy* and, perhaps continuing the allusion, to playwrights who *"write to please"* and are thus lesser playwrights than Massinger.

> *The* Printers *haste calls on; I must not driue*
> *My time past* Sixe, *though I begin at* Fiue.
> *One houre I haue entire; and 'tis enough,*
> *Here are no* Gipsie Iigges, *no* Drumming stuffe,
> Dances, *or other* Trumpery *to delight,*
> *Or take, by common way, the common sight.*
> *The* Avthor *of this* Poem, *as he dares*
> *To stand th' austerest Censure; so he cares,*
> *As little what it is. His owne, Best way*
> *Is to be* Iudge, *and* Avthor *of his* Play.
> *It is his* Knowledge, *makes him thus secure*;
> *Nor do's he write to please, but to endure.*

W[illiam?] B[agnall?]. "The *Authors* Friend to the Reader," commendatory verses to Philip Massinger's *The Bond-Man*. London: Edw. Allde, for John Harison and Edward Blackmore, 1624, sig. A4r.

13. 1624, August 10 The Spanish Ambassador's Indignation

Don Carlos Coloma, Spanish Ambassador to England from 1622 to September of 1624, wrote the Count-Duke of Olivares this outraged account of what he had heard about the performances of Middleton's *A Game at Chess* and what he feared would result: war. Olivares, perhaps the most influential of Philip IV's ministers, had been active in the Spanish side of the English-Spanish marriage negotiations and was satirized in the play as the Black Duke, though Coloma appears to have been unaware of that personal attack or to have been avoiding its mention.

... Since then there has occurred an event that is not unworthy of Your Excellency's, and even of His Majesty's, knowledge, in order that the shamelessness of the English may be plainly seen, if indeed there is still any need of new examples of it. This is what happened:

The actors whom they call here "the King's men" have recently acted, and are still acting, in London a play that so many people come to see, that there were more than 3000 persons there on the day that the audience was smallest. There was such merriment, hubbub and applause that even if I had been many leagues away it would not have been possible for me not to have taken notice of it, and notorious baseness, not merely excessive tolerance, if I had paid no attention to it or neglected it. The subject of the play is a game of chess, with white houses and black houses, their kings and other pieces, acted by the players, and the king of the blacks has easily been taken for our lord the King, because of his youth, dress and other details. The first act, or rather game was played by their ministers, impersonated by the white pieces, and the Jesuits, by the black ones. Here there were remarkable acts of sacrilege and, among other abominations, a minister summoned St Ignatius from hell, and when he found himself again in the world, the first thing he did was to rape one of his female penitents; in all this, these accursed and abominable men revealed the depths of their heresy by their lewd and obscene actions. The second act was directed against the Archbishop of Spalato, at that time a white piece, but afterwards won over to the black side by the Count of Gondomar, who, brought on to the stage in his little litter almost to the life, and seated on his chair with a hole in it (they said), confessed all the treacherous actions with which he had deceived and soothed the king of the whites, and, when he discussed the matter of confession with the Jesuits, the actor disguised as the Count took out a book in which were rated all the prices for which henceforwards sins were to be forgiven. Besides this, those who saw the play relate so many details and such atrocious and filthy words, that I have not thought fit to offend Your Excellency's ears with them. In these two acts and in the third, the matter of which I do not know in detail, they hardly shewed anything but the cruelty of Spain and the treachery of Spaniards, and all this was set forth so personally that they did not even exclude royal persons. The last act ended with a long, obstinate struggle between all the whites and the blacks, and in it he who acted the Prince of Wales heartily beat and kicked the "Count of Gondomar" into Hell, which consisted of a great hole and hideous figures; and the white king {drove} the black king and even his queen {into Hell} almost as offensively. All this has been so much applauded and enjoyed by the mob that here, where no play has been acted for more than one day {consecutively}, this one has already been acted on four, and each day the crowd is greater.

Had I followed the advice of the Marqués de la Hinojosa when he advised me to go away with him, such things would not have reached my ears, nor should I have seen the sacred name of my King outraged in so many ways by such low, vile people, nor his holy and glorious acts so unworthily interpreted; only this was lacking to let me describe my sufferings here as a true Hell. The greatest of these, materially, is to listen to the blasphemies uttered against God; I have been unable, too, to discover during the last two months whether I did right or wrong to stay on here; the question whether I served the King well or ill by so doing keeps me in that uneasiness that Your Excellency will readily understand in this true servant of his. But I leave this to Your Excellency's care, for so great a gentleman and so noble a minister of His Majesty will do me the honour of telling it to his royal ears with the due recognition of the zeal with which I have desired and striven to fulfil my duties. I report, Sir, that when I had received a statement of the shamelessness of the actors, I dispatched the language-secretary to the King of England, who is at present forty miles away, where he is feasting and fawning upon the French Ambassador, with a letter in the following terms:

"Although I have not yet received orders from the King my master to give His Majesty an account of my embassy, which orders I expect to receive at any moment, I cannot refrain from fulfilling the obligations of my post and representing to Your Majesty what seems to be my duty. Yesterday and to-day the players called Your Majesty's men have acted in London a play that is so scandalous, so impious, so barbarous and so offensive to my royal master — if perhaps his known greatness and the inestimable worth of his royal person were capable of receiving offence from any man, least of all from such vile persons as are usually the authors and actors of such follies — that I am compelled to take up my pen and in a few words and with all the humility I owe Your Majesty, to beg Your Majesty one of two things: either that Your Majesty would be pleased to order the authors and actors of the said play to be publicly punished as an example, by which means Your Majesty will satisfy his own honour and the reputation of the English nation which has been so much smirched by actions that are so vile and so unworthy of honourable men; or that Your Majesty would be pleased to order that a ship be given me in which I may cross to Flanders with the necessary guarantees granted to ambassadors of other sovereigns and leave to depart instantly. I await indifferently either decision. I pray God etc."[58]

[Having explained to Olivares why he gave the King of England these options, Coloma recounts the difficulties he has had as Ambassador.] It cannot be pleaded that those who repeat and hear these insults are merely four rogues because during these last four days more than 12,000 persons have all heard the play of *A Game at Chesse*, for so they call it, including all the nobility still in London. All these people come out of the theatre so inflamed against Spain that, as a few Catholics have told me who went

58. For the complete Spanish text of Coloma's letter to King James, see Peter G. Phialas, "An Unpublished Letter About *A Game at Chess*."

secretly to see the play, my person would not be safe in the streets; others have advised me to keep to my house with a good guard, and this is being done. Let Your Excellency consider whether I could pass over this in silence; it is enough to have ignored so many different things that have been said and done, even some filthy songs that Buckingham makes his musicians sing where they now are, which are such that the Marquis of Hamilton, the Earls of Montgomery and Carey, and others left a great reception in order not to hear them, as I have been told in a letter from one who saw them go. Finally, Sir, nothing else but war is to be expected from these people. Let Your Excellency believe me, I beg and pray, even if for certain reasons it suits us to defer it, our best plan is to show bravery and resolution {now}, rather than allow them to increase their strength.[59]

Letter in the Spanish State Archives, Registro de Cartas, libro no. 375, as cited in Edward M. Wilson and Olga Turner, "The Spanish Protest Against *A Game at Chesse*," *Modern Language Review*, 44 (1949): 480-82.

14. 1624, August 11 Sir John Holles Interprets

When John Holles returned from a weekend visit to Robert Carr, he heard about *A Game at Chess* and wrote the discredited Carr this eyewitness account.

My Lord though from Mr. Whittakers, or others, this vulgar pasquin may cum to your eares, yet whether he, or thei saw it, I know not, muche beeing the difference betweene ey=sight, & hear=say: when I returned from your Lordship hither uppon munday, I was saluted with a report of a facetious comedy, allreddy thryce acted with extraordinary applause: a representation of all our spannishe traffike, where Gundomar his litter, his open chayre for the ease of that fistulated part, Spalato &c. appeared uppon the stage. I was invited by the reporter Sr Edward Gorge (whose ballance gives all things waight to the advantage) to be allso an auditor therof, & accordingly yesterday to the globe I rowed, which hows I found so thronged, that by scores thei came away for want of place, though as yet little past one;

59. On the 18th of August, Coloma forwarded a translation of King James's response and told Olivares that only actions would prove whether the King was genuinely angry with the players: "The fact is that this play has run for nine days, to the general applause of bad men and to the grief of those whose intentions are sound, who already thought that we had sufficient cause for complaint in the barbarism and vile behaviour of these people without this additional insult" (Wilson and Turner, 482).

nevertheless lothe to check the appetite, which came so seldome to me (not
having been in a play=house thes 10. years) & suche a daynty not every day
to be found, I marched on, & heard the pasquin, for no other it {was,} which
had been the more complete had the poët been a better states=man: the
descant was built uppon the popular opinion, that the Jesuits mark is to bring
all the christian world under Rome for the spirituality, & under Spayn for the
temporal{i}ty: heeruppon, as a precept, or legacy left those disciples from
their first founder Ignatius Loyola, this their father serves for the prologue,
who admiring no speedier operation of his drugg, is inraged, & desperate, till
cumforted by one of his disciples, the plott is revealed him, prosperously
advanced by their dessigne uppon England: with this he vanisheth, leaving
his benediction over the work. The whole play is a chess board, England the
whyt hows, Spayne the black: one of the white pawns, with an under black
dubblett, signifying a Spanish hart, betrays his party to their advantage,
advanceth Gundomars propositions, works under hand the Princes cumming
into Spayn: which pawn so discovered, the whyt King revyles him, objects
his raising him in wealth, in honor, from meane, next classis to a labouring
man: this by the character is supposed Bristow[60]: yet is {it} is hard, players
should judge him in jest, before the State in ernest. Gundomar makes a large
account of his great feates heer, descrybes in scorne our vanities in dyet, in
apparell, in every other excess, (the symptomes of a falling state) how many
Ladies brybed him to be groome of the stoole to the Infanta, how many to be
mother of the mayds, with muche suche trashe, letters from the nunnry in
Drury lane, from those in Bloomsbury &c. how many Jesuites, & priests he
loosed out of prison, & putt agayn into their necessary work of seducing how
he sett the Kings affayrs as a clock, backward, & forward, made him believe,
& un=believe as stood best with his busines, be the caws never so cleere:
how he covered the roguery of the Jesuits in abusing wemen licentiously:
how he befooled Spalato with a counterfett letter from Cardinall Paolo his
kinsman, promising to leave his Cardinals hatt to him, himself then beeing
elected Pope: with muche suche like stuff, more wittily penned, then wysely
staged: but at last the Prince making a full discovery of all their knaveries,
Ollivares, Gundomar, Spalato, the Jesuite, the spannish bishop, & a spannish
euenuke {eunuch} ar by the Prince putt into the bagg, & so the play ends.
Your Lordship may give to this a morall; me thinks this is a hardy part, &
beyond my understanding: & surely thes gamsters must have a good retrayte,
else dared thei not to charge thus Princes actions, & ministers, nay their
intents: a foule injury to Spayn, no great honor to England, rebus sic

---

60. John Digby, Earl of Bristol, was the person whom Holles believed was being condemned.

stantibus [things thus standing]: every particular will beare a large paraphrase, which I submitt to your better judgment.

Newcastle University Library MS NeC 15405, pp. 3-5, as cited in A. R. Braunmuller, "'To the Globe I Rowed': John Holles Sees *A Game at Chess*," *English Literary Renaissance* 20 (1990): 341-43. Material deleted from the original manuscript is excluded.

15. 1624, August 12   Secretary Conway to the Privy Council

Secretary Conway here passes on King James's instructions to his Privy Council as a result of Coloma's letter. That none of the English nobility had mentioned Middleton's play to the king suggests the degree to which they supported the positions expressed in it.

His Ma[tie] hath receaued informacion from the Spanish Ambassado[r], of a very scandalous Comedie acted publickly by the King's Players, wherein they take the boldnes, and presumption in a rude, and dishonorable fashion, to represent on the Stage the persons of his Ma[tie], the King of Spaine, the Conde de Gondomar, the Bishop of Spalato &c. His Ma[tie] remembers well there was a commaundment and restraint giuen against the representinge of anie modern Christian kings in those Stage-plays, and wonders much both at the boldnes nowe taken by that companie, and alsoe that it hath ben permitted to bee so acted, and that the first notice thereof should bee brought to him, by a forraine Ambassado[r], while soe manie Ministers of his owne are thereaboutes, and cannot but have heard of it. His Ma[ts] pleasure is that yo[r] LL[ps] presently call before yo[u] as well the Poett, that made the comedie, as the Comedians that acted it, And upon examinacion of them to commit them, or such of them as yo[u] shall find most faultie, unto prison, if yo[u] find cause, or otherwise take securitie for their forthcominge. . . .

State Papers (Dom.), James I, vol. 171, no. 39, as cited in R. C. Bald's edition of *A Game at Chesse*. Cambridge: the University Press, 1929, pp. 159-60.

16. 1624, August 13   The Florentine Ambassador's View

Amerigo Salvetti quickly wrote home about the uproar, which he saw as directed against King James and the royal advisors.

For the last eight days here, almost every day the public actors have played a comedy called *A Game at Chess*; in it they present vividly the Count of Gondomar's actions during the time he was Ambassador, not leaving out anything that seems to them worthy of exposure as they denounce his intrigue and falseness, to so great applause and concourse of the people that it is believed they make 300 golden scudi with every performance. In the play they also introduce the character of the Archbishop of Spalatro, and, in short, the play is very satiric and exciting. It is believed nonetheless that the comedy will be prohibited when the king hears about it; because they cannot lacerate the Count of Gondomar in exposing his way of dealing without depicting him as a man of influence against their will, and consequently without reflecting the weak judgment of those who had believed in him and had daily dealings with him.

British Library Add. MS. 27,962, c. p. 189, as cited in Bald, ed., pp. 160-61. Trans. by Patrizia Callahan.

17. 1624, August 14   Sir Francis Nethersole: *A Game at Chess*

Sir Francis Nethersole, a staunch Protestant, agreed with the portrayal of Spanish Catholics as evil. He wrote to Sir Dudley Carleton, who, as ambassador first to Venice and then to the Hague, was rarely in London, but kept himself well informed of London affairs.

. . . Yet we haue now these ten dayes a new play here, the plot whereof js a game of Chesse, vnder wᶜʰ the whole Spanish busines js ripped vp to the quicke, and Gondomar brought on yᵉ Stage in his chayre, wᶜʰ fitteth skorners so well that the players haue gotten 100ˡ the day euer since, for they play no thing els, knowing there time cannot be long.

State Papers (Dom.), James I, vol. 171, no. 49, as cited in Bernard M. Wagner, "New Allusions to *A Game at Chesse*." *PMLA* 44 (1929): 828.

18. 1624, August 20   The Venetian Ambassador: *A Game at Chess*

Alvise Valaresso, who disliked the Spanish as much as had Horatio Busino, wrote the Doge of Venice and the Senate about the furor, distinguishing between the play's literary merit and its political daring.

In one of the public mercenary theatres here they have recently given several representations under different names of many of the circumstances about the marriage with the Infanta. The work is of no great merit from what they say, but it drew great crowds from curiosity at the subject. The Spaniards are touched from their tricks being discovered, but the king's reputation is affected much more deeply by representing the case [ease?] with which he was deceived. The Spanish ambassador has made a remonstrance, and it is thought that they will at least punish the author.

Calendar of State Papers and Manuscripts, Relating to English Affairs, Existing in the Archives and Collections of Venice, and in Other Libraries of Northern Italy. Vol. 18, *1623-1625*. Ed. Allen B. Hinds. London: for His Majesty's Stationery Office, 1912, no. 557, p. 425.

19. 1624, August 21 John Chamberlain to a Friend

For thirty years, from 1597 to 1626, John Chamberlain wrote detailed letters of London affairs to his friend Sir Dudley Carleton. He included whatever he thought would interest Carleton, such as the drunken penance of Moll Cutpurse, the heroine of Middleton and Dekker's *The Roaring Girl*.[61] In this letter, Chamberlain, who normally paid little attention to theater, reports that London's enthusiasm for *A Game at Chess* cut across the usual lines of class and religion.

. . . I doubt not but you have heard of our famous play of Gondomar, which hath ben followed with extraordinarie concourse, and frequented by all sorts of people old and younge, rich and poore, masters and servants, papists and puritans, wise men *et ct.*, churchmen and statesmen as Sir Henry Wotton, Sir Albert Morton, Sir Benjamin Ruddier [Rudyerd], Sir Thomas Lake, and a world besides; the Lady [Judith] Smith wold have gon yf she could have persuaded me to go with her. I am not so sowre nor severe but that I wold willingly have attended her, but I could not sit so long,[62] for we must have ben there before one a clocke at farthest to find any roome. They counterfeited his person to the life, with all his graces and faces, and had gotten (they say) a cast sute of his apparell for the purpose, and his Lytter, wherin the world sayes lackt nothing but a couple of asses to carrie yt, and Sir G. Peter [Petre] or Sir T. Mathew [Matthew] to beare him companie. But the worst is in playeng him, they played sombody els, for which they are forbidden to play that or any other play till the Kings pleasure be further

61. Letter 133. 12 February 1612.
62. Chamberlain was seventy years old and increasingly troubled by illness.

knowne; and they may be glad yf they can so scape scot-free: the wonder
lasted but nine dayes, for so long they played yt.

Letter 457. *The Letters of John Chamberlain.* Ed. Norman Egbert McClure. Vol.
2. Philadelphia: The American Philosophical Society, 1939: 577-78.

20. 1624, August-December   Contemporaries Enjoy *A Game at Chess*

Thomas Salisbury, a Cambridge M.A. and an Anglican priest,
composed this verse letter about the recent news in London sometime
between August and December of 1624, when Sir Thomas Dawes liked the
letter enough to copy it into his commonplace book. Like most Londoners,
Salisbury appreciates the play's general positions — and he is so enthusiastic
about the Black Knight's speeches comparing the Black House's ambitions
of world conquest to a feast (5.3) that he nearly quotes them at the end of this
excerpt.

> the rumor buzzes now in eury eare
> is: bought a Game at Chess but y^t I fear
> to show my small skill in y^t royall play
> I could tell most of y^t, y^t most men say:
> take but y^e [   ]^{63} & Gamesters: mongst ye rest
> ye seuerall dishes of Ambitions ffeast:
> and y^{en} yould wish or y^t ye Scene lay there
> or yo^u were, where ye scene is wth vs heere:
> ffor ye black howse, they chose to represent
> ye King, Queene, Bishop, Knight, Duke, to each lent
> their seuerall Paunes as Guards ye first yo^u knowe
> ye rest to life y^{is} present Verse shall shewe
> ye Bishop stood for Roomes corrupted chayre
> ye Knight for no Knight errant; but a Rare
> subtill Embassadour: ye like o^r shoare
> neuer r^d: nor may it euermore!
> ye Duke for ye Duke ffauorite of Spaine;
> highly belou'd of ye black Soueraigne.
> 3 Paunes were famous: yo^{se} we shall expresse
> ye Bishop: a Shy Jesuite, adde on S
> ye Queenes Paune was a seculare Jesuitesse:

63. Blank in the manuscript.

yᵉ Knights a State-flye: whome he did addresse
to vndermine oʳ Candor: one he tooke
and made an Eunuch: yⁱˢ yᵉ Blackhowse: looke
now to yᵉ white: (uirtues pure sacred Reste)
oʳ maᵗⁱᵉˢ like heauens: are best exprest
in duteous Silence, opposite agen
to yᵉ blacke-house, wee had as many men
one Supernumerus Bishop did appeare
to fill upp a vacante sede there
and did it by Reuolt; Apostates Hire,
their turne once seru'd, they damn him to yᵉ Fire
yᵉ Queenes Paune was a Lady hard besett
to become Nunne: but came off cleerely yet:
but two remaine yᵉ Princely Knight; Lou'd Duke
yᵗ Royall Payre yᵗ a close iourney tooke
vnto Iberia: why? to what successe?
I tell not nowe: I onely haue one messe
was sett before oʳ Knight: to sett to yoᵘ
and I haue sᵈ when I haue sᵈ Adieu.
to compasse his owne ends oʳ valiaunt Knight
pretends himself Ambitious: in such height
yᵗ one might sooner Bound, yᵉ Boundlesse ffire
yᵉⁿ quench yᵒˢᵉ thoughts yᵗ did to rule aspire.
to cure yⁱˢ sore yᵉ Black Knight vndertakes
to cure all els yᵗ fowle disturbance makes
in his greate Harte, yⁱˢ first he slights & sayes
we hold yⁱˢ but for Pufpaste a light Messe.
wᶜʰ eury Cardinals cooke hath skill to dresse.
yᵉⁿ smild & sᵈ: yoᵘ doe not Couet Moe
yᵉⁿ yᵉ whole world white Knight, yᵗ yoᵘ may knowe
w'are 'bout yⁱˢ already; where yᵗ Land
from whence yoᵘ came wᵗʰ vs no more doth stand
yᵉⁿ for a garden whence oʳ Cooke may picke
a sallet for oʳ ffeast.——
Our ffood's Leane Fraunce larded wᵗʰ Germany
but first their enters in yᵉ Graue [   ]
of Venice: Seru'd in (though yᵉ Sirs be Loth)
like to oʳ English Capons in white Broth
Italy's oʳ Ouen: thence oʳ baked meates come
Sauoy oʳ Salt: Geneua pure we doome
for oʳ chip'd Man-cheate: beneath yᵉ Salt doth lye

ye Netherlands, lowe pride will sett y^{em} high
for o^r next Course, there Enters in at dores
for Plouers Portugals for Black-Birds Mores
and last on all handes, least o^r ffeast proue Drye
Holland, for Sauce stands ready melted By.
ye Voyder come, we thus o^r hope suffice
Zealand sayes Grace for fashion then we Rise.
I rise & rest. . . .

British Library Add. MS. 29,492, fos. 33b-35, as cited in Geoffrey Bullough, "*The Game at Chesse*: How It Struck a Contemporary." *Modern Language Review* 49 (1954): 157-58.

21. 1624 The Company Smiles About Its Success

John Fletcher's *Rule a Wife and Have a Wife* was licensed for the King's Men only a little more than two months after their performances of *A Game at Chess*. In the prologue to Fletcher's play, they remind the audience that they were the company who brought an irreverent Spanish play to the boards only a short time ago.

> *Pleasure attend yee, and about yee sit*
> *The springs of mirth fancy delight and wit*
> *To stirre you up, doe not your looks let fall,*
> *Nor to remembrance our late errors call,*
> *Because this day w'are* Spaniards *all againe,*
> *The story of our Play, and our Sceane* Spaine:
> *The errors too, doe not for this cause hate,*
> *Now we present their wit and not their state.*
> *Nor Ladies be not angry if you see,*
> *A young fresh beauty, wanton and too free,*
> *Seeke to abuse your* [her] *Husband, still tis* Spaine,
> *No such grosse errors in your Kingdome raignes,*
> *W'are* Vestalls *all, and though we blow the fire,*
> *We seldome make it flame up to desire,*
> *Take no example neither to beginne,*
> *For some by president delight to sinne:*
> *Nor blame the Poet if he slip aside,*
> *Sometimes lasciviously if not too wide.*
> *But hold your Fannes close, and then smile at ease,*

A cruell Sceane did never Lady please.
Nor Gentlemen, pray be not you displeas'd,
Though we present some men fool'd some[64] diseas'd,
Some drunke, some madde: we meane not you, you'r free,
We taxe no farther then our Comedie,
You are our friends sit noble then and see.

Prologue to John Fletcher's *Rule a Wife and Have a Wife*. Oxford: by Leonard Lichfield, 1640, sig. A2[r].

22. 1626 Ben Jonson on *A Game at Chess*

Jonson appears to have shared Middleton's political views — in *The Staple of News*, he, too, satirizes Gondomar — but he shows little respect for Middleton's "poore *English-play*." He does, however, acknowledge the play as a main topic of conversation (3.2).

<LIC.> Ha' you no *Newes* o'the *Stage?*
They'll aske me abou<t> *new Playes*, at dinner time.
And I should be as dumbe as a fish. THO. O! yes.
There is a *Legacy* left to the *Kings Players*,
Both for their various shifting of their *Scene*,
And dext'rous change o' their persons to all shapes,
And all disguises: by the right reuerend
Archbishop of *Spalato*. LIC. He is dead,
That plai'd him![65] THO. Then, h'has lost his share o' the *Legacy*.
LIC. What newes of *Gundomar?* THO. A second *Fistula*,
Or an *excoriation* (at the least)
For putting the poore *English-play*, was writ of him,
To such a sordid vse, as (is said) he did,
Of cleansing his *posterior's*. LIC. Iustice! Iustice!

The Staple of Newes. In *Ben Jonson*. Vol. 6. Ed. C. H. Herford, Percy Simpson, and Evelyn Simpson. Oxford: Clarendon, 1938: 334.

---

64. Emended from "fome."
65. Refers to the death of William Rowley, who had played the Archbishop of Spalatro.

23. N.D. The Company's Profits from *A Game at Chess*

This manuscript record, unpublished until 1779,[66] probably was written by someone who had heard the actors discuss the play's phenomenal success. In part because fifteen hundred pounds seemed an outlandish figure, some scholars argued that the note was a later forgery, but the discovery of a Renaissance commonplace book with the poem (entry 24) increased the likelihood that the comment in the quarto is, if not accurate in its information, at least authentic.

After nyne dayse wherein I have heard some of the acters say they tooke fiveteene hundred Pounde the spanish faction being prevalent gott it supprest the chiefe actors and the Poett Mr. Thomas Middleton that writt it committed to prisson where hee lay some Tyme and at last gott oute upon this petition presented to King James
> A harmles game: coyned only for delight
> was playd betwixt the black house and the white
> the white house wan: yet stille the black doth bragge
> they had the power to put mee in the bagge
> use but your royall hand. Twill set mee free
> Tis but removing of a man thats mee.

Manuscript note "in an old hand" in a copy of a quarto of the play, Dyce Collection, Victoria & Albert Museum, no. 6561, 25, D. 42, as cited in Bald, ed., p. 166.

24. >1628 Poem from a Commonplace Book

Sir Thomas Dawes, who in 1624 had copied into his commonplace book Salisbury's verse letter on *A Game at Chess*, continued his interest in Middleton and sometime before 1628 entered this epigram, supposedly written by Middleton to King James. Middleton may have been imprisoned, although we have no official corroboration, but because the epigram has survived in two versions without having been published (see entry 23), it likely circulated fairly widely. If Middleton was not incarcerated, many people thought he had been.

> A harmelesse Gaime rais'd meerely for delight
> Was lately plaide bye *black* howse & *White*

66. It first appeared in Edward Capell's *The School of Shakespeare*, 3: 31. See entry 49.

The White side wann but nowe ye black side bragg
They changd ye Gaime & putt me in ye bagg
And y^t wch makes malicios ioy more sweete
I lye nowe vnder hatches in ye ffleete.
Yet vse y^r Royall hand! my hopes are free;
Tis but remouing of one man, that's mee.

British Library Add. 29,492, f. 43, as cited in Bullough, p. 163.

25. 1629 A Richard Brome Allusion

Nearly five years after the performances of *A Game at Chess*, Richard Brome allowed the King's Men to allude in *The Northern Lass* to their most successful play. Bulfinch, the Justice, speaks to a character disguised as a Spaniard (5.8) and mentions Gondomar not by name, but as the "black Knight," the part Middleton had assigned him in *A Game at Chess*.

I do see Signior I thanke the light, that you are a goodly man of outward parts, and except it were the black Knight himselfe, or him with the Fistula, the proprest man I haue seene of your Nation. They are a People of very spare dyet, I haue heard, and therefore seldome fat. Sure you[67] haue had most of your breeding in this Countrey, the dyet whereof you like better then your owne, which makes you linger here, after all your Country men, vpon some vncouth plot.

The Northern Lasse, A Comœdie. London: by Avg. Mathewes, to be sold by Nicholas Vavasovr, 1632, sig. L4^v.

26. c. 1631-32 The Puritan Respónse

Thomas Randolph, poet, dramatist, and one of Jonson's literary sons, lost a finger in a "fray" and wrote poems on the incident. His schoolfriend and fellow dramatist William Hemminge, son of the Shakespeare First Folio editor, responded with the mock-heroic "Elegy on Randolph's Finger" in which over thirty poets solemnly accompany the finger to the classical underworld. In the first section, Middleton is among those Hemminge calls

---

67. Emended from "you you".

"worthyes," and in the second he is portrayed as adored by Puritans for
having written the anti-Catholic *A Game at Chess.*

[After invoking the Muse and setting the scene,
Hemminge describes the procession.]

The fluente Flettcher, Beaumonte riche In sence
for Complement and Courtshypes quintesence,
Ingenious Shakespeare, Messenger that knowes
the strength to wright or plott In verse or prose,
Whose easye pegasus Can Ambell ore
some threscore Myles of fancye In an hower,
Clowd grapling Chapman whose Aeriall mynde
Soares att philosophie and strickes ytt blynd,
Dauborne I had forgott, and lett ytt bee,
hee dyed Amphybion by thy Ministrye,
Siluester Bartas whose Translatinge pate
Twynd or was Elder to our Lawreatt,
Deuyn composing Quarles, whose Lynes asspire
to heauen, and rauysh the Celestiall quire,
The Aprile of all poesy, Tom May
that makes our Englishe speake Pharsalia,
Sandes Metamorphised Into a nother,
wee knowe nott Sandes, nor Ouid from each other,
Hee that soe well on Scoppius playd the Man
the Famous Digges, or Leonard Claudian,
the pithy Danyell whose salt lynes afford
A wayghty sentence In each little word,
Heroicke Drayton, Withers smarte In Ryme,
the verye Poett beadle of the tyme,
Pans Pastorall Browne whose Infante Muse did squeake
At eighteen yeare better then others speake,
Shirlye the Morninge Childe the Muses Breed
and sent hyme vs wth Bayes borne on his head,
Deep In a dumpe Iacke forde alone was gott
W^th folded Armes and Melancholye hatt,
The squoblinge[68] Middelton and Heywood sage
The Apollogetticke Attlas of the stage,

68. "Squoblinge," perhaps one who squabbles, but more likely one who uses squibs; makes
smart, satirical remarks.

well of the goulden world hee could Intreat
but little of the Mettall hee could gett,
fower score sweet babes he fashond from the lumpe,
for he was Christned In parnassus pumpe,
the Muses Gossips to Auroras bedd,
and since that tyme his face was euer redd:
More worthyes Like to thes I could Impart
but that wee are troubled wth a broken hart.

[The poets continue through the "Infernall deeps,"
and we meet more mourning writers. At the
Styx, the procession halts, because Charon demands
money for passage, and poets have no money. John
Taylor, the Thames waterman, tries to convince
Charon to let them cross, but Charon is obdurate.
When three or four Puritans enter, rich from gulling
orphans, the poets present their lines: the Puritans,
however, are not interested and continue on their way.]

Thay Quakte at Iohnson as by hym thay pase
because of Trebulation Holsome and Annanias,
But Middleton thay seemd much to Adore
fors learned Excercise gaynst Gundomore.
To whom thay thus pray, Can you Edifye
our understandinges In this misterye?
wth Teares the storye hee begane whilest thay
prickt vpp thayr eares and did begin to pray.
the sad tale ended, Nosing out 'prophane',
straight for the finger wisht the man weare slayne:
such was thayr Charritye cause his sarsnett hood
so vilye wrote a gaynst the Brotherhood,
And wch was worse that lately he did pen
vyle thinges for pigmeyes gaynst the Sonns of men,
The Righteous man and the regenerate
being laught to scorne thare by the reprobate.
"brother, sayd on, you spurr you^r Zeale to slow
to checke att thes thinges when the learned knowe
Thes arre but scarrs: the woundes dothe deeper lye:
Who knowes but hee wrightes to a Monastarye
and those whome wee call players may In tyme
Luther abuse and fence for Bellermyne [Bellarmine]?

The Pope has Iuglinge trickes and can vse slightes
to Conuerte Players Into Iesuittes.
the Metamorphises wee sees no other
then when A Cobler turnes a preaching brother.
The Catholicke sculls of Spayne and Ittalye
workes all by Vndermining Villanye.
I graunte theyr show is fayre, but this you knowe,
A Papist tutore makes his Pupill soe."

[The poets receive no money, so the Muses are sad
and Minerva sets libraries afire, but Hermes brings
Quicksilver, with which they pay Charon. Chaucer
and Spenser welcome them. The Faerie Queene
transforms the finger to a may-pole, around which
her servants dance and sing.]

William Hemminge's Elegy on Randolph's Finger, *Containing the Well-Known Lines "On the Time-Poets."* Ed. G. C. Moore Smith. Oxford: Basil Blackwell, Shakespeare Head Press, 1923, pp. 11-19.

27. 1635 Thomas Heywood on the Modern Poets

The versatile and prolific Thomas Heywood was called the "Apollogetticke Attlas of the stage" (entry 26), a punning allusion to his *Apology for Actors*, a defense. In *The Hierarchy of the Blessed Angels*, Heywood defends poets, who can through verse keep themselves and others from dying. In past ages, he says, excellent writers were graced with longer names; honor meant adding the city of birth, the country of breeding, or the nature of their work to their names. Their modern counterparts, he notes, are not so graced.

Our moderne Poets to that passe are driuen,
Those names are curtal'd which they first had giuen;
And, as we wisht to haue their memories drown'd,
We scarcely can afford them halfe their sound.
Greene, who had in both Academies ta'ne
Degree of Master, yet could neuer gaine
To be call'd more than *Robin*: who had he
Profest ought saue the *Muse*, Serv'd, and been Free
After a seuen yeares Prentiseship; might haue

(With credit too) gone *Robert* to his graue.
Marlo, renown'd for his rare art and wit,
Could ne're attaine beyond the name of *Kit*;
Although his *Hero* and *Leander* did
Merit addition rather. Famous *Kid*
Was call'd but *Tom*. *Tom. Watson*, though he wrote
Able to make *Apollo's* self to dote
Vpon his Muse; for all that he could striue,
Yet neuer could to his full name arriue.
Tom. Nash (in his time of no small esteeme)
Could not a second syllable redeeme.
Excellent *Bewmont*, in the formost ranke
Of the rar'st Wits, was neuer more than *Franck*.
Mellifluous *Shake-speare*, whose inchanting Quill
Commanded Mirth or Passion, was but *Will*.
And famous *Iohnson*, though his learned Pen
Be dipt in *Castaly*, is still but *Ben*.
Fletcher and *Webster*, of that learned packe
None of the mean'st, yet neither was but *Iacke*.
Deckers but *Tom*; nor *May*, nor *Middleton*,
And hee's now but *Iacke Foord*, that once were *Iohn*.
    Nor speake I this, that any here exprest,
Should thinke themselues lesse worthy than the rest,
Whose names haue their full syllable and sound;
Or that *Franck*, *Kit*, or *Iacke*, are the least wound
Vnto their fame and merit. I for my part
(Thinke others what they please) accept that heart
Which courts my loue in most familiar phrase;
And that it takes not from my paines or praise.
If any one to me so bluntly com,
I hold he loues me best that calls me *Tom*.

The Hierarchie of the Blessed Angells. Their Names, Orders and Offices. The Fall of Lucifer with His Angells. London: by Adam Islip, 1635, sig. S^v.

28. 1640 A Bookseller Speaks

J. S., the stationer, was reprinting *A Mad World, My Masters*, probably because it recently had been successfully revived at Salisbury Court Theatre. In his prefatory note to the reader, he praises Middleton as a writer whose name will "survive to all Posterities," but at the same time fears that Middleton's use of verse may mean that readers will scorn the nearly thirty-five-year-old comedy.

Courteous Reader, let not the Title or Name of this Comedy be any forestalling, or a weakning of the worthy Authors Judgement, whose knowne Abilities will survive to all Posterities, though hee be long since dead. I hope the Reading thereof shall not prove distastefull unto any in particular, nor hurtfull unto any in generall; but I rather trust that the Language and the plot which you shall find in each Scene, shall rather be commended & applauded, than any way derided or scorned. In the action, which is the life of a Comedy, and the glory of the Author, it hath bin sufficiently expressed, to the liking of the Spectators, and commendations of the Actors; who have set it forth in such lively colours, and to the meaning of the Gentleman that true penn d it, that I dare say few can excell them, though some may equall them. In the reading of one *Act* you ghesse the consequence, for here is no bumbasted or fustian stuffe; but every line weighed as with ballance; & every sentence placed with judgement and deliberation. All that you can find in the perusall, I will give you notice of beforehand, to prevent a censure that may arise in thy reading of this Comedy; as also for the excuse of the *Author*; and that is this: here & there you shall find some lines that doe answer in meetre, which I hope will not prove so disdainefull, whereby the booke may be so much slighted, as not to be read; or the *Authors* judgement undervalued as of no worth. Consider (gentle Reader) it is full twenty yeares since it was written, at which time meetre was most in use, and shewed well upon the conclusion of every Act & Scene. My prevalent hope desires thy charitable censure, and thereby drawes me to be

Thy immutable friend.

I. S., "The Printer and Stationer to the Gentle *READER*." *A Mad World My Masters: A Comedy. As It Hath Bin Often Acted at the Private House in Salisbury Court, by Her Majesties Servants.* London: Printed for J. S. and are to be sold by James Becket, 1640, sigs. A3r-A4r.

29. 1640 An Epigram in Praise

This anonymous epigram from *Wits Recreations*, sometimes attributed to John Mennes or James Smith, corroborates Hemminge's indication that Middleton was esteemed for his clever barbs (entry 26). The epigram appears among hundreds of such epigrams, whose dedicatees include

Beaumont and Fletcher, Jonson, Shakespeare, Chapman, Randolph, Shirley, Massinger, Ford, and Heywood.

> ### 48 To Mr. Thomas Middleton.
> Facetious *Middleton* thy witty Muse,
> Hath pleased all, that books or men peruse
> If any thee dispise, he doth but show,
> Antipathy to wit, in daring so:
> Thy fam's above his malice and 'twilbe,
> Dispraise enough for him, to censure thee.

Witts Recreations. Selected from the Finest Fancies of Modern Muses. With a Thousand Outlandish Proverbs. London: for Humph. Blunden, 1640, sig. B7ᵛ.

30. 1654 Edmund Gayton on Two Middleton Plays

Edmund Gayton was one of Jonson's literary sons and at least once an actor, when he played a role in a 1637 St. John's college performance for the king and queen. He also studied medicine and was a beadle at Oxford until he was among the Royalists removed from their positions by parliament. During the interregnum, he wrote *Pleasant Notes upon* Don Quixote, four lighthearted books of prose and verse commentary on Cervantes's *Don Quixote*, and a treasure-trove of tales, jokes, and literary allusions.

Gayton's two references to *The Mayor of Quinborough* confirm the announcement of the play's publisher that Simon the rustic Mayor was famous; the character was so successful, in fact, that Gayton expected his readers to understand quips about a decades-old play that would not be published until 1661. The first allusion is in the early description of Don Quixote himself, and the second occurs in a discussion of the Barber's plans for vengeance against Don Quixote, who was wearing the Barber's brass shaving basin as the Golden Helmet of Mambrino. In Gayton's version, the Barber thinks of blowing meal in the Don's eyes to confuse him and regain the basin, just as Middleton's pickpocket threw meal in Simon's eyes to escape with a purse.

The allusion to *The Changeling* suggests that play, too, was well known and loved. Gayton uses the name Tony, from Rowley's subplot, as a synonym for simpleton; and the *OED*, where Gayton is among those cited, lists *The Changeling* as the probable source of that usage.

His Wardrobe not much exceeding the *Maior of Quinboroughs*, though for the thrift lesse notorious. The Frugality of the Canvasse back to the Velvet fore-body, being not then known at *Madrid*, and so could not possibly arrive at the *Mancha*.[69]

But if all these miscarried, this *Machavillian* at a strategem, never went without a small Box of Powder, or dryed Meale, and his Puffings, which if he could but advance to the *Dons* eyes, hee doubted not to spoile him for all Adventures, and to punish him in's *kinde* for that of the *Winde-mill*, and regaine his *Bason*, leaving the *Vnmambryno-helmeted Don* in as confounded a case, as the Mayor of *Quinborough* after the Encounter with PICKPOCKETO of *Nov. Hispaniola*, or *Nov. Anglia*,[70] which you please.

Humours are sodainly imitated, especially if there be any life and fancy in 'um. Many have by representation of strong passions been so transported, that they have gone weeping, some from Tragedies, some from Comedies; so merry, lightsome and free, that they have not been sober in a week after, and have so courted the Players to re-act the same matters in the Tavernes, that they came home, as able Actors as themselves; so that their Friends and VVives have took them for Tonies or Mad-men.

Pleasant Notes upon Don Quixot. London: William Hunt, 1654, pp. 2, 111, 140-141.

31. 1657 A Publisher on Middleton's Sales Record

Ordinarily, praise from one's publisher would not be taken too seriously, but Humphrey Moseley was the foremost publisher of fine literature in his day. He was apt to recognize good writing and to know authors' reputations and sales records. In publishing *More Dissemblers Besides Women* and *Women Beware Women*, he had experience to rely on, since he had published Middleton before and would again.

WHen these amongst others of Mr. *Thomas Middleton's* Excellent Poems, came to my hands, I was not a little confident but that his name would prove as great an Inducement for thee to Read, as me to Print them: Since those Issues of his Brain that have already seen the Sun, have by their

---

69. Simon's costume in Act 5 was, according to the stage directions, satin in front and canvas in back.

70. Gayton suggests that Simon's pickpocket was one of the disappointed adventurers who returned from the new world, whether New Spain or New England, and lived by their wits.

worth gained themselves a free entertainment amongst all that are ingenious: And I am most certain, that these will no way lessen his Reputation, nor hinder his Admission to any Noble and Recreative Spirits. All that I require at thy hands, is to continue the Author in his deserved Esteem, and to accept of my Endeavors which have ever been to please thee.

Humphrey Moseley, "To the Reader," *Two New Playes. Viz.* More Dissemblers Besides Women. Women Beware Women. London: for Humphrey Moseley, 1657, sig. A3r-v.

32. 1657 Nat Richards on *Women Beware Women*

In these commendatory verses, poet and dramatist Nathanael Richards places Middleton among the best of his age. One would like to believe, however, that others in Middleton's audiences saw *Women Beware Women* as more than a homily on the evils of "Women crost."

> *WOmen beware Women*; 'tis a true Text
> Never to be forgot: Drabs of State vext,
> Have Plots, Poysons, Mischeifs that seldom miss,
> To murther Vertue with a venom kiss.
> Witness this worthy *Tragedy*, exprest
> By him that well deserv'd among the best
> Of *Poets* in his time: He knew the rage,
> Madness of Women crost; and for the Stage
> Fitted their humors, Hell-bred Malice, Strife
> Acted in State, presented to the life.
> I that have seen't, can say, having just cause,
> Never came *Tragedy* off with more applause.

"Upon the Tragedy of My Familiar Acquaintance, *Tho. Middleton*," *Two New Playes. Viz.* More Dissemblers Besides Women. Women Beware Women. London: for Humphrey Moseley, 1657, sig. A4r.

33. 1661-68 Samuel Pepys on Four Middleton Plays

Whatever else he was or was not, Samuel Pepys was a theater-goer, attending over three hundred performances in one nine-year period of his life. He read plays, knew the performers, and talked with the managers. He saw *The Widow* soon after the theaters re-opened, spent his twenty-eighth birthday with *The Changeling*, read *The Spanish Gypsy* and *The Mayor of Quinborough* as he tried to sort out business affairs, and attended a revival of *The Spanish Gypsy*, recording his responses in his diary.

8 Jan. 1660/1

After dinner I took my Lord Hinchingbrooke and Mr. Sidny [Sidney] to the Theatre and showed them *The Widdow*, an indifferent good play, but wronged by the womens being much to seek in their parts [poor memorization].

23 Feb. 1660/1

Then by water to White-fryers to the play-house, and there saw *The Changeling*, the first time it hath been acted these 20 yeeres — and it takes exceedingly.

16 June 1661

But am not yet come to a resolucion, but am at very great loss and trouble in mind what in the world to do herein. The afternoon, while Will is abroad, I spent in reading *The Spanish Gypsy*, a play not very good, though commended much.

16 June 1666

At noon home to dinner, and then down to Woolwich and Deptford to look after things, my head akeing from the multitude of businesses I had in my head yesterday in settling my accounts. All the way down and up, reading of *The Mayor of Quinborough*, a simple play.

7 Mar. 1667/8

At noon home to dinner, where Mercer with us; and after dinner, she, my wife, Deb and I to the King's playhouse and there saw *The Spanish Gypsy*, the second time of acting, and the first that I saw it — a very silly play; only, great variety of dances, and those most excellently done, especially one part by one Hanes, only lately come thither from the Nursery.[71]

The Diary of Samuel Pepys. Ed. Robert Latham and William Matthews. 11 vols. Berkeley: University of California Press, 1970-83, 2: 8, 41, 122-23; 7: 168-69; 9: 107.

---

71. Joseph Haynes, later a popular comedian, had been with Hatton Garden Theatre, a training-ground for younger actors.

34. 1661 A Publisher on *The Mayor of Quinborough*

The degree to which *The Mayor of Quinborough*'s comic sub-plot with
Simon overshadowed the tragic action is reflected in the title page, where
publisher Henry Herringman calls the play a comedy, and in his description
of the play. Herringman suggests that the play's wit will be a welcome relief
after the difficult years under Oliver Cromwell, when theaters were closed
and characters like Simon could not "*walk abroad.*"

GENTLEMEN,
YOu have the first flight of him I assure you; this Mayor *of* Quinborough
*whom you have all heard of, and some of you beheld upon the Stage, now
begins to walk abroad in Print; he has been known sufficiently by the
reputation of his Wit, which is enough (by the way) to distinguish him from
ordinary Mayors; but Wit you know, has skulk'd in Corners for many years
past, and he was thought to have most of it that could best hide himself: Now
whether this Magistrate fear'd the decimating times, or kept up the state of
other Mayors, that are bound not to go out of their Liberties during the time
of their Mayoralty, I know not; 'tis enough for me to put him into your hands,
under the title of an honest man, which will appear plainly to you, because
you shall find him all along to have a great picque to the Rebel* Oliver; *I am
told his drollery yields to none the* English Dramma *did ever produce; and
though I would not put his modesty to the blush, by speaking too much in his
Commendation, yet I know you will agree with me, upon your better
acquaintance with him, that there is some difference in point of Wit, betwixt
the* Mayor *of* Quinborough, *and the* Mayor *of* Huntingdon.[72]

Publisher's Epistle, *The Mayor of Quinborough: A Comedy. As It Hath Been Often
Acted with Much Applause at Black-Fryars, by His Majesties Servants.* London: for
Henry Herringman, 1661, sig. A2r.

35. 1662 John Evelyn on *The Widow*

Though John Evelyn occasionally attended plays, he was not as involved
with theater as was his friend Pepys. Almost exactly a year after Pepys had
seen *The Widow*, Evelyn mentions in his diary that it had been played before
Charles II. The royal performance and the number of other Restoration
productions suggest that initial post-war audiences were reasonably amused,
but Evelyn's succinct response is unfavorable.

72. Huntington was Oliver Cromwell's birthplace.

16 Jan. 1661/2

This night was acted before his Majestie the *Widow*, a lewd play.[73]

The Diary of John Evelyn. Ed. E. S. de Beer. Oxford: Clarendon, 1955, 3: 313.

36. 1663 William D'Avenant Alludes to *A Game at Chess*

That D'Avenant would have alluded to *A Game at Chess* is not surprising; at the time of the scandal in August of 1624, he was eighteen years old and only a few years from seeing a play of his own produced. What is revealing in terms of Middleton's reputation is that D'Avenant would expect the members of his audience to remember the celebrated play in 1663, nearly forty years later.

In D'Avenant's *Play-House to be Let*, the playhouse is to be rented for the vacation, and an overwhelming number of performers respond.

[Tiring Woman] There's such a crowd at door, as if we had
A new Play of *Gundamar*.

The Play-House To Be Lett, in *The Works of Sr William Davenant K^t*. London: by T. N. for Henry Herringman, 1673, 2: 73.

37. 1670 A Jest in a Commonplace Book

The character of Simon, the Mayor of Quinborough, had become a part of seventeenth-century popular culture, or so it would seem when Henry Newcome, an Oxford student in his late teens or early twenties, enters a joke like this one into the humorous section at the back of his commonplace book some fifty years after the play's first production.

The Major of Quinborough (before his inchoation) read ye statutes, & amongst ye rest yt hee yt fired a Becon [beacon] should bee so punished, & hee reading false apprehanded ones, wm hee found frying Bacon.

Henry Newcome. Commonplace Book. Begun in Sept. 1669. Folger MS. V. a. 232, jest #146.

---

73. "Lewd" may have meant poor as well as its surviving sense of obscene.

38. 1675 Middleton Enters the Theatrical Histories

Edward Phillips, nephew of John Milton and tutor to John Evelyn's son, wrote poetry, novels, and history, as well as his *Theatrum Poetarum*, a collection of literary biographies. Like Pepys, Phillips is among the first generation of writers who would have known Middleton only from the Restoration revivals or the printed texts, because they were born a few years after his death and were still children when the theaters closed in 1642.

Tho. Middleton, a copious Writer for the English Stage, Contemporary with *Johnson* and *Fletcher*, though not of equal repute, and yet on the other side not altogether contemptible, especially in many of his Plays: his Comedies were *Blurt Mr Constable, the Chast Maid in Cheapside, More dissemblers then Women, the Game at Chesse*; *A mad World my Masters, Michaelmas Term*; *the Phœnix, A Trick to catch the old ones:* His Tragedies *The Mayor of Queenborough*, besides what he wrote associated with *W. Rowly*.

Edward Phillips, *Theatrum Poetarum, or a Compleat Collection of the Poets, Especially the Most Eminent, of All Ages*. London: for Charles Smith, 1675, p. 180.

39. 1687 The Historians Continue

William Winstanley was a barber who early turned to letters and is known primarily for his biographies in *The Lives of the Most Famous English Poets*. He has been accused of being a plagiarist — according to the peevish Anthony Wood, he continued to use his scissors when he took up the pen[74] — and it is true that when he writes of Middleton, he draws on Phillips; but he also supplements Phillips. (Many of the titles he lists, however, are slightly wrong.) This first critical response to *Michaelmas Term* indicates that the play was still valued some eighty years after its only known performances (c. 1605).

THomas Midleton was one who by his Industry added very much to the *English* Stage, being a copious Writer of Dramatick Poetry. He was Contemporary with *Johnson* and *Fletcher*, and tho' not of equal Repute with them, yet were well accepted of those times such Plays as he wrote; namely, *Blurt Mr. Constable, the chaste Maid in* Cheapside, *Your fine Gallants*,

74. See Winstanley's entry in the *Dictionary of National Biography*.

Family of Love, More Dissemblers than Women, the *Game at Chess*, the *Mayor of* Quinborough, *a mad world my Masters, Michaelmas Term, No Wit like a womans*, the *Roaring Girl, any thing for a quiet Life*, the *Phenix* and *a new Trick to catch the old one*, Comedies; *The world toss'd at Tennis*, and *the Inner Temple*, Masques; and *Women beware Women*, a Tragedy. Besides what, he was an Associate with *William Rowley* in several Comedies and Tragi-Comedies; as, *the Spanish Gypsies, the Changling, the Old Law, the fair Quarrel, the Widow*: Of all which, his *Michaelmas-Term* is highly applauded both for the plot and neatness of the style.

William Winstanley, *The Lives of the Most Famous English Poets, or the Honour of Parnassus*. London: for Samuel Manship, 1687. Reprint. Gainesville, Florida: Scholars' Facsimiles and Reprints, 1963, pp. 135-36.

40. 1688   Gerard Langbaine on Plagiarists

Gerard Langbaine loved theater. He says in this preface to *Momus Triumphans; or, The Plagiaries of the English Stage* that he not only has seen as many plays as possible, but he also owns over 980 English plays and masques, and has read most of them. In *Momus Triumphans*, his intention is less to indict plagiarists than to point out indebtedness in a scholarly way. He would prefer that borrowers acknowledge their debts to writers like Middleton, who are no longer as well known as Shakespeare and Fletcher.

'Tis true indeed, what is borrow'd from Shakspeare *or* Fletcher, *is usually own'd by our Poets, because every one would be able to convict them of Theft, should they endeavour to conceal it. But in what has been stolen from Authors not so generally known, as* Murston, Middleton, Massenger, &c. *we find our Poets playing the parts of* Bathyllus *to* Virgil, *and robbing them of that Fame, which is as justly their due, as the Reward the Emperour* Augustus *had promised to the Author of that known* Distich *affixed on the Court Gate, was to* Virgil.[75]

"Preface," *Momus Triumphans; or, The Plagiaries of the English Stage*. London: for Nicholas Cox, 1688, sig. [a3r].

75. The plagiarism and Virgil's retaliation are recounted in "Virgils Life, Set Foorth, as It Is Supposed, by Aelius Donatus, and Done into English," in *The Whole. XII. Bookes of the AEneidos . . . Newly Set Forth, by Thomas Twyne, Gentleman*, sig. ☾iiiᵛ.

41. 1691 Langbaine: Middleton in the Second Rank

Gerard Langbaine used his fine library and the work of Phillips and Winstanley to produce *An Account of the English Dramatick Poets*, a collection of critical reviews with bibliographical citations. Because he owned a copy of *The Widow* that attributed it to Middleton, Jonson, and Fletcher, he assumed they had been friends and congenial colleagues; and since Langbaine was often consulted by later compilers, Middleton's connection with Jonson and Fletcher became one of the few personal "facts" the eighteenth-century historians knew.

Langbaine's bibliographical citations, which were in most cases transcribed from the title pages of the published texts, are omitted here, but the sections relevant to reception are included.

Thomas MIDDLETON.

An Author of good Esteem in the Reign of King *Charles* the First. He was Contemporary with those Famous Poets *Johnson, Fletcher, Massinger* and *Rowley*, in whose Friendship he had a large Share; and tho' he came short of the two former in parts, yet like the *Ivy* by the Assistance of the *Oak*, (being joyn'd with them in several Plays) he clim'd up to some considerable height of Reputation. He joyn'd with *Fletcher* and *Johnson*, in a Play called *The Widow*, of which we have already spoken . . .; and certainly most Men will allow, That he that was thought fit to be receiv'd into a *Triumvirate*, by two such Great Men, was no common Poet. He club'd with *Massinger* and *Rowley* in Writing the *Old Law*, as before I have remarked already. . . . He was likewise assisted by *Rowley* in three Plays, of which we shall presently give an Account; and in those Plays which he writ alone, there are several Comedies; as *Michaelmass-Term, Mayor of Quinborough, &c.* which speak him a Dramatick Poet of the Second Rank. [Here Langbaine begins his bibliography.]

[*Anything for a Quiet Life*] This Play being One of those Manuscripts published by *Kirkman*, I suppose was in Esteem on the Stage, before the Breaking out of the Civil Wars.

[*Blurt, Master Constable*] There is no Name affix'd to this Play, and several others, which are ascribed to our Author by Mr. *Kirkman;* as *The Phœnix, Game at Chess,* and *The Family of Love;* but knowing his Acquaintance with Plays to have been very considerable, I have plac'd them to their Reputed Author.

[*The Family of Love*] This Play is mentioned by Sir *Thomas Bornwel*, in *The Lady of Pleasure*, Act I. Sc. I.[76]

[*A Trick to Catch the Old One*] This is an Excellent Old Play.

[*The Triumphs of Love and Antiquity*, listed by its full title] This Piece consists only of Speeches, addrest to his Lordship, at his *Cavalcade* thro' the City, and I think no ways deserv'd either the Title of a *Masque*, under which Species it has been hitherto rank'd; nor so pompous a Title, as the Author has prefix'd.

[*Women Beware Women*] This *Drama*, if we give Credit to Mr. *Richards*, a Poet of that Age, was acted with extraordinary applause, as he says in his Verses on that Play:

> *I that have seen't, can say, having just cause,*
> *Ne're Tragedy came off with more Applause.*

[*A Mad World, My Masters*] This Play was writ twenty Years before 'twas publish'd, as the *Printer* and *Stationer* inform the *Reader;* and appeared with Applause on the Stage. The Language and Plot of this Comedy are very diverting; and the former is so little obsolete, that Mrs. *Behn* has transplanted part of it into her *City Heiress*.

An Account of the English Dramatick Poets. Oxford: by L. L. for G. West and H. Clements, 1691, sigs. Aa^v-Aa4^r, Oo2^v.

42. 1708 A Former Prompter Remembers *The Changeling*

When *The Changeling* was revived on the early Restoration stage, to Pepys's enjoyment, John Downes was a prompter and keeper of books for D'Avenant's Duke's Servants. In fact, he continued as a prompter until just a few years before he published his information and reminiscences in 1708 as *Roscius Anglicanus, or an Historical Review of the Stage.* He reminds eighteenth-century readers that Thomas Betterton and Thomas Sheppy had become famous for their roles in *The Changeling*. (One wonders whether Massinger's friend would have been happy to see *The Bondman* still coupled with a Middleton play. See entry 12.)

76. The reference in *The Lady of Pleasure* is to Shirley's *The Ball*.

*M*r. *Betterton*, being then but 22 Years Old, was highly Applauded for his Acting in all these Plays, but especially, For the Loyal Subject; The *Mad Lover*; *Pericles*; The Bondman: *Deflores*, in the Changling; his Voice being then as Audibly strong, full and Articulate, as in the Prime of his Acting.

*M*r. *Sheppy* Perform'd *Theodore* in the Loyal Subject; Duke *Altophil*, in the Unfortunate Lovers; *Asotus*, in the Bondman, and several other Parts very well; But above all the Changling, with general Satisfaction.

John Downes, *Roscius Anglicanus, or an Historical Review of the Stage*. London: H. Playford, 1708, pp. 18-19.

43. 1719 A Follower of Langbaine

Giles Jacob trained in law, and most of his published works are law compilations, although twice he did try his hand at drama. He confesses in his preface to *The Poetical Register* that he has drawn on Langbaine; in fact, his entry is largely an abridgment. Jacob demonstrates the extent to which, through Langbaine, Middleton came to be seen primarily in relation to Jonson and Fletcher.

*M*r. THOMAS MIDDLETON.

A POET in the Reign of King *Charles* I. He was Contemporary with *Ben Johnson, Fletcher, Massinger*, &c. by the two first of which he was thought fit to be receiv'd into a Triumvirate in the Writing of Plays, which shew'd him to be no mean Poet; and tho' he fell short of those celebrated Writers, yet by their Assistance, he attain'd a pretty considerable Reputation. [Here begins the list of works.]

G[iles] J[acob], *The Poetical Register: Or, The Lives and Characters of the English Dramatick Poets*. London: for E. Curll, 1719, pp. 181-82.

44. 1747 Langbaine's Influence Continues

Seventeen years after Thomas Whincop's death, his widow Martha obtained subscribers and published his tragedy, *Scanderbeg*, with a list of dramatic biographies. (In her research, Whincop was assisted by John Mottley, who is believed responsible only for a few of the modern descriptions, including his own.) Whincop's Middleton biography draws again on Langbaine, likely by way of Jacob, and perhaps on Phillips. Although her publication indicates that at least one woman was studying the early modern playwrights, it unfortunately tells us nothing of what she read or of her personal reactions.

Mr. THOMAS MIDDLETON.

Our Author, who lived in the Reign of King *Charles* I. and was Contemporary with *Ben Johnson* and *Fletcher*, with whom he joined in writing several Plays, which shews he was not contemptibly thought of. He also joined with *Philip Massinger* in the same Business. [Here begins the list of plays.]

Thomas Whincop, *Scanderbeg: Or, Love and Liberty. A Tragedy. To Which Are Added a List of All the Dramatic Authors, with Some Account of Their Lives; And of All the Dramatic Pieces Ever Published in the English Language, to the Year 1747.* London: for W. Reeve, 1747, pp. 131-32.

45. 1750 The Infamous W. R. Chetwood

William Rufus Chetwood, a prompter at Drury Lane theater and later a Dublin dramatist and bookseller, spent many years in debtors' prisons and often wrote there. Sometimes he simply made up facts for his biographies, a few of which, like his Shakespeare in *The British Theatre* and his Middleton here, seem pleasantly fanciful now that they no longer confuse. In this note prefixed to an edition of *Blurt, Master Constable*, Chetwood is either deceived or deceiving about Middleton's longevity; then he incorporates his vision of the aged Middleton into verses he attributes to dramatist William Lower, verses meant to illustrate to eighteenth-century readers the high esteem in which Middleton's "brother poets" held him. There is no record of a 1663 edition of *Michaelmas Term*, and Lower died in 1662.

MR. *THOMAS MIDDLETON*, the author of the following comedy, was born in the reign of queen *Elizabeth*, and lived to a very great age, cotemporary with *Shakespear, Beaumont, Fletcher, Massenger, Haywood*, &c. We may judge of his *longaevity*, by his works; since his first play was acted in 1601, and his last in 1665. He was one of the earliest poets that gave us comedy unmix'd with tragedy, and author of twenty three dramatick pieces.

That he was much esteem'd by his brother poets, we may judge by four lines of sir *William Lower* upon his comedy, call'd, *A Michaelmas Term*, 1663.

> *Tom Middleton*, his numerous issue brings,
> And his last *muse* delights us when she sings:
> His halting age, a pleasure doth impart;
> And his white locks, shews *master* of his *art*.

W[illiam] R[ufus] Chetwood, "An Account of the Author," prefixed to *Blurt, Master Constable*, in his edition of *A Select Collection of Old Plays*. Dublin: by the Editor, 1750, sig. A6ʳ.

46. 1753 Theophilus Cibber and Robert Shiels

The Lives of the Poets of Great Britain and Ireland, a volume of literary biographies that appeared under Theophilus Cibber's name, was actually researched and written by Robert Shiels, Scottish amanuensis to Dr. Johnson, and rewritten and corrected by Cibber, an actor and playwright famous for his stage roles and notorious for his off-stage behavior. The Middleton entry is based again on Langbaine and suggests the difficulties of finding information on a writer like Middleton.

Thomas Middleton
Lived in the reign of King Charles I. he was cotemporary with Johnson, Fletcher, Massinger and Rowley, in whose friendship he is said to have shared, and though he fell much short of the two former, yet being joined with them in writing plays, he arrived at some reputation. He joined with Fletcher and Johnson in a play called The Widow, and the highest honour that is known of this poet, is, his being admitted to make a triumvirate with two such great men: he joined with Massinger and Rowley in writing the Old Law; he was likewise assisted by Rowley in writing three plays. We have not been able to find any particulars of this man's life, further than his friendship and connection already mentioned, owing to his obscurity, as he was never considered as a genius, concerning which the world thought themselves interested to preserve any particulars. [Here follows the list of plays.]

[Theophilus] Cibber, *The Lives of the Poets of Great Britain and Ireland, to the Time of Dean Swift*. London: for R. Griffiths, 1753, I: 352-54.

47. 1764 Early Romanticism: "Considerable Genius"

David Erskine Baker was the grandson of Daniel Defoe and a published translator in his teens. His father had expected him to pursue science, but Baker instead turned to acting and to compiling *The Companion to the Play-House*, a reference guide to the theater. Baker draws on various sources, including Chetwood, Cibber, and especially Langbaine, whose enthusiasm for theater he shares. Baker's interest lies in Middleton's reception: Middleton seems to have been well known as a result of his collaborations, Baker says, but little regarded for his individual efforts, which was a mistake, since his collaborators would not have worked with him had he not been a fine writer. In Baker's use of language and his sense of Middleton's "considerable Genius," he foreshadows the Romantic response. Included here are the sections that indicate evaluations of Middleton and the plays.

MIDDLETON, Mr. *Thomas*, was a very voluminous Writer, and lived so late as the Time of *Charles* I. yet I can meet with very few Particulars relating to him; for, notwithstanding that he has certainly shewn considerable Genius in those Plays, which are unquestionably all his own, and which are very numerous, yet he seems in his Life-Time to have owed the greatest Part of the Reputation he acquired, to his Connection with *Jonson*, *Fletcher*, *Massinger* and *Rowley*, with whom he was concerned in the writing of several dramatic Pieces, but to have been consider'd in himself as a Genius of a very inferior Class, and concerning whom the World was not greatly interested in the pursuing any Memoirs. — Yet, surely it is a Proof of Merit sufficient to establish him in a Rank far from the most contemptible among our dramatic Writers, that a Set of Men of such acknowledged Abilities consider'd him as deserving to be admitted a joint Labourer with them in the Fields of poetical Fame; and more especially by *Fletcher* and *Jonson*, the first of whom, like a Widow'd Muse, could not be supposed readily to admit another Partner after the Loss of his long and well-beloved Mate *Beaumont*; and the latter, who entertained so high an Opinion of his own Talents as scarcely to admit any Brother near the Throne, and would hardly have permitted the clear Waters of his own *Heliconian* Springs to have been muddied by the Mixture of any Streams, that did not apparently flow from the same Source, and, however narrow their Currents, were not the genuine Produce of *Parnassus*. [Here follows Baker's list of plays.]

[*Anything for a Quiet Life*, confused with *A Game at Chess*] It was printed before, under the Title of *A Game at Chess*. — It was often performed with great Applause; and, by it's being one of the Manuscripts published by *Kirkman*, it is probable that it was in Esteem on the Stage before the breaking out of the civil Wars.

[*The Changeling*] *Rowley* join'd with our Author in this Play, which met with very great Success.

[*A Mad World, My Masters*] This is a very good Play, and has been since borrowed from by many Writers; particularly by Mrs. *Behn* in her *City Heiress*, and by *C. Johnson* in his *Country Lasses*.

[*Michaelmas Term*] This Play was sundry Times acted.

[*The Phoenix*] This is a good Play.

[*A Trick to Catch the Old One*] This is an excellent old Play, and appears to have been greatly in vogue at the Time it was written.

[*Women Beware Women*] How high a Rank of Estimation this Piece stood in with the Public at its first coming out, may be gather'd from the Words of Mr. *Richards*, a Cotemporary Poet, who closes a Copy of Verses in Praise of it, with these Words, "*Ne'er Tragedy came off with more Applause.*"

[David Erskine Baker,] *The Companion to the Play-House: Or, An Historical Account of All the Dramatic Writers (and Their Works) That Have Appeared in Great Britain and Ireland, from the Commencement of Our Theatrical Exhibitions, Down to the Present Year 1764.* London: for T. Becket, *et al.*, 1764, II: X6ᵛ; I: B6ᵛ, D4ʳ, N2ᵛ, O3ʳ, Q5ʳ, Y5ᵛ, Bb1ᵛ.

48. 1778 *Macbeth* and *The Witch*

The publication in 1778 of the rediscovered *Witch* manuscript, with its full versions of the songs in *Macbeth*, would raise the question of whether Shakespeare or Middleton had written the witch passages in *Macbeth*. For decades afterwards, many pieces written about Middleton would result from interest in Shakespeare and this controversy.

This comment by Edmond Malone is the first on the issue and appeared in the prefatory materials to George Steevens's edition of Shakespeare; it gives some sense of the tone of what is coming later. Steevens, whose accompanying notes follow Malone's comments, had just discovered the manuscript of *The Witch* that would soon be privately printed for Isaac Reed.

Mr. Steevens has lately discovered a Ms. play, entitled THE WITCH, written by Thomas Middleton, which renders it questionable, whether Shakspeare was not indebted to that author for the first hint of the magic introduced in this tragedy. The reader will find an account of this singular curiosity in the note[a]. — To the observations of Mr. Steevens I have only to add, that the songs, beginning, *Come away*, &c. and *Black spirits*, &c. being found at full length in *The Witch*, while only the two first words of them are printed in *Macbeth*, favour the supposition that Middleton's piece preceded that of Shakspeare; the latter, it should seem, thinking it unnecessary to set down verses which were probably well known, and perhaps then in the possession of the managers of the Globe theatre. The high reputation of Shakspeare's performances (to mention a circumstance which in the course of these observations will be more than once insisted upon) likewise strengthens this conjecture; for it is very improbable, that Middleton, or any other poet of that time, should have ventured into those regions of fiction, in which our author had *already* expatiated:

— "Shakespeare's magick could not *copy'd* be,
Within that circle none durst walk but he."[77]

[a][Steevens discusses parallels between *The Witch* and *Macbeth*, then goes on to the question of originality.]

From the instances already produced, perhaps the reader would allow, that if *Middleton*'s piece preceded *Shakespeare*'s, the originality of the magic introduced by the latter, might be fairly questioned; for our author (who as actor, and manager, had access to unpublished dramatic performances) has so often condescended to receive hints from his contemporaries, that our suspicion of his having been a copyist in the present instance, might not be without foundation. . . . I must observe at the same time, that *Middleton*, in his other dramas, is found to have borrowed little from the sentiments, and nothing from the fables of his predecessors. He is known to have written in concert with *Jonson*, *Fletcher*, *Massinger*, and *Rowley*; but appears to have been unacquainted, or at least unconnected, with *Shakespeare*.

[Steevens speculates about *The Witch*'s date of composition and James I's response to the witches in the two plays.] The witches of *Shakespeare* (exclusive of the flattering circumstance to which their prophecy alludes) are solemn in their operations, and therefore behaved in conformity to his majesty's own opinions. On the contrary, the hags of *Middleton* are ludicrous in their conduct, and lessen, by ridiculous combinations of images, the solemnity of that magic in which our scepter'd persecutor of old women most reverently and potently believed.

---

77. Malone changed his mind and argued in a revision of this essay that *The Witch* was written after *Macbeth*. See *The Life of William Shakspeare*, 420-440.

[Steevens lastly argues that William D'Avenant's additions to *Macbeth* are plagiarized from Middleton, as will be clear when *The Witch* is published.]

Edmond Malone, "An Attempt to Ascertain the Order in Which the Plays Attributed to Shakespeare Were Written," in *The Plays of William Shakespeare. . . To Which Are Added Notes by Samuel Johnson and George Steevens.* Edited by George Steevens. 2nd. ed, rev. and aug. London: for C. Bathurst, *et al.*, 1778, I: [324-330].

49. 1779 Middleton as a Way to Understand Shakespeare

Edward Capell was a Shakespeare editor and commentator who, like Steevens, read Middleton to better understand Shakespeare in the context of his time. *The School of Shakespeare* is a collection of bibliographical citations and brief extracts from the works of Shakespeare's contemporaries. In his selections, Capell emphasizes Middleton's comedies, as he does in this brief evaluation, which occurs with the selections from *Anything for a Quiet Life*.

The author of this play was no mean comick genius; and has left us a number of plays, some of which (as title-pages and catalogues tell us) were written in conjunction with other poets, as — *Fletcher, Jonson, Massinger*, and *Rowley.* One of his plays, "*A Game at Chess*," cost him his liberty: as appears from the following anecdote, enter'd upon the first blank leaf of a copy of that play, in a hand seemingly of the same age with it. [Here follow the note and poem from entry 23.]

[Edward Capell,] *The School of Shakespeare: Or, Authentic Extracts from Divers English Books, That . . . Contribute to a Due Understanding of His Writings, or Give Light to the History of His Life, or to the Dramatic History of His Time.* Vol. 3 of *Notes and Various Readings to Shakespeare.* London: by Henry Hughs, for the Author, [1779], pp. 30-31.

50. 1784 Richardson, Young, and Hayley

William Hayley was a poet and playwright whose friends describe in glowing terms his temperament and his goodness. There is no hint that he could perpetrate the slightest fraud. Yet when his *Marcella*, an adaptation of *The Changeling*, was published, he went to some lengths to disguise the degree of his indebtedness.

In the preface to *Plays of Three Acts*, which contains three of his comedies and two of his tragedies, he says "I am not conscious of having borrowed a single character or situation from any comic writer whatever, either foreign or domestic" (p. xi), somewhat disingenuously forgetting to acknowledge how much he has borrowed from a tragic writer. Then, in the preface to *Marcella* cited here, he explains how the plot came to him — in a sketch from Samuel Richardson, to Edward Young, to Young's son, and through a neighbor to Hayley — all of which may be true. Richardson probably had thought well of the morality in the main plot of *The Changeling* and encouraged his friend Young to make a play of it. But Hayley's play, though devoid of Middleton's complexity, parallels *The Changeling* closely enough to make it likely that Hayley worked directly from the play.[78] His verses offer fitting clues to the kinds of alterations he made.

THE following Tragedy may perhaps attract the notice of the curious reader, more by a literary anecdote relating to its subject, than by any intrinsic merit as a dramatic composition.

The story was recommended to YOUNG by the Author of Clarissa. — The poet adopted it, and wrote a single act; but this shared the fate of his other unfinished manuscripts, and, according to the direction of his will, was committed to the flames.

These particulars, with a concise sketch of the story as related by RICHARDSON, were communicated to Mr. THORNTON by the poet's very liberal and amiable Son, the neighbour and the much-esteemed relation of my dear departed friend, who wished me to build a tragedy upon this foundation.

Some particular circumstances prevented me at that time from executing the desire of a person, who, from the integrity of his judgment, and the uncommon warmth of his friendship, had an undisputed title to influence my studies. — Other works had engaged me, and this dramatic story lay for some years neglected: but in looking over the letters of my still-valued, though lost correspondent, it struck me with new force. As the distress, with which it abounds, is of a private nature, it appeared to me singularly calculated for my purpose of forming a drama for a domestic theatre. I have therefore, with some considerable alterations in the principal incident, raised from it a tragedy of three acts; with what success, it is now the privilege of my readers to pronounce.

I will not attempt to influence their decision by any arguments in its behalf; but let me be allowed to close this short preface with a little poetical

78. See Marston Stevens Balch, "The Dramatic Legacy of Thomas Middleton," chapter 9.

acknowledgment to the two literary illustrious friends, who first marked the story for the tragic Muse, and from whom it has accidentally descended to me.

SONNET.

BLEST Authors! with whose fame the world has rung,
Immortal minds, of philanthropic mold!
Pathetic RICHARDSON! sublimer YOUNG!
To you let me inscribe the leaves, that hold
A theme, ye once consulted to unfold!
Fairer its fortune, had not death's despite
Torn from the silenc'd bard this tale half-told!
O could I blend those beams, whose sep'rate light
Forms each a glory round your rival brows,
Sublimity and Pathos! effluence bright
Of highest genius! — but in vain such vows:
Yet in the reach of emulation's flight
One eminence ye share: — be that my end!
Teach me to rank with you, as Virtue's friend!

William Hayley, Preface to *Marcella*, in *Plays of Three Acts; Written for a Private Theatre*. London: for T. Cadell, 1784, pp. [95-97].

51. 1789 An Adaptation Fails and Succeeds

In November of 1789, William Hayley's *Marcella*, an adaptation of *The Changeling*, played at Drury Lane and Covent Garden in the same week, failing at the former, where it had opened without sufficient rehearsal, and succeeding at the latter. In this letter to his wife Eliza, Hayley describes his experience.

BARNARD'S-INN, Saturday, *November* 15, 1789.
Here I am at last; and I thank you for the kind and comfortable letter I found on my arrival. A severe inflammation of the eyes, united to some disagreeable dramatic news, from Drury-Lane, prevented my setting forth till yesterday. Never was any thing more strange or illiberal, than the conduct of the Drury managers, respecting my poor *Marcella*. They seem to have played it only on a few hours' preparation, to get the start of [Thomas] Harris, and prevent his success by having the play damned in their own theatre. Long and Romney, who were at Drury-Lane on the Saturday, say,

nothing could be more infamous than their mode of exhibiting the piece: but on the Tuesday following, as you have seen in the papers, *Marcella*, in spite of her premature supposed death, revived and triumphed at Covent-Garden. On my arrival last night, I was hurried, perforce, to the theatre, and saw my dwarfish tragedy played indeed most admirably, but to a house rather thin; it was received, however, with unchequered applause; and will be occasionally repeated; but, as I told Harris this morning, it is not calculated to be a popular play. He is very angry at the base treatment he received from the rival house, and the more so, as [Richard Brinsley] Sheridan had promised, when he applied to him on the subject, that he would prevent the unworthy manœuvre he apprehended.

So much for dramatic matters, in which you know, I have had *twenty years' seasoning*, to make me a *sound philosopher;* and, in truth, no events of this kind can wound me deeply.

William Hayley, *Memoirs of the Life and Writings of William Hayley, Esq.* Ed. John Johnson. London: for Henry Colburn, *et al.*, 1823, I: 398-399.

52. 1800 Charles Dibdin: Dramatist and Musician

By the time *A Complete History of the English Stage* appeared, Charles Dibdin had been involved with the theater for forty years as singer, actor, dramatist, and songwriter; in fact, the five-volume work had to be written in short sections while he was composing theatrical sketches and travelling in Scotland. Dibdin uses the works of his predecessors thoughtfully, sometimes correcting their errors of fact; he provides personal responses to what he has read, and admits he enjoys *A Mad World, My Masters* even if it is not "correctly chaste."

To MIDDLETON very little more has been attributed but that he wrote in conjunction at times with JONSON, FLETCHER, MASSINGER, and others; and this has been quoted as a proof that he could not be destitute of merit. A better proof, however, are his own plays, some of which are now in print and well known; among these are *A Mad World my Masters*, *The Mayor of Queenborough*, &c. and they rank his reputation about on a par with DECKER'S.

The Old Law, a comedy brought out in 1656, is by no means a good play, though parts of it are admirable. MASSINGER was here assisted by MIDDLETON and ROWLEY. Perhaps it would have been better if he had been let alone; certainly neither of these writers was by any means equal to MASSINGER.

MIDDLETON, who produced one play in the reign of ELIZABETH, wrote sixteen dramatic productions afterwards, and in six more he was concerned with JONSON, FLETCHER, ROWLEY, and others.

The *Phœnix*, a tragi-comedy, performed in 1607, is well spoken of. The plot is taken from a Spanish novel called The *Force of Love*. *Michaelmas Term* is a mere undigested sketch. *Your Five Gallants* was printed, but probably never performed. The *Family of Love*. All we know of this play is that SHIRLEY makes one of his characters speak of it in his *Lady of Pleasure*.[79] *A Trick to Cheat the Old One*, performed in 1608. This comedy was a great favourite when it first came out, and is esteemed, among those who are in possession of old plays, as a piece of considerable merit.

A Mad World my Masters, performed in 1608, was also a popular play. It is certainly a strange thing but it has a great deal of whim and humour of that broad latitude that, though it may not be correctly chaste, is, nevertheless, provokingly laughable. Mrs. BEHN, however, had no objection to this rich vein of humour, and has borrowed some of the most luscious parts of it for her *City Heiress*, and CHARLES JOHNSON, who, however, was contented with that part which was less offensive, availed himself of a part of the plot for his *Country Lasses*. Other authors have also gone to this source for materials.

The *Inner Temple Masque*, was one of those temporary things which were at that time performed upon some public occasion. It has been supposed to have furnished the hint of *Comus*, how truly it is difficult to say.

The *Game of Chess*. This was any thing you please but a play. It was symbolical of a dispute between the Church of ENGLAND and the Church of ROME, wherein, of course, the former was conqueror. It was a stupid impolitic business, and ended, though in other respects it was very successful, in the author's losing the game, for he was sent to prison.[a]

A Chaste Maid in Cheapside, appeared and was soon forgotten. *No Wit, no Help like a Woman's* is a play of which there is no trace but the title. *Woman beware Woman*. This is a tragedy, and has for its date 1657, which is eight years after the Restoration. It must, however, have been originally performed in 1630 at latest, and it was probably, revived 1657 by sir WILLIAM DAVENANT, whose restoration of the stage has no doubt caused so many mistakes, his copies only being extant which writers have taken for

---

79. The reference in *The Lady of Pleasure* is not to *The Family of Love*, but to Shirley's *The Ball*.

originals. At this time it was known and greatly received. What was its original success cannot be known.[b]

More dissemblers besides Women. This play is extant but no author pretends to say any thing about its success. *Any thing for a quiet Life.* From this play, of which we know nothing but that it was printed in 1662, I shall take a hint and content myself once for all with setting down dates, and leaving the reader to consider of the probability of whether the plays they are prefixed to were originally performed at that time or not.

[Dibdin continues to discuss the difficulty of dates, and asks that he be "acquitted of intentional error whenever I set down any thing that nobody can possibly believe, such as that MIDDLETON produced one play in the forty-third year of ELIZABETH's reign, and another in the fourteenth year of the reign of CHARLES the second."[80] He reminds readers, using Langbaine as an authority, that Middleton was contemporary with Shakespeare, not Dryden.]

The pieces in which MIDDLETON was joined by other writers are The *Roaring Girl,* The *Fair Quarrel,* The *Widow,* The *Changling,* The *Spanish Gipsey,* and The *Old Law;* all which, except the *Changling,* which we are told met with considerable applause, are very little spoken of by the various writers on the drama.

There are other things attributed to MIDDLETON, but with nothing like certainty, and in particular that in a piece, called The *Witch,* he furnished SHAKESPEAR with the hint of his witches in *Macbeth;* but when we recollect how very poorly JONSON imitated them, we can hardly suppose our great poet, in his own particular province, where he upon every occasion so completely left all the world behind him, stood in need of a cue from MIDDLETON; who, though he was a respectable writer, and made no mean stand as a dramatist, had nothing in his genius that could furnish instruction to SHAKESPEAR.

[a] [Dibdin reprints the note and poem that are entry 23.]

[b] RICHARDS, a writer in the reign of CHARLES the second, speaks in the highest terms, but in curious language by the bye, of this play in a poem he had written expressly to praise it. He finishes thus:

> I that have seen't, can say, having just cause,
> Ne'er tragedy came off with more applause.

Now, though this is bad poetry, it may be good truth, and if literally so, this

80. Chetwood's "facts" in *The British Theatre,* 32.

play must have been popular, for he does not pledge himself, but the audience.

[Charles] Dibdin, *A Complete History of the English Stage*. London: for the Author, [1800], 3: 112, 241, 265-70.

53. 1804 Walter Scott's Knowledge and Response

As a child, Sir Walter Scott loved Shakespeare, as he loved hearing the stories of his own family history, which was closely tied to the Stuart cause. Scott's notes to *Sir Tristrem* reveal that by his thirties he had read some Middleton as well, and been impressed by *The Changeling*. In addition to the notes below, he quotes *The Roaring Girl* to clarify the meaning of *umbles* (p. 262).

[Scott is discussing the ingredients used in witches' potions and quotes *The Witch* 1.2.204-212 and 2.2.27-31.] This curious old play afforded the songs and choruses for Macbeth. It only existed in MS., till Mr Read printed a few copies for the use of his friends.

The barbarous ingratitude of the queen of Cornwal resembles that of the heroine in Middleton's *Changeling*, an old play, which contains some passages horribly striking.

Sir Tristrem; A Metrical Romance of the Thirteenth Century. Ed. Walter Scott. Edinburgh: James Ballantyne, for Archibald Constable and Longman and Rees, 1804, pp. 294, 300.

54. 1805 A Note of Praise from William Gifford

Poet, editor, and critic William Gifford was older and more conservative than most of the Romantics and antagonistic to what he saw as Romantic radicalism. He shared with the Romantics, however, an enthusiasm for the Elizabethan dramatists. In his introduction to *The Plays of Philip Massinger*, he comments on Middleton's power.

The Old Law, which was not printed till many years after Massinger's death, is said to have been written by him in conjunction with Middleton and Rowley. The latter of these is ranked by the Author of *the Companion to the Play House*, in the third class of dramatick writers; higher it is impossible to

place him: but the former was a man of considerable powers, who has lately
been the object of much discussion, on account of the liberal use Shakspeare
is supposed to have made of his recently discovered tragi-comedy of *the
Witch.*

"Introduction." *The Plays of Philip Massinger.* Vol. 1. London: G. and W. Nicol,
et al., 1805, xxi-xxii.

55. 1808 Charles Lamb: An Energizing Voice

Appreciation of the early dramatists was already on the increase when
Charles Lamb published *Specimens of English Dramatic Poets*; at least the
plays were being made available and thus were being read again. But
Lamb's excerpts and ardent commentary energized that movement. Lamb
saw the plays as living literature, not simply "old plays," and he made
Middleton and Middleton's contemporaries relevant to a literary generation
inspired by the American and French Revolutions and impatient with the
limits of rationality and analysis. The excerpts are omitted here.

[On *A Fair Quarrel*] The insipid levelling morality to which the modern
stage is tied down would not admit of such admirable passions as these
scenes are filled with. A puritanical obtuseness of sentiment, a stupid
infantile goodness, is creeping among us, instead of the vigorous passions,
and virtues clad in flesh and blood, with which the old dramatists present us.
Those noble and liberal casuists could discern in the differences, the
quarrels, the animosities of man, a beauty and truth of moral feeling, no less
than in the iterately inculcated duties of forgiveness and atonement. With us
all is hypocritical meekness. A reconciliation scene (let the occasion be
never so absurd or unnatural) is always sure of applause. Our audiences
come to the theatre to be complimented on their goodness. They compare
notes with the amiable characters in the play, and find a wonderful similarity
of disposition between them. We have a common stock of dramatic morality
out of which a writer may be supplied without the trouble of copying it from
originals within his own breast. To know the boundaries of honor, to be
judiciously valiant, to have a temperance which shall beget a smoothness in
the angry swellings of youth, to esteem life as nothing when the sacred
reputation of a parent is to be defended, yet to shake and tremble under a
pious cowardice when that 'ark of an honest confidence is found to be frail
and tottering, to feel the true blows of a real disgrace blunting that sword
which the imaginary strokes of a supposed false imputation had put so keen

an edge upon but lately: to do, or to imagine this done in a feigned story, asks something more of a moral sense, somewhat a greater delicacy of perception in questions of right and wrong, than goes to the writing of two or three hackneyed sentences about the laws of honor as opposed to the laws of the land, or a common place against duelling. Yet such things would stand a writer now a days in far better stead than Captain Ager and his conscientious honor; and he would be considered a far better teacher of morality than old Rowley or Middleton if they were living.

[On *Women Beware Women*'s chess game] This is one of those scenes which has the air of being an immediate transcript from life. Livia the "good neighbour" is as real a creature as one of Chaucer's characters. She is such another jolly Housewife as the Wife of Bath.

[On *The Witch*] Though some resemblance may be traced between the Charms in Macbeth, and the Incantations in this Play, which is supposed to have preceded it, this coincidence will not detract much from the originality of Shakspeare. His Witches are distinguished from the Witches of Middleton by essential differences. These are creatures to whom man or woman plotting some dire mischief might resort for occasional consultation. Those originate deeds of blood, and begin bad impulses to men. From the moment that their eyes first meet with Macbeth's, he is spell-bound. That meeting sways his destiny. He can never break the fascination. These Witches can hurt the body; those have power over the soul. — Hecate in Middleton has a Son, a low buffoon: the hags of Shakspeare have neither child of their own, nor seem to be descended from any parent. They are foul Anomalies, of whom we know not whence they are sprung, nor whether they have beginning or ending. As they are without human passions, so they seem to be without human relations. They come with thunder and lightning, and vanish to airy music. This is all we know of them. — Except Hecate, they have no names; which heightens their mysteriousness. The names, and some of the properties, which Middleton has given to his Hags, excite smiles. The Weird Sisters are serious things. Their presence cannot co-exist with mirth. But, in a lesser degree, the Witches of Middleton are fine creations. Their power too is, in some measure, over the mind. They raise jars, jealousies, strifes, *like a thick scurf o' er life.*

[On *The Old Law*] There is an exquisiteness of moral sensibility, making one to gush out tears of delight, and a poetical strangeness in all the improbable circumstances of this wild play, which are unlike any thing in the dramas which Massinger wrote alone. The pathos is of a subtler edge.

Middleton and Rowley, who assisted in this play, had both of them finer geniuses than their associate.

Specimens of English Dramatic Poets, Who Lived About the Time of Shakspeare. London: for Longman, Hurst, Rees, and Orme, 1808, pp. 136, 155, 174, 453.

56. 1817 A Physician and Essayist Speaks

Nathan Drake was a practicing physician and a scholar. *Shakspeare and His Times*, his magnum opus, was very well reviewed, although its reputation has lessened over the years. Drake is most impressed with what he sees as the romantic in Middleton's works.

"If there be a class of writers, of which, above all others," observes Mr. Gilchrist, "England may justly be proud, it is of those, for the stage, coeval with and immediately succeeding Shakspeare;"[81] an observation which the names alone of Fletcher and Massinger would sufficiently justify; but when to these we are enabled to add such fellow-artists as Ford, Webster, Middleton, &c. we are astonished that even the talents of Shakspeare should, for so long a period, have eclipsed their fame.

[Here Drake discusses, in order of importance, Ford and Webster.]

Not less than twenty-four plays are ascribed to THOMAS MID-DLETON, of which, sixteen at least, appear to owe their existence entirely to himself: the rest are written in conjunction with Jonson, Fletcher, Massinger, Decker, and Rowley. Middleton, it is probable, began to compose for the stage shortly after Shakspeare, for one of his pieces was *published* as early as 1602, and eight had passed the press before 1612. His talents were principally directed towards comedy, only two tragedies, *The Changeling*, and *Women beware Women*, and two tragi-comedies, *The Phœnix* and *The Witch*, being included in the list of his productions.

Humour, wit, and character, though in a degree inferior to that which distinguishes the preceding poets [Beaumont and Fletcher, Massinger, Ford, Webster], are to be found in the comedy of Middleton; and, occasionally, a pleasing interchange of elegant imagery and tender sentiment. His tragedy is not devoid of pathos, though possessing little dignity or elevation; but there is, in many of his plays, and especially in the tragi-comedy of *The Witch*, a strength and compass of imagination which entitle him to a very respectable rank among the cultivators of the *Romantic* drama.

81. Octavius Gilchrist, *A Letter to William Gifford, Esq.*, p. 7.

A more than common celebrity has attached itself to this last-named composition, in consequence of the conjecture of Mr. Steevens, that it preceded *Macbeth*, and afforded to Shakspeare the *prima stamina* of the supernatural machinery of that admirable play.[82] This may readily be granted, without aspersing the originality of the Bard of Avon; for if we except the mere idea of the introduction of such an agency into dramatic poetry, there is little beside a few verbal forms of incantation, and two or three metrical invocations, of singular notoriety perhaps at the period, which can be considered as betraying any marks of imitation. In every other respect, affinity or resemblance there is none; for the Witches of Middleton and of Shakspeare are beings essentially distinct both in origin and office. The former are creatures of flesh and blood, possessing power, indeed, to inflict disease, and to execute more than common mischief, but very subordinate instruments of evil, when compared with the spiritual essence and mysterious sublimity of the *Weird Sisters*, who are the authors not only of nameless deeds, but who are nameless themselves, who float upon the midnight storm, direct the elemental strife, and, more than this, who wield the passions and the thoughts of man.

The hags of Middleton are, however, drawn with a bold and creative pencil, and seem to take a middle station between the terrific sisterhood of Shakspeare, and the traditionary witch of the country-village. They are pictures full of fancy, but not kept sufficiently aloof from the ludicrous and familiar.

[Drake goes on to discuss Dekker, whom he sees as equal to Middleton in "dramatic merit," but of less "imagination" and "fancy."]

Nathan Drake. *Shakspeare and His Times.* Vol. 2. London: for T. Cadell and W. Davies, 1817, pp. 563-67.

57. 1819 Errors of the Past and a Distaste for Bawdry

Thomas Campbell was a popular poet who never quite fulfilled the promise that his contemporaries saw in him. Scott and others encouraged him in his project of collecting excerpts of the British poets, and Campbell devoted years to his seven-volume *Specimens of the British Poets*. In his essay on Middleton, he uncritically accepts eighteenth-century "facts" from Chetwood and scorns Middleton's urban comedies. His excerpts, with titles like "Fathers Comparing Sons. Benefit of Imprisonment to a Wild Youth" and "Indignation at the Sale of a Wife's Honour," are excluded here.

82. See entry 48.

The dates of this author's birth and death are both unknown, though his living reputation, as the literary associate of Jonson, Fletcher, Massinger, Dekker, and Rowley, must have been considerable. If Oldys be correct,[83] he was alive after Nov. 1627. Middleton was appointed chronologer to the city of London in 1620, and in 1624 was cited before the privy council, as author of The Game of Chess. The verses of Sir W. Lower, quoted by Oldys, allude to the poet's white locks,[84] so that he was probably born as early as the middle of the 16th century. His tragicomedy, The Witch, according to Mr. Malone,[85] was written anterior to Macbeth, and suggested to Shakspeare the witchcraft scenery in the latter play. The songs beginning "Come away," &c. and "Black spirits," &c. of which only the two first words are printed in Macbeth, are found in the Witch. Independent of having afforded a hint to Shakspeare, Middleton's reputation cannot be rated highly for the pieces to which his name is exclusively attached. His principal efforts were in comedy, where he deals profusely in grossness and buffoonery. The cheats and debaucheries of the town are his favourite sources of comic intrigue. With a singular effort at the union of the sublime and familiar, he introduces, in one of his coarse drafts of London vice, an infernal spirit prompting a country gentleman to the seduction of a citizen's wife.

Thomas Campbell, *Specimens of the British Poets; With Biographical and Critical Notices, and an Essay on English Poetry.* London: John Murray, 1819, 3: 118-19.

58. 1819 William Hazlitt: Rebuilding the Temple of Fame

Until June or July of 1819, William Hazlitt had read little by Renaissance dramatists other than Shakespeare. He devoted that summer to a dozen volumes recommended by his friends Charles Lamb and Barry Cornwall. In November, he opened his third series of lectures for the Surrey Institution with tributes to those solid English geniuses who "sought for truth and nature, and found it in themselves" (p. 2) and discussed the playwrights' distinguishing characteristics — the "sweetness" of Dekker, the learning of Jonson, "the flowing vein of Middleton" (p. 14). In the second lecture, he provided a more specific introduction to Middleton.

. . . To these, however, might be added others not less learned, nor with a scarce less happy vein, but less fortunate in the event, who, though as

---

83. In his manuscript notes on Langbaine in a copy at the British Library.
84. The poem originated with Chetwood. See entry 45.
85. See entry 48.

renowned in their day, have sunk into "mere oblivion," and of whom the only record (but that the noblest) is to be found in their works. Their works and their names, "poor, poor dumb names," are all that remains of such men as Webster, Deckar, Marston, Marlow, Chapman, Heywood, Middleton, and Rowley! "How lov'd, how honour'd once, avails them not:" though they were the friends and fellow-labourers of Shakespear, sharing his fame and fortunes with him, the rivals of Jonson, and the masters of Beaumont and Fletcher's well-sung woes! They went out one by one unnoticed, like evening lights; or were swallowed up in the headlong torrent of puritanic zeal which succeeded, and swept away every thing in its unsparing course, throwing up the wrecks of taste and genius at random, and at long fitful intervals, amidst the painted gewgaws and foreign frippery of the reign of Charles II. and from which we are only now recovering the scattered fragments and broken images to erect a temple to true Fame! How long, before it will be completed?

The names of Middleton and Rowley, with which I shall conclude this Lecture, generally appear together as two writers who frequently combined their talents in the production of joint-pieces. Middleton (judging from their separate works) was "the more potent spirit" of the two; but they were neither of them equal to some others. Rowley appears to have excelled in describing a certain amiable quietness of disposition and disinterested tone of morality, carried almost to a paradoxical excess, as in his Fair Quarrel, and in the comedy of A Woman never Vexed, which is written, in many parts, with a pleasing simplicity and naiveté equal to the novelty of the conception. Middleton's style was not marked by any peculiar quality of his own, but was made up, in equal proportions, of the faults and excellences common to his contemporaries. In his Women Beware Women, there is a rich marrowy vein of internal sentiment, with fine occasional insight into human nature, and cool cutting irony of expression. He is lamentably deficient in the plot and denouement of the story. It is like the rough draught of a tragedy, with a number of fine things thrown in, and the best made use of first; but it tends to no fixed goal, and the interest decreases, instead of increasing, as we read on, for want of previous arrangement and an eye to the whole. We have fine studies of heads, a piece of richly-coloured drapery, "a foot, an hand, an eye from Nature drawn, that's worth a history;" but the groups are ill disposed, nor are the figures proportioned to each other or the size of the canvas. The author's power is in the subject, not over it; or he is in possession of excellent materials, which he husbands very ill. This character, though it applies more particularly to Middleton, might be applied generally to the age. Shakespear alone seemed to stand over his work, and to do what he pleased with it. He saw to the end of what he was about, and with the same faculty of lending himself to the impulses of Nature and the impression of the moment, never forgot that he himself had a task to perform, nor the place which each figure ought to occupy in his general design. — The characters of Livia, of Bianca, of Leantio and his Mother, in the play of which I am speaking, are all admirably drawn. The art and malice of Livia shew equal want of principle and acquaintance with the world; and the scene in which she holds the mother in suspense, while she betrays the daughter into the power of the profligate Duke, is a master-piece of dramatic skill. The proneness of Bianca to tread the primrose path of pleasure, after she has made the first false step, and her sudden transition from unblemished virtue to the most abandoned vice, in which she is notably seconded by her mother-in-law's ready submission to the temptations of wealth and power, form a true and striking picture. The first intimation of the intrigue that follows, is given in a way that is not a little remarkable for simplicity and acuteness. Bianca says,

"Did not the Duke look up? Methought he saw us."

To which the more experienced mother answers,

"That's every one's conceit that sees a Duke.
If he look stedfastly, he looks straight at them,
When he perhaps, good careful gentleman,
Never minds any, but the look he casts
Is at his own intentions, and his object
Only the public good."

It turns out however, that he had been looking at them, and not "at the public good." The moral of this tragedy is rendered more impressive from the manly, independent character of Leantio in the first instance, and the manner in which he dwells, in a sort of doting abstraction, on his own comforts, in being possessed of a beautiful and faithful wife. As he approaches his own house, and already treads on the brink of perdition, he exclaims with an exuberance of satisfaction not to be restrained —

" How near am I to a happiness
That earth exceeds not! Not another like it:
[3.1.82-109]."

This dream is dissipated by the entrance of Bianca and his Mother.

"*Bian.* Oh, sir, you're welcome home.
Moth. Oh, is he come? I am glad on't.
[3.1.109-177]."

The Witch of Middleton is his most remarkable performance; both on its own account, and from the use that Shakespear has made of some of the characters and speeches in his Macbeth. Though the employment which Middleton has given to Hecate and the rest, in thwarting the purposes and perplexing the business of familiar and domestic life, is not so grand or appalling as the more stupendous agency which Shakespear has assigned them, yet it is not easy to deny the merit of the first invention to Middleton, who has embodied the existing superstitions of the time, respecting that anomalous class of beings, with a high spirit of poetry, of the most grotesque and fanciful kind. The songs and incantations made use of are very nearly the same. The other parts of this play are not so good; and the solution of the principal difficulty, by Antonio's falling down a trap-door, most lame and impotent. As a specimen of the similarity of the preternatural machinery, I shall here give one entire scene.

[Hecate with other witches and Firestone, 3.3]

The Incantation scene at the cauldron, is also the original of that in Macbeth, and is in like manner introduced by the Duchess's visiting the Witches' Habitation.

[Duchess's visit to the witches, 5.2]

I will conclude this account with Mr. Lamb's observations on the distinctive characters of these extraordinary and formidable personages, as they are described by Middleton or Shakespear. [See entry 55.]

Lectures Chiefly on the Dramatic Literature of the Age of Elizabeth. Delivered at the Surry Institution. London: Stodart and Steuart, 1820, pp. 2-3 (from Lecture 1), 78-92 (from Lecture 2).

59. 1820-21 Percy Bysshe Shelley's Reading of Middleton

It is difficult to know how far to trust Thomas Medwin's *Life of Percy Bysshe Shelley.* Medwin went to school with Shelley, spent a great deal of time with him, and was an author with whom Shelley shared interests.

Medwin also was an opportunist who sometimes invented stories and once tried to blackmail Mary Shelley. Medwin would seem unlikely, however, to have lied about what books he and Percy Shelley discussed during the winter of 1820-21.

... indeed he was continually reading the Old Dramatists — Middleton, and Webster, Ford and Massinger, and Beaumont and Fletcher, were the mines from which he drew the pure and vigorous style that so highly distinguishes *The Cenci.*

Thomas Medwin, *The Life of Percy Bysshe Shelley.* Introd. by H. Buxton Forman. London: Humphrey Milford, Oxford University Press, 1913, p. 256.

60. 1823 *The Retrospective Review*: Women Who Rebel

The avowed aim of the *Retrospective Review* was to increase public interest in the "old" writers, particularly those of the sixteenth and seventeenth centuries. In the early 1820s, the *Review* published a series of articles on the Elizabethan and Jacobean playwrights, including this one on Middleton.[86] The essay is particularly interesting in its critical perspective: the author disavows hierarchical rankings, because evaluative criteria may differ from reader to reader. When Middleton's witches are compared to Shakespeare's, then, Middleton's may be discussed not as lesser, but as different, and excellent "in their way."

It has been said, often enough, that the lives of authors present but slender materials for biography; and that, in fact, their histories (which are rather histories of thoughts than actions) should be read where they are best recorded, — in their works. The first part of this assertion is well borne out by the life of Middleton. He is almost entirely unknown. The public, at least that part of the public who turn over now and then the leaves of our old dramatic writers, know that such a person existed; that he wrote, singly, and in conjunction with great associates, some memorable matter; but nothing further. None even of the editors of our old plays, can give any material account of this author; and we ourselves are unable to add any thing to the

86. N. W. Bawcutt suggests that the author was C. W. Dilke, who had edited six volumes of *Old English Plays* in 1814-15 ("The Revival of Elizabethan Drama and the Crisis of Romantic Drama," 102). An abridgment of the *Retrospective Review* article was published in *Dramatic Magazine* (May 1830) under the initials T. H. K.

scanty statements which are already before the public. Middleton is said to have been appointed chronologer to the city of London in the year 1620, and to have been cited before the privy council, on the 30th August, 1624, as the writer of "*The Game of Chess;*" and there his biography ends.

Thomas Middleton was the sole author of about sixteen or eighteen regular dramatic works, and four pageants, besides being concerned in different plays jointly with Rowley, Dekker, Webster, Massinger, and even with Fletcher and Ben Jonson. It is said that during his life he owed the greatest part of his reputation to his connexion with his celebrated contemporaries; yet, as is well remarked by the author of the *Biographia Dramatica* [David Erskine Baker], it is surely "a proof of merit sufficient to establish him in a rank far from the most contemptible of our dramatic writers, that a set of men of such acknowledged abilities considered him as deserving to be admitted a joint labourer with them in the fields of poetic fame; and more especially by Fletcher and Jonson, the first of whom, like a widowed muse, could not be supposed readily to admit another partner after the loss of his long and well-beloved mate, Beaumont; and the latter, who entertained so high an opinion of his own talents as scarcely to admit any brother near the throne, and would hardly have permitted the clear waters of his own Heliconian springs to have been muddied by the mixture of any streams, that did not apparently flow from the same source."

The truth is, that Middleton was a man of *very* "considerable power."[87] It is difficult to assign him any precise station among the remarkable men who were his contemporaries. Indeed, nothing is more unsafe than to gauge[88] the comparative merits of authors by the depth of one's own personal admiration; especially where, as in dramatic writing, the individual claims to excellence are so various, as to make it almost impossible to institute any very close comparison among them. Besides, one critic may prefer tragedy, another comedy, another pastoral; a fourth may value only the truth of character; while a fifth may be careless of it, and esteem little else beyond the vigour of the diction, or the melodious flow of the verse. Dekker, Webster, Middleton, Ford, were all men of excelling talent. The first had the best idea of character; the second was the most profound; the third had most imagination; and the last equalled the others in pathos, and surpassed them in the delineation of the passion of love. — Yet these particular points were not all by which these writers caught the attention of critics, and retained the admiration of their readers. They had other qualities, differing in shade and varying in colour, which it would be difficult to contrast with any useful

87. See Gifford, entry 54.
88. An emendation of *guage*.

effect. Dekker was sometimes as profound as Webster, and Middleton as passionate as Ford. Again, the verse of Ford is, generally speaking, musical; while that of Webster is often harsh, but it is more pregnant with meaning, shadowy, spectral, and fuller of a dark and earthy imagination. So it is that Middleton, although he has drawn no sketches, perhaps, so good as Matheo or Friscobaldo, lets fall nevertheless, occasionally, shrewd observations, and displays a wealth of language, which would illuminate and do honour to the better drawn characters of Dekker. In short, one was often rich in qualities, of which another possessed little or nothing; while he, on his part, could retort upon his rival a claim to other excellencies, to which the first did not affect to have even a pretension. It seems, therefore, almost idle to determine the rank and "classes" to which these old writers should respectively belong. We can no more accomplish this, than we can determine upon the positive beauty of colours, or fix the standard of metals, whose durability or scarcity is utterly unknown. Independently of all these reasons, it is invidious, and not very grateful in us, who profess ourselves idolators, to anatomize the remains of our gods, or to impale the reputations of these old fathers of poetry (sacrificing them face to face with each other), upon the hard and unrelenting spikes of modern criticism. They had faults which we have not — and excellencies which we do not possess. They were a fresh, shrewd, vigorous people, — full of fire, and imagination, and deep feeling. They were not swathed and swaddled in the bands by which we cramp the thoughts, and paralyze the efforts of *our* infant poets; but they were rioters in their fancy, — bold, unfettered writers, whom no critics, monthly or quarterly, watched over for the benefit of the time to come. Accordingly, they dared to think, — they wrote what they thought — and their thoughts were generally strenuous, and often soaring, and sometimes even rich in wisdom.

With respect to Middleton, whom we have now more particularly to deal with; — he was, as we have said, a man of very considerable powers, and possessed a high imagination. The reader who is not intimately acquainted with his works, will recognize him, perhaps, when we mention him as the author of *The Witch*, from which Shakspeare is said to have collected his idea of the witches in *Macbeth*. This drama, indeed, is not a production of the highest character, but the witches themselves are worth any thing. The story, which involves a double plot, cannot be unravelled very briefly; nor is there anything in it of sufficient merit to compensate for the tediousness, which a detail of it would force upon the reader. It is sufficient to say, that a Duke of Ravenna, by cruel insults, drives his wife to wish for his death. She accomplishes his murder, as she conceives, by means of a fantastical courtier called Almachildes; and when she supposes that the deed is perpetrated, she is desirous of getting rid of her instrument. — For this purpose, she consults the witches. The superstition which is referred to in the beginning of the following scene [a wax doll that will cause death], is (notwithstanding it has a somewhat Gothic look) as old as Theocritus.

[The Duchess's visit to Hecate and the charm-song — most of 5.2.]

This scene, the reader will perceive, must (if written before *Macbeth*, and generally known amongst the writers of the time,) have been the origin of one of the scenes in that celebrated play. With regard to the witches themselves, an eminent critic (Mr. Charles Lamb) has shewn the difference between Shakspeare's witches and those of Middleton; and he has awarded the palm, perhaps deservedly, in favour of the creations of Shakspeare.[89] Nevertheless — with deference to such authority, which, in fact, we are not aware that we materially oppose — we think, that the hags of Middleton, if not so sublime, are, at the least, as true — *more* true to our pre-conceived notions of those sinful elders, than even the sexless fictions of Shakspeare himself. The witches of our great poet, as pieces of *imagination*, must rank perhaps above the mere earthy superstitions of Middleton. They have neither sex nor name, parents nor children; they have no occupation but as ministers of evil; no habitation, save the blasted heath and the haunted cavern. They have nothing in common with humanity; but stand forth, phantoms, as false, though less attractive, than the fabled cloud which arrayed itself in shape and dazzling beauty to tempt the raging love of Ixion. The creatures of Shakspeare are like the Furies, or the Fates of Greek mythology. They seem born of cloud and storm: they come with the tempest, freighted and full of evil, and dissolve in lightning and thunder. The witches of Middleton, on the other hand, seem compounded of earth. They are akin to Caliban, though scarcely so romantic, being dwellers in the neighbourhood of villages, blasters of corn and maimers of cattle, as hate or interest or the love of mischief prompts them. Nevertheless, with all their drawbacks, they are excellent people in their way; and the freshness and truth of some of the scenes wherein they figure are — it is a bold word — not inferior to those of *Macbeth*. They are altogether a *Midsummer Night's Dream*, — airy as Titania or Oberon, — buoyant as the winds on which they ride. We will give our readers one of these scenes. To us it seems perfect in its way. We have the sense of the "rich evening" upon us — the moonlight — the owl hooting in the copse — the mounting into air: — How light is the dialogue between Hecate and her sisters who are aloft: — We hear them shouting and call-

89. See entry 55.

ing — descending and ascending — and loitering for their mistress on the wind: — They speak of the "dainty pleasure" of riding in the air — in the white moonshine — over woods and hills — steeple-tops and turrets — beyond the sound of bells or the howling of the midnight wolves, and we cannot refuse them our belief.

[3.3]

In this play there is a thought —

"Nothing lives
But has a joy in somewhat" —

which will remind the poetical reader of Mr. Wordsworth. The words themselves would form a good text for all the "Loves" — from the 'Angels,' and 'Plants,' and 'Minerals,' &c. down to (almost) the 'Triangles' themselves.

The next play, from which we select a passage, is the tragedy of *The Changeling*, which Middleton wrote in conjunction with Rowley. And here we may observe a peculiarity which occurs frequently in Middleton's plays, which is, that his heroines, in contradiction to custom, are generally women faithless and abandoned. As other poets seem to raise for themselves a standard of excellence, and appear to be for ever moulding characters and images to approach their ideal model of perfection; so, on the other hand, Middleton seems to have continually contemplated an opposite model — a standard of treachery and infidelity. His worship was like an Egyptian's, and his idols are all moral deformities — monsters and hideous creatures, whom no pure and healthy imagination could consent perpetually to cherish. His Dutchess, in *The Witch* — Biancha, (or Brancha,) in *Women beware of Women* — Beatrice, in *The Changeling* — are women who rebel against the conjugal duties, and conspire against their husbands' lives — and, indeed, there is scarcely a single instance of one of his females possessing real virtue, or any share of gentle affection. They are almost all lascivious, faithless, or cruel. His best personages (where none are good) are amongst the men; for though the titles of Middleton's dramas may seem occasionally to convey a compliment to 'the sex,' as it is called — (as *More dissemblers besides Women*, and *A Woman never vext*) — yet the detail but seldom answers to the heading of the chapter of praise. In the play called *More dissemblers besides Women* there are (independantly of a waiting-woman) three female characters, two of whom are of the frailest possible material, and the third but little better, if at all.

But, with respect to our extract from *The Changeling* — Beatrice Joanna, the heroine, is married to Alonzo de Piracquo: she dislikes him, and employs Deflores, a deformed dwarf, to kill him. The deed is effected, and the following is the first interview between the guilty parties, — the beautiful Beatrice and the hideous dwarf. It contains a lesson for ladies.

[3.4.21-73, 78-89, in which Beatrice offers DeFlores
gold and discovers he wants her body instead]

The tragedy of *Women beware of Women* is on the whole, we think, Middleton's finest play. It is founded on the story of *Biancha Capello*, long since translated into our language from the Italian. The heroine was a beautiful Venetian who married a native of Florence, and accompanying him to that city, was seen and admired by the reigning Duke, one of the family of the De Medici. Biancha yielded to the Duke's passion, and finally conspired with him to put an end to her husband's life. This is the principal vein that runs through the play; though there is an underplot also, and they both branch out into other unexpected, but not unnatural consequences, making the whole as full of incident as any play in the English language. — The drama opens with the arrival of Leantio and his wife Biancha at his poor cottage at Florence. He consigns her to his mother's care, and resolves, after one day of enjoyment, to return to the labour which is necessary for his own and his wife's support. Leantio exults exceedingly in his wife's personal perfections, and she, on her part, rates as nothing the ordinary evils of poverty. She is compensated by the entire love of her husband, whose fondness breaks out upon all occasions.

> "Oh, fair-ey'd Florence!
> Didst thou but know what a most matchless jewel
> Thou now art mistress of, a pride would take thee,
> Able to shoot destruction through the bloods
> Of all thy youthful sons: but 'tis great policy
> To keep choice treasures in obscurest places:
> Should we show thieves our wealth, 'twould make 'em bolder:
> Temptation is a devil will not stick
> To fasten upon a saint; take heed of that;
> The jewel is cas'd up from all men's eyes.
> Who could imagine now a gem were kept,
> Of that great value under this plain roof?"

Nevertheless, it is necessary, as we have said, that he should leave her to follow his occupations. He resolves upon this, while she, on her part, endeavours to detain him.

> "*Bian.* I perceive, sir,
> You're not gone yet; I have good hope you'll stay now.
> *Lean.* Farewell; I must not.
> *Bian.* Come, come, pray return!
> To-morrow (adding but a little care more)
> Will dispatch all as well; believe me 'twill, sir.
> *Lean.* I could well wish myself where you would have me;
> But love that's wanton, must be rul'd awhile
> By that that's careful, or all goes to ruin:
> As fitting is a government in love,
> As in a kingdom."

And now for a change, to startle the simple reader and to tickle the ear of a woman-hater. Biancha, (she is called '*Brancha*' throughout the play, but it is evidently wrong, that name coinciding neither with the fact, nor being sufficient to complete the line,) — Biancha is seen at her window by the Duke of Florence. He contrives to meet her, by the agency of a dissolute lady, (Livia,) and effects her ruin. The change of Biancha's character, consequent upon her seduction, is admirably managed. The scene is altogether very dramatic; and the contrast between the cold, impudent, dissatisfied wife, and the anticipating, confiding husband, is striking and appalling. We give the scene entire.

> [3.1.82-225, Leantio's return home, with
> a few of the "racier" lines excised]

Our last extract commenced with a beautiful eulogy upon marriage. Let us now hear what the more experienced husband has to say upon this fertile subject.

> "*Lean.* Oh, thou the ripe time of man's misery, wedlock,
> When all his thoughts, like over-laden trees,
> Crack with the fruits they bear, in cares, in jealousies!
> Oh! that's a fruit that ripens hastily,
> After 'tis knit to marriage: it begins,
> As soon as the sun shines upon the bride,
> A little to show colour. Blessed powers!
> Whence comes this alteration? the distractions,

The fears and doubts it brings, are numberless,
And yet the cause I know not. What a peace
Has he that never marries! if he knew
The benefit he enjoy'd, or had the fortune
To come and speak with me, he should know then
The infinite wealth he had, and discern rightly
The greatness of his treasure by my loss."

The reader may now take an extract from a banquet scene, where
Biancha glitters as the duke's mistress, and her husband, the melancholy
Leantio, mourns over her defection.

[3.2.235-262]

They afterwards meet together at the lady's lodgings, when Leantio's
anger overcomes his grief. The taunting which passes between them is very
spirited.

"*Lean.* You're richly plac'd.
Bian. Methinks you're wond'rous brave, sir.
[4.1.52-103, with excisions]."

One more quotation, and we have done. It is where the Cardinal de
Medici reproves his brother, the Duke of Florence, for his misdoings. The
scene, though on the whole a little tedious, is impressive. We give a part of
it only:

[4.1.181-250].

"Art. VII: *The Witch, The Changeling, Women Beware of Women,*" *Retrospective
Review* 8 (1823): 125-45.

61. 1831 John Payne Collier and a Street Ballad

In 1617, the apprentices "or rather the unruly people of the suburbs"[90]
attacked the Cockpit playhouse, ostensibly to protest the immorality there.
They fought with the guards, destroyed costumes and props, and burned the
playbooks. (Middleton alluded to the apprentices' Shrove Tuesday behavior
in *The Inner-Temple Masque*.)

90. Chamberlain, I: 22.

In *The History of English Dramatic Poetry to the Time of Shakespeare*, John Payne Collier says that the ballad in praise of the apprentices from which this verse is taken came from a seventeenth-century manuscript; however, Collier's forgeries appear to have begun with this volume and the manuscript has never been recovered, so this ballad, too, is likely a Collier re-creation.[91]

> Books olde and young on heap they flung,
> And burnt them in the blazes,
> Tom Dekker, Haywood, Middleton
> And other wandring crazyes:
> Poor Daye that daye not scapte awaye;
> And what stil more amazes,
> Immortall Cracke was burnt all blacke,
> Which every bodie praises.

The History of English Dramatic Poetry to the Time of Shakespeare: And Annals of the Stage to the Restoration. London: John Murray, 1831, I:404.

62. 1835 George Darley: Middleton as a British Poet

George Darley was a mathematician, a poet, and the dramatic reviewer for *The Athenaeum.* He described himself as a "stern Elizabethan" (p. 208) whose "mind was born among the rude old dramatists" (p. 149); as a reviewer, he attacked the drama of his age for its lack of Elizabethan energy. On 14 July he wrote to Allan Cunningham about the writers he felt should be included in Cunningham's projected *Lives of the Poets* if the volume were to represent the best of English poets.

You conceive yourself no doubt obliged to exclude from your List all who have never written any but dramatic Poetry. Else wherefore omit such names as Marston, Middleton, Heywood, Decker, Webster & others? For my own part I do not see why certain scores of the Ducks [Duchesses] and Dukes should not give place to our Early Dramatists, and so furnish out indeed a complete as well as unblotted scroll of British Poets.

---

91. His forgery of other ballads is explored in Dawson, "John Payne Collier's Great Forgery." Bullen also thought this ballad might be fraudulent ("Introduction," *The Works of Thomas Middleton*, xcii).

Claude Colleer Abbott, *The Life and Letters of George Darley, Poet and Critic.*
London: Humphrey Milford, Oxford University Press, 1928, p. 121.

63. 1837 Middleton as a Character in a Tragedy

In his one-act play *The Death of Marlowe*, Richard Henry Horne
recreates Christopher Marlowe's death, compressing time to make Marlowe
close friends with Middleton and Thomas Heywood. Horne's Middleton is
a strong character, more aware of reality than Marlowe, though lacking
Marlowe's passion, and more philosophical than Heywood. Some critics,
like Algernon Charles Swinburne, thought the play was rubbish (see entry
82), but the tragedy was printed in several editions and was still being
praised many decades later.

In the first excerpt, Middleton accurately assesses the character of
Jacconot, the tavern-pimp who will stab Marlowe. In the second selection,
a fan, pleased to find himself in a tavern with Middleton, Heywood, and
Marlowe, offers a toast to these "choicest spirits of the age." In the last,
Middleton has been asked the identity of the dead man.

MID. Your weighty-pursed knowledge of women, balanced against
your squinting knowledge of honesty, Master Jack-o'-night, would come
down to earth, methinks, as rapid as a fall from a gallows-tree.

JAC. Well said, Master Middleton — a merry devil and a long-lived one
run monkey-wise up your back-bone! May your days be as happy as they're
sober, and your nights full of applause! May no brawling mob pelt you when
throned, nor hoot down your plays when your soul's pinned like a cock-
chafer on public opinion! May no learned or unlearned calf write against
your knowledge and wit, and no brother paper-stainer pilfer your pages, and
then call you a general thief! Am I the only rogue and vagabond in the
world?

MID. I'faith, not: nay, an' thou wert, there would be no lack of them
i'the next generation. Thou might'st be the father of the race, being now the
bodily type of it.

JAC. That, for your type!

> A GENT[LEMAN]. I do rejoice to find myself among
> The choicest spirits of the age: health, sirs!
> I would commend your fame to future years,
> But that I know ere this ye must be old
> In the conviction, and that ye full oft

With sure posterity have shaken hands
Over the unstable bridge of present time.
   MAR. Not so: we write from the full heart within,
And leave posterity to find her own.
Health, sir! — your good deeds laurel you in heaven!
   MID. 'Twere best men left their fame to chance and fashion
As birds bequeath their eggs to the sun's hatching,
Since genius can make no will.
   MAR. Troth, can it!
But, for the consequences of the deed,
What fires of blind fatality may catch them!

   MID. He who erewhile wrote with a brand of fire,
Now, in his passionate blood, floats tow'rds the grave!
The present time is ever ignorant —
We lack clear vision in our self-love's maze;
But Marlowe in the future will stand great,
Whom this — the lowest caitiff in the world —
A nothing, save in grossness, hath destroy'd.

R[ichard] H[enry] Horne. *The Death of Marlowe: A Tragedy.* London: Saunders and Otley, 1837, pp. 11-12, 14-15, 21.

64. 1839 A Literary Historian Provides a Mixed Review

   Henry Hallam was already a well-known historian when he published *Introduction to the Literature of Europe in the Fifteenth, Sixteenth, and Seventeenth Centuries.* It was reviewed as "the most important contribution to literary history which English libraries have received for many years"[92] and was a standard reference work for decades. Hallam ranks Middleton below Shakespeare, Jonson, Massinger, and Webster and follows the lines of eighteenth-century studies in emphasizing Middleton as a writer of comedy and a collaborator with his betters.

   . . . Middleton belongs to this lower class of dramatic writers [with Marston, Chapman, Rowley, Tourneur, and Dekker]; his tragedy entitled "Women beware Women" is founded on the story of Bianca Cappello; it is full of action, but the characters are all too vicious to be interesting, and the

92. [Herman Merivale?], *Edinburgh Review*, 194.

language does not rise much above mediocrity. In comedy, Middleton deserves more praise. "A Trick to catch the Old One" and several others that bear his name are amusing and spirited. But Middleton wrote chiefly in conjunction with others, and sometimes with Jonson and Massinger.

Henry Hallam, *Introduction to the Literature of Europe in the Fifteenth, Sixteenth, and Seventeenth Centuries.* Vol. 3. London: John Murray, 1839: 622.

65. 1840 Alexander Dyce Introduces Middleton's Works

Alexander Dyce took religious orders rather than comply with his father's wishes and join the East India Company. He served only two curacies, however, before resigning his clerical work to dedicate himself to literature. Dyce devoted two years to preparing Middleton's complete works; as a result, he presents a far more complete introduction than any earlier biographer or historian. While Dyce values Middleton's talent, he is not ready to rank Middleton with writers like Webster and Ford, whose reputations had risen more quickly in the nineteenth century than had Middleton's.

[Dyce has been discussing the controversy about whether *Macbeth* preceded *The Witch* or vice versa.] . . . and whichever of the two may have been the copyist, he owes so little to his brother-poet, that the debt will not materially affect his claim to originality. Concerning the tragi-comedy *The Witch*, I have only to add, that its merit consists entirely in the highly imaginative pictures of the preternatural agents, in their incantations, and their moonlight revelry: the rest of it rises little above mediocrity.

In the estimation of an anonymous critic, *Women beware Women* is "Middleton's finest play,"[93] and perhaps he has judged rightly. It is indeed remarkable for the masterly conception and delineation of the chief characters, and for the life and reality infused into many of the scenes; though the dramatis personae are almost all repulsive from their extreme depravity, and the catastrophe is rather forced and unnatural. In this tragedy, says Hazlitt, there is "a rich marrowy vein of internal sentiment, with fine occasional insight into human nature, and cool cutting irony of expression."[94] To his subsequent observation, that "the interest decreases, instead of increasing, as we read on," I by no means assent.

93. See entry 60.
94. See entry 58.

The Changeling affords another specimen of Middleton's tragic powers. If on the whole inferior to the piece last mentioned, it displays, I think, in several places, a depth of passion unequalled throughout the present volumes. According to the title-page, William Rowley, who was frequently his literary associate, had a share in the composition; but I feel convinced that the terribly impressive passages of this tragedy, as well as those serious portions of *A Fair Quarrel* which Lamb has deservedly praised,[95] and the pleasing characters of Clara and Constanza in *The Spanish Gipsy*, are beyond the ability of Rowley.

Among our author's works there are few more original and ingenious than *A Game at Chess*. By touches of sweet fancy, by quaint humour, and by poignant satire, he redeems the startling absurdities in which the plan of the drama had necessarily involved him.

Middleton's "principal efforts," says an accomplished writer, "were in comedy, where he deals profusely in grossness and buffoonery. The cheats and debaucheries of the town are his favourite sources of comic intrigue."[96] *A Mad World, my Masters*, and *A Trick to catch the Old One*, are the most perfect of the numerous comedies which Mr. Campbell has dismissed with so slight and unfavourable a notice; and next to them may be ranked *The Roaring Girl, A Chaste Maid in Cheapside, Michaelmas Term*, and *No Wit, no Help like a Woman's*. The dialogue of these pieces is generally spirited; the characters, though their peculiarities may be sometimes exaggerated, are drawn with breadth and discrimination; and the crowded incidents afford so much amusement, that the reader is willing to overlook the occasional violation of probability. As they faithfully reflect the manners and customs of the age, even the worst of Middleton's comedies [*Your Five Gallants* and *The Family of Love*] are not without their value.

A critic, whom I have already quoted, after observing that "it is difficult to assign Middleton any precise station among the remarkable men who were his contemporaries,"[97] proceeds to compare him with Webster and Ford, who were assuredly poets of a higher order. The dramatists with whom, in my opinion, Middleton ought properly to be classed — though superior to him in some respects and inferior in others — are Dekker, Heywood, Marston, and Chapman: nor perhaps does William Rowley fall so much below them that he should be excluded from the list.

---

95. See entry 55. Dyce assumes that Lamb is so well known that he need not be cited, an assumption Dyce rarely makes.
96. See entry 57.
97. See entry 60.

"Some Account of Middleton and His Works," in *The Works of Thomas Middleton*.
London: Edward Lumley, 1840, 1: liv-lvii.

66. 1840 *The Gentleman's Magazine* Reviews Dyce

This anonymous reviewer of Dyce's edition praises Middleton as a
genuine artist and poet, but also sees him as a lesser genius whose work is
marred by coarseness and low humor. In the sections that deal with the
individual plays, I have included criticism, but omitted the textual
discussions that compose a large part of the review.

[The author opens with a discussion of those "highly gifted poets" of the
Renaissance theater, who "plunged into the ocean of human passion" and
drew from the "poetic atmosphere" of life around them.]
In the rich catalogue of dramatic writers, many names of higher fame
than that of Middleton occur. But as all who love and practise art with
success cannot be first-rate, so are we capable of receiving delight from
works of inferior genius, if the writer does not attempt greater things than he
can attain, and knows the limits of his own power. Middleton had assuredly
a genius for dramatic imitation and characterisation; and he well understood
the principles of theatrical success and effect. Mr. Dyce says, that his
"characters are drawn with breadth and discrimination." If so, this is as high
praise as can be bestowed on the successful efforts of genius; for it may be
said, that in poetry as in the sister arts, the great difficulty is to unite breadth
to accuracy of detail, and to truth and variety of character; and to succeed in
uniting these, is the sure mark of a great and genuine artist. Another writer
observes, "Dekker, Webster, Middleton, Ford, were all men of excelling
talent. The first had the best idea of character; the second was the most
profound; *the third had most imagination;* and the last equalled the others in
pathos, and surpassed them in the delineation of the passion of love." Again,
"He was a man of very considerable powers, and possessed a high
imagination."[98]
Middleton appears

> "In scenes like these, which, daring to depart
> From sober truth, are still to nature true,"

to have relied on his own observation and strength for such representations
as would be acceptable and effective. There is a fulness and freshness in his

98. See entry 60.

delineations that speak them to be the production of original observation and thought. His characters are drawn with sufficient fulness and spirit, without being, like those of Jonson, very skilfully but artificially and minutely laboured. The general conduct of his dialogue — its various and conflicting passion — its coarse raillery — its broad humour — its comic force — its gay and sportive fancies — its rapid turns — its ingenious and remote allusions — shew much fertility of thought, extent of knowledge, and readiness of application. His plots also afford a sufficient variety of incident, degree of emotion, and contrast of situation, and present a moving picture of the agitated surface of social life. We will now make a few observations on each separate play as it occurs; and if our critical notices are not so numerous, as from the state of the text in the old editions might have been expected, it has arisen from the admirable manner in which the present editor has performed his duty. [Here follow comments on Dyce's editing, a biographical sketch of Middleton, and Dyce's summary comments from entry 65.]

[*The Old Law*] Mr. C. Lamb says, "There is an exquisiteness of moral sensibility making one to gush out tears of delight, and a poetical strangeness in all the improbable circumstances of this wild play, which are unlike anything in the dramas which Massinger wrote alone. The pathos is of a subtler edge. Middleton and Rowley, who assisted in this play, had both of them finer geniuses than their associates."[99] The plot is very wild and strange, and the low comic characters disgusting; but some of the passages have great poetical merit. Cleanthes is an amiable character; the great defect is, a want of progression in the plot. We will give a specimen or two of the poetical conception and versification.

> *Creon.* "———— In my youth
> I was a soldier; no coward in my age:
> [1.1.220-240]."

From Act iv. sc. 2, we take the opening speech of Cleanthes:

> *Cleanth.* — What's that? oh! nothing but the whispering wind
> Breathes thro' yon churlish hawthorn, that grew rude,
> [4.2.1-22].

[*The Mayor of Quinborough*] This play is no favourite of ours. The story

99. See entry 55.

is from Higden's Polychronicon. The comic parts are full of coarse, low ribaldry, and suburb humour. The character of Roxana disagreeable and disgusting. The violation of Castiza is a wild unnatural act of violence and baseness. The brutal villany of Horsus, and the murders and mutual recriminations at the end, form a fit termination of the guilty intrigues and wickedness in the preceding parts. . . .

There is merit both in the coarse drollery of the comic parts, and in the poetical sentiments and expressions of the tragic; but the former sinks into buffoonery, and in the latter, except in depicting the purity and sorrow of Castiza, the poet has drawn with too dark a pencil the progress of guilty passions, criminal desires, and perfidious intrigues; the whole ending in the mutual reproaches of disappointed villany, and the view of sin perishing in the destruction which it bred in its own bosom. We give Constantius's speech as a specimen of the style. . . .

> "——— Oh! blessed creature!
> And does too much felicity make you surfeit?
> [1.2.151-168]."

[*Blurt, Master Constable*] There is in this play a sufficient variety of incident and much comic humour of a coarse kind. The character of Imperia is drawn with a fullness of detail, and many amusing circumstances, that contrasts well with the innocent sprightliness of Violetta.

[*The Phoenix*] As a specimen of this play, we give the following speech of Phoenix.

> "Thou angel sent among us, sober Law,
> Made with meek eyes, persuading action,
> [1.4.197-227]."

[*A Trick to Catch the Old One*] This is an amusing and clever tragedy, in which the progress of the plot is ingeniously sustained, and the curiosity kept awake. Perhaps the natural consternation, surprise, and grief of Hoard at the termination, is scarcely given with adequate force, and seems to fall somewhat flat. But there is something pleasing in the repentance and recantation of the countryman and of Witgood, which gives a calm satisfaction to the mind, after the scenes of villany and fraud which have hung like dark clouds over the progress of the plot.

[*The Family of Love*] In this play there is much coarse indelicate humour, relieved by the love of Maria and Gerardine. Middleton well understood the power of *contrast*, though he too frequently has substituted the sudden repentance of a frail and guilty woman, for the uniform loveliness of virtue, for undeviating rectitude of conduct, and the charms of moral beauty.

[*Your Five Gallants*] In this play there is much humour, but more ribaldry — no characters to interest, nor incidents to surprise; but the dialogue, though low, is clever, and the numerous allusions to the customs and manners of the times afford amusement.

[*A Mad World, My Masters*] This is one of the most lively and entertaining of this species of comedy, descriptive of the vices and follies of the times, which we have of Middleton. The humour is broad and coarse enough, and the wit often of the lowest kind; but there is cleverness in the dialogue, and a succession of fanciful incidents which would delight an audience not over sensitive nor squeamish. The sudden repentance of the ladies (the frail and fair) at the end of these plays, is very edifying, and is no doubt intended as a sufficient moral to obliterate the impressions made by the former part of their conduct.

[*The Roaring Girl*] There is much family likeness between the plot and character of these comedies of Middleton. The sharper, the countryman, the bully, and the wittol are prominent persons, to which if we add the Citizen's Wife and the Country Knight, we have a fair outline of the materials of which these comedies are formed; but there is often, to balance defects, great ingenuity in the allusions, wit in the conceits, and humour in the language: for they were written "before the little art that fools have was silenced." The present play is superior to some of the others in liveliness of interest and situation.

[*The Honest Whore, Part 1*] In this play the comic parts resemble those of the others, but there is a higher tragic strain or elevation of fancy, and a richer vein of ideal poetry. The introduction of the Mad House and of its fearful grotesque incidents, (the man in a net) is a wild burst of imaginative power, producing an effect which a less daring attempt could not have reached. Here the ludicrous and sublime — the sublime of terror — were in close and dangerous contact.

[*The Witch*] Mr. C. Lamb has rightly observed the distinction between the Witches of Shakspere and of Middleton: "The names and some of the properties which Middleton has given to the hags excite smiles. The Weird

Sisters are serious things, their presence cannot co-exist with mirth; but in a lesser degree the Witches of Middleton are fine creations, &c."[100] Shakspere has, in fact, separated all that could either merely amuse or distract the mind of the spectator, all that was common with humanity, and has selected what was awful, unearthly, and supernatural, 'la terribil' via' of the true sublime, as far removed from Middleton's hags, as the Satan of Milton from the devil of Tasso.

[*The Widow*] This is a pleasing comedy, much raised in poetical taste and expression above the usual style of Middleton. Mr. Collier thinks that there is internal evidence that Ben Jonson contributed to the play, and is surprised that Gifford did not trace his pen through the whole of the fourth act. Gifford says, "The comedy was popular, and not undeservedly, for it has considerable merit."[101]

[*More Dissemblers Besides Women*] There is nothing very engaging in the plot of this play or in the delineation of the characters; but there is a vein of good poetry, with good language and versification.

[*The Spanish Gypsy*] There is an agreeable plot and much fine poetry in this play.

[*The Changeling*] It has been rightly observed, that the heroines of Middleton are generally women faithless and abandoned; formed after a standard of treachery and infidelity. They are almost all lascivious, faithless, and cruel.[102] The Dutchess in the Witch, Biancha in Women beware Women, and Beatrice in the present play, are strong examples of the poet's models of female character. In the Changeling the delineation of guilty passions and the terrific punishments awaiting their possessor, is coarsely but most powerfully drawn, with a fearful energy of language and thought. What a scene is that between De Flores and Beatrice in the last part of the third and the first of the fourth act — with what malicious and cruel levity, with what cool and fiend-like irony he addresses his victim — knowing that her destiny is in his hands, and that she is hastening without a possibility of escape into the net that he has so skilfully spread for her. Again, see the subsequent interview between Beatrice and her injured husband. Indeed, the progress of her ruin, from her first avowed hatred of De Flores to her becoming the

100. See entry 55.
101. Reprinted in "Memoirs of Ben Jonson," *The Works of Ben Jonson*, 42n.
102. See entry 60.

wretched partner of his crimes, is drawn with a most powerful and masterly pencil — by the Hogarth of the pen. At a time when an audience was not fastidious about incident or expression — would not object to some extravagance of character, and would hear without wincing any allusions however gross, and listen willingly to a plot formed of the most fearful and complicated crimes — the impression must have been deeply and fearfully thrilling which was produced in the latter part of this play, where the plot is apparently rushing headlong to its fearful consummation; and after every form of distress and anguish has been exhausted, every subterfuge has failed, every artifice of escape in vain attempted, and threats, reproaches, and recriminations have been exhausted in vain; final and unavoidable ruin is at last met with the expiring struggle of nature — the dreadful audacity of despair, and so ends this history of guilt — misery — and death. The only passages in any other play of our author that can compete with the above, are those scenes between Leantio and Bianca in Women beware Women, which are of the same kind and of very high excellence.

[A Game at Chess] Of this political and allegorical drama, Mr. Dyce says, "by touches of sweet fancy, by quaint humour, and by poignant satire, Middleton relieves the startling adventures in which the plan of his drama had necessarily involved him."

[Anything for a Quiet Life] In Malone's Shakspeare, by Boswell, vol. x. p. 156, note, this play is called a silly comedy, by Anmer (i.e. by Steevens). This character is unkindly, perhaps unjustly awarded. There is nothing masterly in the conduct of the plot, or clever in the succession of incidents, but the dialogue is not inferior to that of others, and the poetry is good in its way: the sentiments are suitable to the characters, and fairly imitate the realities of life. Mr. Dyce says, "There is every reason to believe that the text is greatly corrupted." Knavesby, the lawyer, is a pander to his honest wife. In Middleton's Chaste Maid in Cheapside, Allwit is a character of the same kind, who voluntarily consents to and contributes to his own dishonour, but then his wife is not a consenting party.

[Women Beware Women] There is a great deal of fine poetry in this play, of elegant expression, and just reflections and sentiments expressed in good versification. There is sufficient variety of characters and passion; but the plot is hurried up abruptly at the close, and a violent death saves the trouble of a more ingenious unravelment and a better designed catastrophe.

"The Works of Thomas Middleton," The Gentleman's Magazine 14 (1840): 563-87.

67. 1843 James Russell Lowell: The U.S. Enters

The versatile James Russell Lowell — poet, critic, editor, anti-slavery advocate, professor, and diplomat — shared the English Romantics' love of Renaissance writers. As a critic, he said he deplored Romantic egotism and sentimentality, but he was a Romantic in his idealism and eagerness to deal with life at its most serious. In this article in *The Pioneer*, a product of his mid-twenties, Lowell promotes Middleton as a tragedian and an eloquent tenderer of what Lowell, a religious mid-nineteenth-century American, views as unchanging emotional and spiritual truths, such as the democracy of soul that supersedes class and rank, or the natural modesty of women.

[Lowell discusses poets as the "prophets of changes in the moral world."]
Of Thomas Middleton little is known. Indeed it seems to be the destiny of poets that men should not be familiar with their personal history — a destiny which to the thoughtful has a true and beautiful meaning. For it seems meant to chide men for their too ready preference of names and persons to *things*, by showing them the perishableness of the one, and the immortality of the other, and to give to those divine teachings of theirs which remain to us, something of a mysterious and oracular majesty, as if they were not truly the words of men, but only more distinct utterances of those far-heard voices which, in the too fleeting moments of a higher and clearer being, come to us from the infinite deep with a feeling of something heard in childhood, but long ago drowned in the din of life. It is a lesŝon also, for those who would be teachers of men that theirs must be rather the humbly obedient voice than the unconquerable will, and that he speaks best who has listened longest. And yet there is something beautiful, too, in the universal longing which men feel to see the bodily face of that soul whose words have strengthened or refreshed them. . . .
It is of Middleton's tragedies chiefly that we shall speak, both because they are very fine ones, and because from them we can more safely draw an estimate of his character. A good tragedy is, perhaps, the hardest thing to write. Nothing is easier than to draw tears from the reader; nothing surely is more rare than the power of drawing them rightly, or of touching that deepest string of our being which God, that he might give us the most meaning lesson of universal brotherhood, has ordained should never quiver at the touch of our private sorrows, how soul-piercing soever. There are a thousand who can write pathetically, for one who has in any measure of fullness the tragic faculty. Many may touch the heart, but none save a master can bring up for us the snowy pearls which sleep in the deep abysses and

caverns of the soul. . . . To write a good tragedy, therefore, demands, if not the greatest of poets, certainly some of the highest elements of one.

The plot of "The Changeling," the most powerful of Middleton's tragedies, is briefly this. De Flores, a deformed and ugly villain, loves Beatrice, the heroine of the play, who has an unconquerable loathing of him. She has been betrothed by Vermandero her father, to Alonzo de Piracquo, a noble gentleman, but whom she cannot love, having already given all her heart to Alsemero. De Flores first tempts her to the murder of Piracquo, and then offers himself as the instrument of that hideous guilt. The murder is successfully accomplished without the knowledge of Alsemero, and Beatrice, no obstacle now remaining, is married to him. On the day of her wedding she deems it high time to get De Flores out of the way, but he refuses any other reward than the satiation of his hellish passion for Beatrice, to the gratification of which he compels her by a threat of disclosing all to her husband. Alsemero at length is led to suspect his wife, the whole ghastly story is laid bare, and De Flores, after slaying his unwilling paramour, prevents the revenging steel of Tomaso, Piracquo's brother, by stabbing himself to the heart. The tragedy takes its name from the chief character in an under-plot, which, as is usually the case in the old drama, has nothing whatever to do with the action of the piece.

In the opening of the play, Beatrice thus strongly expresses her aversion to De Flores.

> —'t is my infirmity;
> Nor can I other reason render you
> Than his or hers of some particular thing
> They must abandon as a deadly poison,
> Which to a thousand other tastes were wholesome;
> Such to mine eyes is that same fellow there,
> The same that report speaks of the basilisk.

It was a fine thought in our author thus to give a dim foreshadowing of that bloody eclipse of her better nature which Beatrice was to suffer from De Flores. It is always an unacknowledged sense of our own weaknesses that gives birth to those vague feelings and presentiments which warn us of an approaching calamity, and when the blow has fallen, we soothe our wounded self-respect by calling it Fate. We cheat our sterner reason into a belief that some higher power has interfered to bring about that blight in us whose steady growth always circles outward from some hidden meanness in our own souls. Our woes are our own offspring, and we feed our hungry brood, as was once fabled of the pelican, with our best heart's-blood; — alas, they never become fledged, like hers, and fly away from us, but raven till the troubled fountain runs dry! The shafts of destiny never rend through buckler and breast-plate, but reach our hearts with an awful and deadly certainty, through any chink in our armor which has been left unbraced by our own sin or recklessness. Beatrice would make us believe that she has a natural antipathy to De Flores. But antipathies are only so many proofs of something wanting in ourselves, whereby we are hindered of that perfect sympathy with all things, for which we were created, and without which that life, which should be as harmonious as the soft concent of love, becomes harsh and jarring. The thought of De Flores is to Beatrice what the air-drawn dagger was to Macbeth; she foresees in her own heart the crime yet uncommitted, and trembles at the weapon even while she stretches her quivering hand to grasp it. A terrible fascination seems to draw us on to the doing of ill deeds, the foreconsciousness whereof, graciously implanted in our natures by God as a safeguard, we misconstrue into the promptings of our evil demon. We brood over the gloomy thought in an agony of fierce enjoyment. Infidels to our own holy impulses, we blaspheme the eternal benignity which broods forever on its chosen nest in the soul of man, giving life to all beauty and all strength. We go apart from the society of men that we may hold converse with our self-invoked and self-created tempter. Always at our backs it dogs us, looming every hour higher and higher, till the damp gloom of its shadow hems us wholly in. We feel it behind us like the fearful presence of a huge hand stretched forth to gripe us and force us to its withering will. One by one the dark, vague fingers close around us, and at last we render ourselves to its fancied bidding in a gush of wild despair which vibrates in us with a horrible delight. We sign our deeds of sale to the fiend with a feather self-torn from our own wings. It is the curse of Adam in us that we can no longer interpret the tongue of angels, and too often mistake the tender forethought of our good spirit concerning us, for the foul promptings of an evil demon which we would fain believe is permitted to have dominion over us. In another place Beatrice says of De Flores,

> I never see this fellow but I think
> Of some harm towards me; danger's in my mind still;
> I scarce leave trembling for an hour after.

Here we have a still clearer omen of what is to follow.

Our poet drops a few "lilies in the mouth of his Tartarus," but there is ever a dark sprig of nightshade among them. In the scene we next quote, the bloody dawning of the thought of Piracquo's murder in the soul of Beatrice, blots out luridly the tender morning-star of love which still trembles there,

making us feel yet more thrillingly the swiftly nearing horrors which it
betokens. The scene is between Beatrice and Alsemero.

> *Beat.* I have within mine eyes all my desires:
> Requests, that holy prayers ascend heaven for,
> [2.2.8-28].

With what exquisite naturalness is this drawn! The heart of Beatrice,
afraid of itself, would fain cheat itself into the belief that Alsemero gave it
that dark hint which its own guilty wishes had already forestalled. To
return —

> *Beat.* How? call you that extinguishing of fear,
> When 't is the only way to keep it flaming?
> Are not you ventured in the action,
> That's all my joys and comforts? pray, no more, sir:

Though she seemingly rejects the offer, yet she goes on weighing the
risk in her own mind.

> Say you prevailed, you're danger's and not mine then;
> The law would claim you from me, or obscurity
> Be made the grave to bury you alive.
> *I'm glad these thoughts come forth;* oh keep not one
> Of this condition, sir! here was a course
> Found to bring sorrow on her way to death;
> The tears would ne'er have dried till dust had choked them.
> Blood-guiltiness becomes a fouler visage; —

Thus she works herself up to a pitch of horror at the fancied guilt of
Alsemero, and with half-conscious cunning renders her own plot, (which she
now for the first time acknowledges to herself,) less full of loathsomeness.
She continues, (*aside.*)

> *And now I think on one:* I was to blame,
> I've marred so good a market with my scorn;
> It had been done, questionless: the ugliest creature
> Creation framed for some use; yet to see
> I could not mark so much where it should be!

How full of doubt and trembling hesitation is the broken structure of the verse, too, and how true to nature the lie in the last line and a half, which she will persist in telling herself!

> *Als.* Lady —

But she does not hear him; she is too fearfully intent with watching a murder even now adoing in her own heart.

> *Beat.* (*aside.*) Why, men of art make much of poison,
> Keep one to expel another; where was my art?

The scene which follows, between Beatrice and De Flores, is a very powerful one. Not powerful in the same degree with Lear and Othello, but yet in the same kind, for as much power is needful to the making of a violet as of an oak. It is too long for us to copy the whole of it. She strives to persuade herself that De Flores is not so hideous to her after all, like a child talking aloud in the dark to relieve its terrors.

> When we are used
> To a hard face it is not so unpleasing;
> It mends still in opinion, hourly mends,
> I see it by experience. . . . .
> Hardness becomes the visage of a man well;
> It argues service, resolution, manhood,
> If cause were of employment.

De Flores is led on gradually to the desired end, and when he has sworn to devote himself to whatever service she may lay upon him, she exclaims, not daring to hear the name of "her murdered man," on her lips, till emboldened by slow degrees,

> Then take *him* to thy fury!
> *De F.* I thirst for him!
> *Beat.* Alonzo de Piracquo!

De Flores murders Piracquo, and brings one of his fingers with a ring upon it, as a token of the deed, to Beatrice. She is startled at sight of him.

> *Beat.* De Flores!
> *De F.* Lady?

She will not trust her tongue with anything more than an allusion to what she so eagerly longed for.

> *Beat.* Thy looks promise cheerfully.
> *De F.* All things are answerable, time, circumstance,
> Your wishes, and my service.
> *Beat.* Is IT done then?
> *De F.* Piracquo is no more.
> *Beat.* My joys start at mine eyes; *our sweet'st delights*
> *Are evermore born weeping.*
> *De F.* I've a token for you.
> *Beat.* For me?
> *De F.* But it was sent somewhat unwillingly:
> I could not get the ring without the finger.
> *Beat. Bless me, what hast thou done!*

Exclaims the horror-stricken Beatrice, the woman reviving again in her. She had hardened herself to the abstract idea of murder, but revolts at this dreadful material token of it.

> *De F.* Why is that more
> Than killing the whole man? I cut his heart-strings.

How finely is the contemptuous coolness of De Flores, the villain by calculation, set off by the shrinking dread of Beatrice, whose guilt is the child of a ravished intercourse between her passions and her affections. The sight of the ring carries her and us back to the sweet days of her innocency, and the picture is complete.

> *'Tis the first token my father made me send him.*

She sighs, remembering the calm purity from which she has fallen, and yet, at the same time, with the true cunning of a guiltiness which only half repents, strives to palliate the sin of whose terrible consciousness she must evermore be the cringing bondslave, by thinking of her father's tyranny. The horror which a murderer feels of the *physical fact* of murder, and the dread which creeps over him from the cold corpse of his victim, exemplified by Beatrice in the above quotation, seem, at first thought, strange phenomena in nature. But are they not in truth unwitting recognitions of the immortality of the soul, as if the wrong done were wholly to the body and had no terrors for the spiritual part of our being? This feeling may be well called *bodily remorse*, being clearly of a grosser and more outward nature than that strong agony which shakes us inwardly when we have done a murder upon the soul of our brother, and have been marked on our foreheads as spiritual Cains, by ingratitude, hypocrisy, mistrust, want of faith, or any other lie against God.

The remainder of this scene between De Flores and Beatrice is all of it striking, but we have not room to quote it all. De Flores tells her the loathsome price at which she has bought Piracquo's death and she exclaims,

> Why, 't is impossible thou canst be so wicked,
> Or shelter such a cunning cruelty,
> To make his death the murderer of my honor!
> Thy language is so bold and vicious,
> I cannot see which way I can forgive it
> With any modesty.

No guilt can ever sear out of a woman's soul the essential tenderness and purity of its nature. Desecrated as its dwelling may be by infamy and shame, with meek and silent forgiveness it comes home again to its ruined cell, and gently effaces, as far as it can, the ruthless traces of the destroyer. Alas! where the celestial whiteness of woman's nature is most bedimmed, she stands most in need of the uplifting sympathy of her sisters, who only give her scorn or a distant pity which makes her but the more an outcast. How more ennobling and worthy of us, it is to seek out and cherish the soiled remnant of an angelic nature in the lepers of sin against whom the hard world has shut its iron doors, than to worship it (which we are not over-ready to do) where it shines unclouded in the noble and the wise.

This modesty of Beatrice is one of the most touchingly natural traits in her character. De Flores spurned it as he would a worthless flower,

> Pish! you forget yourself;
> A woman dipped in blood, and talk of modesty!
> *Beat.* O, misery of sin! would I'd been bound
> Perpetually unto my living hate
> In that Piracquo, than to hear these words!
> Think but upon the distance that creation
> Set 'twixt thy blood and mine, and keep thee there.

She shrinks behind her pride, but the next speech of De Flores drives her forth from her flimsy shelter. The speech is a very vigorous one and full of moral truth.

De F. Look but into your conscience, read me there,
'T is a true book; *you'll find me there your equal:*
Pish! fly not to your birth, but settle you
In *what the act has made you, you're no more now;*
You must forget your parentage to me;
You are the deed's creature: by that name
You lost your first condition, *and I challenge you,*
As peace and innocency have turned you out,
And made you one with me.
    Beat. With thee, foul villain!
De F. Yes, my fair murderess, do you urge me?

Yes, there are no bounds of caste, no grades of rank, in sin. If we may be born again in virtue, so also may we be in sin, and we bear some trace of the hideous features of our second mother to our graves.

A very striking and forcible line is put into the mouth of De Flores when he first meets Tomaso, Piracquo's brother, after the murder.

I'd fain get off, this man's not for my company,
I smell his brother's blood when I come near him.
    Tom. Come hither, kind and true one; I remember,
My brother loved thee well.
    De F. O, purely, dear sir!
Methinks I'm now again a killing him,
He brings it so fresh to me. (*aside.*)

In another scene between Beatrice and De Flores, she is made to say something which is full of touching pathos. She suspects her maid of having betrayed her to her husband. De Flores asks,

Who would trust a waiting-woman?
    Beat. I must trust somebody.

How truly is here expressed the wilderness of bleak loneliness into which guilt drives those it possesses, forcing them, when that sweet spring of peacefulness, which bubbles up so freshly in the open confidingness of joy, is cut off, to seek a sympathy in their degradation, and in the bewildering darkness of doubt and suspicion, to *trust* some one, even though it be only with the story of their shame. In its lowest and most fallen estate, the spirit of man cannot shake off its inborn feeling of brotherhood, which whispers it to seek for that sympathy which in happier days it was perhaps too slow to grant. It is sorrow which teaches us most nearly how full of sustainment and help we may be to our fellows, and how much we in our turn stand in need of them; and that when once selfishness has rusted apart that chain which binds us so closely to man, it has also broken the supporting tie which links us with uplifting trustfulness to the all-enfolding sympathy of God.

In the last act Beatrice confesses her crime to her husband, and he cries bitterly

> O, thou art all deformed!
> *Beat.* Forget not, sir,
> It for your sake was done: shall greater dangers
> Make the less welcome?
> *Als. O, thou should' st have gone*
> *A thousand leagues about to have avoided*
> *This dangerous bridge of blood!* here we are lost!

There is a sternly truthful naturalness in these words of Alsemero. To a soul highly wrought up, language resolves itself into its original elements, and the relations and resemblances of things present themselves to it rather than the things themselves, so that the language of passion, in which conventionality is overwhelmed by the bursting forth of the original savage nature, is always metaphorical.

The tragic depth of the climax of this drama can only be thoroughly felt in a perusal of the whole. We can only quote a few sentences. There is much pathos in what the broken-hearted Beatrice says to her father, as she is dying.

> O, come not near me, sir, I shall defile you!
> I am that of your blood was taken from you
> For your better health; look no more upon it,
> But cast it to the ground regardlessly,
> Let the common sewer take it from distinction,
> Beneath the stars, upon yon meteor
> Ever hung my fate, 'mongst things corruptible;
> *(Pointing to De Flores.)*
> I ne'er could pluck it from him; my loathing
> Was prophet to the rest, but ne'er believed:
> Mine honor fell with him, and now my life.

The concluding words of the play which Alsemero addresses to his bereaved father-in-law, are fragrant with beautiful and sincere humanity.

Sir, you have yet a son's duty living,
Please you, accept it; let that your sorrow,
As it goes from your eye, go from your heart;
Man and his sorrow at the grave must part.
All we can do to comfort one another,
To stay a brother's sorrow for a brother,
To dry a child from the kind father's eyes,
Is to no purpose, it rather multiplies:
Your only smiles have power to cause re-live
The dead again, or in their rooms to give
Brother a new brother, father a child;
If these appear, all griefs are reconciled.

The dramatic power of Middleton is rather of the suggestive kind, than of that elaborately minute and finished order, which can trust wholly to its own completeness for effect. Only Shakespeare can so "on horror's head horrors accumulate," as to make the o'ercharged heart stand aghast and turn back with trembling haste from the drear abyss in which it was groping bewildered. Middleton has shown his deep knowledge of art and nature, by that strict appreciation of his own weakness, which is the hardest wisdom to gain, and which can only be the fruit of an earnest, willing, and humble study in his own heart, of those primitive laws of spirit which lie at the bottom of all hearts. It is much easier to feel our own strength than our want of it; indeed a feeling of the one blinds us to the other. Middleton is wise in choosing rather to give mysterious hints which the mind may follow out, than to strive to lead the imagination, which is most powerful in conjuring up images of horror, beyond where he could guide it with bold and unwavering certainty. With electric sympathy we feel the bewilderment of our guide's mind through the hand with which he leads us, and refuse to go farther, when, if left to ourselves, our very doubt would have enticed us onward.

To show our author's more graceful and delicate powers, we copy the following from another tragedy:

How near am I now to a happiness
The earth exceeds not! not another like it
[Leantio, *Women Beware Women*, 3.1.82-106].

Another, from the same play:

O, hast thou left me, then, Bianca, utterly?
Bianca, now I miss thee! O, return,
[Leantio, *Women Beware Women*, 3.2.241-48, 252-56].

We shall copy a few scattered passages, and conclude. [Here Lowell cites a variety of Middleton passages, under the following titles: The Sins of Great Men, Charity, Honor, Want of Nobleness, Sense of Guilt, Prudence, Patience, A Happy Man, Twilight, The World, The Body, Over-Cunning.]

There is a simplicity and manly directness in our old writers of tragedy, which comes to us with the more freshness in a time so conventional as our own. In their day, if the barrier between castes was more marked than it is now, that between hearts was less so. They were seers, indeed, using reverently that rare gift of inward sight which God had blessed them with, and not daring to blaspheme the divinity of Beauty, by writing of what they had not seen and truly felt in their own hearts and lives. . . .

"The Plays of Thomas Middleton," *The Pioneer* 1 (1843): 32-39.

68. 1844 Leigh Hunt: Tempered Enthusiasm

Leigh Hunt, critic, essayist, dramatist, and poet, was nearing sixty when he published *Imagination and Fancy*. His goals were to explain the nature and principles of poetry and to present with brief commentary some of the finest passages of poetry written in English. Those he chose as the greats among English poets were Spenser, Marlowe, Shakespeare, Jonson, Beaumont and Fletcher, Middleton, Dekker, Webster, Milton, Coleridge, Shelley, and Keats. From Middleton, he cited *The Witch*, 3.3.

Middleton partakes of the poetry and sweetness of Decker, but not to the same height: and he talks more at random. You hardly know what to make of the dialogue or stories of some of his plays. But he has more fancy; and there is one character of his (De Flores in the "*Changeling*") which, for effect at once tragical, probable, and poetical, surpasses anything I know of in the drama of domestic life. Middleton has the honour of having furnished part of the witch poetry to Macbeth, and of being conjoined with it also in the powerful and beautiful music of Locke.[103]

103. Matthew Locke, the seventeenth-century composer thought to have written the *Macbeth* music now usually attributed to Henry Purcell.

Imagination and Fancy; Or Selections from the English Poets. London: Smith, Elder, 1844, p. 222.

69. 1845 Dead to All But a Few

George L. Craik, a professor of English literature and history at Queen's College, Belfast, was a friend of Leigh Hunt, but he did not share Hunt's interest in Shakespeare's contemporaries. Should one begin to think that everyone shared the Romantics' enthusiasm, Craik's *Sketches of the History of Literature and Learning in England* is a good antidote: only Shakespeare, Craik believed, had risen above the rudeness of his era.

Where are now the best productions even of such writers as Greene, and Peele, and Marlow, and Decker, and Marston, and Webster, and Thomas Heywood, and Middleton? They are to be found among our 'Select Collections of Old Plays,' — publications intended rather for the mere preservation of the pieces contained in them, than for their diffusion among a multitude of readers. Or, if the entire works of a few of these elder dramatists have recently been collected and republished, this has still been done only to meet the demand of a comparatively very small number of curious students, anxious to possess and examine for themselves whatever relics are still recoverable of the old world of our literature. Popularly known and read the works of these writers never again will be; there is no more prospect or probability of this than there is that the plays of Shakspeare will ever lose their popularity among his countrymen. In that sense, everlasting oblivion is their portion, as everlasting life is his. In one form only have they any chance of again attracting some measure of the general attention — namely, in the form of such partial and very limited exhibition as Lamb has given us an example of in his 'Specimens.' And herein we see the first great difference between the plays of Shakspeare and those of his predecessors, and one of the most immediately conspicuous of the improvements which he introduced into dramatic writing. He did not create our regular drama, but he regenerated and wholly transformed it, as if by breathing into it a new soul. We possess no dramatic production anterior to his appearance that is at once a work of high genius and of anything like equably sustained power throughout. Wonderful bursts of poetry there are in many of the pieces of our earlier dramatists; but the higher they soar in one scene, the lower they generally seem to think it expedient to sink in the next. Their great efforts are made only by fits and starts: for the most part it must be confessed that the best of them are either merely extravagant and absurd, or do nothing but trifle or dose away over their task with the expenditure of hardly any kind of faculty at all. This may have arisen in part from their own want of judgment or want of painstaking, in part from the demands of a very rude condition of the popular taste; but the effect is to invest all that they have bequeathed to us with an air of barbarism, and to tempt us to take their finest displays of successful daring for mere capricious inspirations, resembling the sudden impulses of fury by which the listless and indolent man of the woods will sometimes be roused for the instant from his habitual laziness and passiveness to an exhibition of superhuman strength and activity. From this savage or savage-looking state our drama was first redeemed by Shakspeare. [Craik goes on to praise Shakespeare and criticize his colleagues, since "the generality of the dramatic writers who were contemporary with Shakspeare still belong to the semi-barbarous school which subsisted before he began to write" (p.187). He follows with sketches of the playwrights.]

Thomas Middleton is the author, in whole or in part, of between twenty and thirty dramatic pieces; his associates in those which he did not write entirely himself being Decker, Rowley, Jonson, Fletcher, and Massinger. One of his plays, a comedy called The Old Law, which he wrote in conjunction with Rowley (and which was afterwards improved by Massinger), appears to have been acted so early as 1599; and another was published in 1602. The greater number of his pieces are comedies, and, compared with most of his contemporaries, he has a good deal of comic talent; but his most noted dramatic production is his tragi-comedy of The Witch, which remained in manuscript till a small impression of it was printed, in 1778, by Isaac Reed, after it had been suggested by Steevens that it had probably been written before Macbeth, and might have been the source from which Shakspeare borrowed his Witches in that play.[104] The commentators would have everything, in Shakspeare and everybody else, to be borrowed or stolen: they have the genius and the zeal of thief-catchers in ferreting out and exposing all transferences among writers, real and imaginary, of thoughts, words, and syllables; and in the present case, as in many others, their professional ardour seems to have made a great deal out of very little. Lamb, in an admirable criticism, has pointed out the essential differences between the witches of Shakspeare and those of Middleton, from whose play, however, Shakspeare appears to have taken a few lines of his incantations; unless, indeed — which we think not improbable — the verses in question were common popular rhymes, preserved among the traditions of the nursery or the country fireside. Middleton's witches have little of the

104. See entry 48.

supernatural awfulness of Shakspeare's. [He goes on to quote Lamb, see entry 55.]

Geo[rge] L. Craik. *Sketches of the History of Literature and Learning in England.* Vol. 3, *From the Accession of Elizabeth to the Revolution of 1688.* London: Charles Knight, 1845, 179-80, 190-92.

70. 1853 What a Student Might Learn

Students were to have little knowledge of Middleton from William Spalding's popular *History of English Literature*, which was still used in classes in Britain and the United States at the turn of the next century. Even though Spalding was a specialist in the Renaissance and might be expected to encourage students to love that era, he argues that writings so licentious as early seventeenth-century dramas should be "passed over very cursorily," because the "pleasure which their genius gives can be safely enjoyed only by minds mature and well trained" (p. 262). As a result, he devotes but a sentence to Middleton, in the section on the audiences to which various dramatists appealed.

Jonson might be held to have written chiefly for men of sense and knowledge, Fletcher and his friend for men of fashion and the world. A similar audience to that of Jonson may have been aimed at in the stately, epical tragedies of Chapman. The other class of auditors, or one a step lower, would have relished better such plays as those of Middleton and Webster: the former of whom is chiefly remarkable for a few striking ideas imperfectly wrought out. . . .

William Spalding. *The History of English Literature.* Edinburgh: Oliver & Boyd, 1853, p. 265.

71. 1859 E. P. Whipple: "Oppressive and Impressive"

Edwin Percy Whipple was a noted Massachusetts author and speaker who, during the lyceum period, addressed a thousand audiences. This lecture on Heywood, Middleton, Marston, Dekker, Webster, and Chapman was given before the Lowell Institute in 1859; later it was printed in the *Atlantic Monthly* (under the editorship of James Russell Lowell, see entry 67) and incorporated into Whipple's 1869 *Literature of the Age of Elizabeth.* To Whipple, a writer should be sympathetic, tender, genial, and sentimental, and

Middleton's plays, because they lack warmth, make depressing reading. Like many nineteenth-century male critics, Whipple identifies strongly with Leantio and his "agonizing complaint," demonstrating again that cultural values, here on the nature of women, marriage, and sexuality, shape one's readings.

With less fluency of diction, less skill in fastening the reader's interest to his fable, harsher in versification, and generally clumsier in construction [than Heywood's], the best plays of Thomas Middleton are still superior to Heywood's in force of imagination, depth of passion, and fulness of matter. It must, however, be admitted that the sentiments which direct his powers are not so fine as Heywood's. He depresses the mind, rather than invigorates it. The eye he cast on human life was not the eye of a sympathizing poet, but rather that of a sagacious cynic. His observation, though sharp, close, and vigilant, is somewhat ironic and unfeeling. His penetrating, incisive intellect cuts its way to the heart of a character as with a knife; and if he lays bare its throbs of guilt and weakness, and lets you into the secrets of its organization, he conceives his whole work is performed. This criticism applies even to his tragedy of "Women beware Women," a drama which shows a deep study of the sources of human frailty, considerable skill in exhibiting the passions in their consecutive, if not in their conflicting action, and a firm hold upon character; but it lacks pathos, tenderness, and humanity; its power is out of all proportion to its geniality; the characters, while they stand definitely out to the eye, are seen through no visionary medium of sentiment and fancy; and the reader feels the force of Leantio's own agonizing complaint, that his affliction is

> "Of greater weight than youth was made to bear,
> As if a punishment of after-life
> Were fall'n upon man here, so new it is
> To flesh and blood, so strange, so insupportable."

There is, indeed, no atmosphere to Middleton's mind; and the hard, bald caustic peculiarity of his genius, which is unpleasingly felt in reading any one of his plays, becomes a source of painful weariness as we plod doggedly through the five thick volumes of his works. Like the incantations of his own witches, it "casts a thick scurf over life." It is most powerfully felt in his tragedy of "The Changeling," at once the most oppressive and impressive effort of his genius. The character of De Flores in this play has in it a strangeness of iniquity, such as we think is hardly paralleled in the whole range of the Elizabethan drama. The passions of this brute imp are not human. They are such as might be conceived of as springing from the union of animal with fiendish impulses, in a nature which knew no law outside of its own lust, and was as incapable of a scruple as of a sympathy.

"Minor Elizabethan Dramatists," *Atlantic Monthly* 20 (1867): 693-94.

72. 1873-78 Anthony Trollope: A Novelist's Condemnation

Anthony Trollope read Middleton's plays during his late fifties and early sixties when, according to his autobiography, he was searching the Elizabethan and Jacobean dramatists for plots and characters. Though his *Ralph the Heir* (1871) draws on *Michaelmas Term*[105] and his *Fixed Period* (1882) is based on *The Old Law*, his notes in his copy of Dyce's edition indicate that he finds little to admire in Middleton's technique or morality. In many ways, Trollope is the stereotypical Victorian. He applauds the moral progress England has made since the vulgar Renaissance: Middleton's plays too much reflect his vicious age. To Trollope, a "good" writer promotes virtue through sentimental and "poetic" language, through the depiction of irreproachable people — especially women[106] — who make honorable choices, and through the "poetic" justice of the plot. In all three, Middleton's plays too often fall short for Trollope, hence his animosity.

August 1873 and later, undated, *The Roaring Girl* (2:559):
A most unintelligible gallimafrey, unreadable as a whole and but little worth the labour of the attempt; but with sparkles of such wit as was then popular. It is not divided into acts and therefore the more confused. This and many plays of James I were probably written in great haste to satisfy the demands of the Stage. They are hardly worth looking at except as giving pictures of the period.
[Later]
In the above note I have spoken of this play as not divided into acts and scenes, — whereas it has been so divided, by Dyce, in this volume. But the note is extracted from Dodsley, in whose edition I read the play. In Pearsons edition of Dekkers works this piece is again given undivided; but with that work no trouble whatever was taken —

---

105. See Geoffrey Harvey, "Trollope's Debt to the Renaissance Drama."
106. Trollope measured writers by their virtuous female characters (Elizabeth R. Epperly, *Anthony Trollope's Notes on the Old Drama*, 29-33), which reflects his sense that his female readership should find respectable role models in his novels.

3 March 1874, *The Mayor of Quinborough* (1: [222]):

This play is very bad reading, but is interesting as shewing what a gallimafrey of plot was pleasing to the frequenters of plays in the reign of James I. There is such a variety of incident that it can all be included in the one piece only by the insertion of dumb shews between the acts; and yet, with even that aid, it must have been very long. I cannot but think that it must also have been very tedious.

Simon the Mayor has but very little to do with the play, the connexion between him and the Vortigern plot being maintained only by the thongs of leather the Mayor cut. He seems to have been introduced simply that the horse play of the cheaters and the clown might be introduced on the stage. The present name has grown on to the play probably because his portion of the action best pleased the audience —

29 May 1874, *Blurt, Master Constable* (1: 308-[309]):

It is impossible to criticise this play by any laws of literature as they exist now; — as it is also absurd to judge it by the taste of the present age.

From the days of Marlowe and Shakespeare downwards the dramatists gradually fell from poetry and charm of character-painting to quaintness of language and intricacy of plot, garnished with bawdry, till at last they brought plays to the birth so garbled in language and so confused in incident as to be almost unintelligible to the reader of the present day. Middleton, who was late among the lot, was about the most offensive. Nevertheless there is in this comedy a certain spirit which makes it readable.

Why it should have been called by the Constable's name I cannot say, unless it had first some other name and then was known by the special acting of one person, as Greenes Tu Quoque, and Lord Dundreary[107] in our own time.

8 July 1876, *The Old Law* (1: 120):

See Massingers works.[108] [In Dyce's introduction (1: 57), where Lamb is cited on *The Old Law* (entry 55), Trollope responds to Lamb's comment that Middleton and Rowley had "finer geniuses" than Massinger by noting, "But neither of them Massingers ear for poetry & melody — ."]

---

107. Edwin Askew Sothern was famed for his interpretation of this character in Tom Taylor's *Our American Cousin.*

108. Epperly cites Trollope's note from his copy of *The Plays of Philip Massinger*: "The fun of Middleton (or Rowley) — for I do not distinguish between them is dirty and commonplace, but is often very funny. With old Agatha there is even a touch of true pathos" (105-106).

8 October 1876, *Women Beware Women* (4: [635]):
The execution of the 3 first acts of this play is so good as to make the critic feel that Middleton, had he given himself fair chance by continued labour, might have excelled all the Elizabethan dramatists except Shakespeare. But the plot is so detestable, there not being a single part which is not abhorrent to the reader, that the same critic is driven to acknowledge that, with all his power of language, this author could never have become a great poet.

That Bianca and Livia should have been abominable one could have endured, had not Isabella have been equally bad. Her conscience was soon made easy when she was brought to think that her paramour was not quite her uncle.

The execution of the last portion of the play is as bad as the plot.

But it has to be acknowledged that there is wonderful work in the first three acts.

15 January 1877, *A Trick to Catch the Old One* (2: 99):
I cannot call this a good play, though I can understand that it should have been lively on the stage. The fun is all low in its nature, and of poetry there is little or none. As to the morality the less said the better.

January 1877, *The Witch* (3: 335):
This play is for the most part confused outrageous and uninteresting, nor is there anything to recommend it to special attention but the fact that it contains certain expressions which make it not improbable that Shakespeare borrowed from it. It may have been written before Macbeth; — though not before Othello — and there is a passage in Act IV s iii which seems to shew that one poet must have known the work of the other. There is no other interest in Middletons Witch, which is very inferior to the work generally of the Elizabethan dramatists.

17 February 1877, *The Phoenix* (1: 409):
This is an intricate uninteresting vulgar play, written altogether for the audience and not for the closet, — and which I should think must have been dull even to an audience. Tangle who goes mad over his law has the best of it.

4 March 1877, *The Family of Love* (2: 209):
The wit of this play, or rather I should say the fun, is much too poor to excuse the dullness and the coarseness together. When it breaks into verse the verses are more prosaic than the prose. See the dialogue between Geraldine and Maria Act III. Sc. I than which nothing can be worse.

10 March 1877, *No Wit, No Help Like a Woman's* (5: 131):
This is a bad play all round; — bad in language, bad in character, and bad in plot. And yet there is a certain activity about it that may have made it attractive on the stage to an audience devoid of all taste. The people with whom the reader is intended to sympathise are all bad; — and then there is not a single scene that is not badly writ.

31 March 1877, *A Chaste Maid in Cheapside* (4: 88):
Middletons plays are all bad to me. The system on which he plans them disgusts me. Every character here is vitious. — except that of the girl Moll, who consequently has little to do. And then his sudden repentances are as bad as his successful rascals. But all this is not the worst. When he is funny, — in prose, — his fun is always dull. When he rises to poetry, — or attempts to rise, he cannot get his feet off the ground. This is the case in this play when the author attempts to become serious. The lines which Moll sings p. 88 would make a pretty song.

4 April 1877, *A Game at Chess* (4: 412):
I have found that it was impossible to read this piece. There is a certain interest in the allusions to the religious feuds of the time; and the language in which these are described is sometimes good; — the abominations of the Papacy are well put forth; — but the dramatic form, with the personages of the pawns etc, is so unreal, and so antipathetic to dramatic effect, that the piece is to me so dull as to be unreadable.

9 April 1877, *Anything for a Quiet Life* (4: 509-510):
    This play is readable; which is more than can be said of some of Middleton; and the character of Mrs Knavesby, when she refuses to become a w---- at her husbands order, is well, and in one or two lines, finely portrayed. But all the other characters are vapid and meaningless, bad or good as the special scenes may require.

27 April 1877, *More Dissemblers Besides Women* (3: [645]):
    This play like most of Middleton is very hard reading. I can understand that there should have been amusement from the acting. According to the fun of the time there would have been fun in the singing master and dancing master giving lessons to the poor mock page, when she was just about to fall into the straw, and in the dignity of the Duchess, and the hypocrisy of the Cardinal there may have been amusement. All the serious underplots no doubt served, though each severally is poor. But as a play for the closet there

is nothing in it. It never rises to poetry though there is much easy versification —

6 February 1878, *Michaelmas Term* (1: 514):
The grains of wheat are so few that it is hard indeed to pick them out of the chaff. There are a few grains, but the chaff is overwhelming. That such a play should ever have pleased a large audience is the marvel.

26 March 1878, *Your Five Gallants* (2: 323):
    This piece is so tedious, so perplexed so uninteresting and so bad, that one is at loss to conceive how such a man as Dyce could have given up his time to editing it. To have read it is a sin, in the wasting of time.

31 March 1878, *A Fair Quarrel* (3: 549):
This is a very good play, but surely Middleton never wrote it. The play, no doubt, was Rowleys, with the parts of the roarers and street-walkers put in by Middleton. C. Lamb in his criticism . . . is quite correct as to the excellence of the main plot as shewn in the characters of Ager and Ager's mother,[109] but has not seen, or has not been careful to mark, the difference between the work of the two dramatists to whom the play has been attributed. Middleton never did such work as that of the scenes in which Ager is concerned; — never wrote such poetry or conceived such characters. Rowley is called a third rate dramatist; — perhaps correctly if Shakespeare is to form the 1st class and Fletcher the second; — but Rowley was a poet and understood a plot. Middleton understood only the appetite of his audience for low buffoonery.

20 April 1878, *The Changeling* (4: 300):
There is much movement in this play and there are scenes of interest. But it is so confused and inconsequent that the reader can too readily perceive the quick unmatured way in which the dramatists of James I. worked with the plots which fell in their way. There is, however, more good work in this play than ever came from Middletons hands.

April 1878, *A Mad World, My Masters* (2:422):
This is a good rattling comedy of the time, with more of true fun in it than many, — but still without anything in it worthy of mention. It is Middleton, perhaps at his best, — but only Middleton.

109. See entry 55.

April 1878, *The Spanish Gypsy* (4: 202):
This play is often tedious and sometimes obscure; but there is much in it good in action and something of real poetry. The humour, like all that of Middleton, is none for this age. It perhaps tricked a time in which men were less impatient and more easily pleased. The poetry we may be sure did not come from Middleton. It was probably written by Rowley. Someone says that Rowley was a third rate dramatist. To what class then must Middleton be relegated.

Ms. Notes in Trollope's set of *The Works of Thomas Middleton*, edited by Alexander Dyce. Folger Shakespeare Library, PR 2711 .D8 As. Col.

73. 1874 William Minto: Still Funny to Someone

William Minto was versatile: critic, editor, journalist, professor (at Aberdeen), and novelist. His goal in *Characteristics of English Poets from Chaucer to Shirley*, written when he was nearly thirty, was to reveal the person behind the works — as Minto phrased it, to answer the question, "What sort of man was he?" Minto is particularly interesting because the evolution of his thinking can be traced; he revised this analysis for the book's second edition in 1885 (see entry 76) and reviewed Bullen's 1885 edition of Middleton's works (see entry 79). In Minto's defense of Middleton, he answers critics like Trollope (see entry 72).

Middleton's comedies come nearer than Dekker's to Hazlitt's idea of "making human nature look as mean, as ridiculous, and as contemptible as possible;"[110] and they also put human nature into very laughable situations. Middleton, whose birth Mr. Dyce fixes at a date not earlier than 1570, began like Marston as a satirist, publishing 'Microcynicon,' "six snarling satires," in couplets, in 1599; and followed up this with a prose satire, called the 'Black Book,' in 1604. But he achieved no great success in this fashionable and artificial line of composition: his rhymed satire is inferior to Marston's or Donne's, and his prose very inferior to Dekker's 'Seven Deadly Sins of London.' These performances, however, sufficiently show the character of the man — his broad, clever, unsentimental humour, and shrewd common-sense.
  Middleton was formally conjoined with Dekker in the composition of

110. "Lecture II: On Shakspeare and Ben Jonson," *The Complete Works of William Hazlitt*, 35.

"The Honest Whore," though his share is not conspicuous; and he would seem in his earliest work to have looked up to Dekker as a friend and master. His Simon the Tanner, the "Mayor of Quinborough," is an imitation of Dekker's Simon Eyre the shoemaker, Mayor of London. But the romantic and tragic element in that play is very coarse compared with the serious side of Dekker's plays; and Middleton found a more congenial field in the unmixed comedy of Jonson and Chapman. "A Trick to Catch the Old One," and "A Mad World, my Masters," were apparently written at the instigation of Chapman's "All Fools," the great exemplar and archetype of the English comedy of "gulling." In this type of comedy Middleton is exceedingly happy, and surpasses his masters in ingenuity of construction and easy accumulation of mirthful circumstances. The fun begins early, and goes on to the end with accelerating speed. He excels particularly in making his gulls accessory to their own deception, and in putting into their mouths statements that have, to those in the secret, a meaning very much beyond what they intend. From the preface to "The Roaring Girl" — which was written in conjunction with Dekker, and bears marks of his hand in the shopping and gallanting scenes, if not also in the character ascribed to Moll, and some of the speeches put into her mouth — we learn that Middleton prided himself on the construction of his comedies. There is an alteration, he says, now in the fashion of playmaking: "your huge bombasted plays, quilted with mighty words to lean purpose," have gone out of fashion, and neater inventions, with single plots and quaint conceits, have been set up. He professes also to be more decent than some of his predecessors, and has a gird apparently at Marston or Jonson, as some obscene fellow, who cares not what he writes against others, yet rips up the most nasty vice in his own plays, and presents it to a modest assembly. It is the excellency of a writer, says Middleton, to leave things better than he finds them.[111] According to this principle, in the "Trick to Catch the Old One," and the "Mad World," the courtesans are married and made honest women — the rakes are reclaimed; and though no lesson is weightily inculcated, there is less indecency than in the works of more pretentious moralists.

Middleton's genius — and genius he did possess in no small measure — was essentially comical and unromantic. If Middleton "is admired for a certain wild and fantastic fancy, which delights in portraying scenes of witchcraft and supernatural agency,"[112] the admiration must come from people who have read only the witch-scenes in "The Witch," and have not quite appreciated even them. Middleton's witches, which Malone first held,

111. See entry 2.
112. A variety of writers express this idea, but I have not identified the source of this wording.

and then did not hold, to have been created before Shakespeare's,[113] exist more for comic and spectacular purposes than as an integral part of a tragic conception. Familiarity breeds contempt: if they had been consulted only by the Duchess, with a view to the murder of her husband, they might have kept up an appearance of dignity and terror; but when the drunk Almachildes staggers in among them, upsets some of the beldams, and is received by Hecate as a favoured lover, we cease to have much respect for them, even though they do profess to exercise the terrible power of raising jars, jealousies, strifes, and heart-burning disagreements like a thick scarf o'er life. The visit of the fantastical gentleman whom Hecate has thrice enjoyed in incubus, is a very happy inspiration in the same vein as Tam o'Shanter's admiration of the heroine of Alloway Kirk:[114] the scene is a fine opportunity for a comic actor; but it is damaging to the respectability of the dread Hecate. The tragedy of "Women Beware Women," the last act of which makes a quick dispatch of all the chief actors after the model of the Spanish Tragedy, is sadly wanting in dignity of character. The characters are all so vile that the pity and terror produced by their death is almost wholly physical. Tragedy, as I have said, was not Middleton's *forte*.

Characteristics of English Poets from Chaucer to Shirley. Edinburgh and London: W. Blackwood and Sons, 1874, pp. 453-56.

74. 1875 A Modern Historian: Vivacious and Moral

Adolphus William Ward, for many years a professor of history and literature, is perhaps best remembered as co-editor of the *Cambridge History of English Literature.* His *History of English Dramatic Literature to the Death of Queen Anne* is the first systematic and in-depth "modern" history of the Elizabethan and Jacobean playwrights; and his lengthy analysis of Middleton reflects his belief that Middleton may be of interest to a wider audience. Although Ward shares some of Trollope's literary values, he disagrees with Trollope about Middleton.

THOMAS MIDDLETON was born about 1570, or rather later, the son of a gentleman settled in London. In the Introductory Epistle to his mask of *A World Tost at Tennis* he speaks of himself as 'born on the bank-side of Helicon, brought up amongst noble gentle commons and good scholars of all

113. For Malone's argument in favor of Middleton's precedence and a citation to his counter-argument, see entry 48.
114. Tam o'Shanter admired the witch Cutty Sark in Robert Burns's *Tam o'Shanter* (1791).

sorts, where, for his time, he did good and honest service beyond the small seas.' These expressions would seem to indicate that he was born in South London (he is also described as of Newington in the county of Surrey), that he enjoyed the education of a gentleman, and that he served for a short time in the wars in the Netherlands or in France. It may be unhesitatingly affirmed that he was at one time a member of Cambridge University, to the life at which he frequently refers in his plays with the easy but not unconscious familiarity of the old University man. Moreover, his works are, notwithstanding their frequent coarseness, distinguished by a general flavour of good-breeding from those of such an author as Dekker. [Ward continues to discuss Middleton's life.]

Of Middleton's relations to his more prominent literary contemporaries we know little or nothing; except that Jonson in the *Conversations* set him down as 'a base fellow,' while Thomas Heywood mentions him, without any special tribute of praise, among the dramatists of the age.[115] Three of his plays were brought on the stage after the Restoration; but he has since been less remembered than his deserts would have warranted. At the same time, as will appear from the following brief review of his works, he was perhaps happiest in a branch of dramatic literature which more than any other addresses itself in the first instance to the sympathies of a particular age. But he has merits which seem to call for a fuller record than has usually fallen to his lot in surveys of the Elisabethan drama.

[On *The Mayor of Quinborough*] It is in the manner of the Chronicle Histories, though written with far greater ease and freedom of diction than these . . . but as a whole the piece seems hardly to deserve perusal.

[On *The Old Law*] The play is a romantic comedy on a sufficiently extravagant theme; but this being once allowed as admissible, the execution must be described as both facile and felicitous. 'Evander, duke of Epire' has promulgated a law ordaining that all old men living to the age of fourscore years, and all women to that of threescore, are to be cut off as useless members of the commonwealth. With the exception of one dutiful son and his wife, who hide their aged father till he is discovered by the wiles of a female hypocrite to whom they have revealed their secret, this law is universally welcomed and put into execution with extreme eagerness. In the end it appears that the good Duke has merely intended to test the virtue of his subjects; the supposed victims of the law are made to sit in judgment on its supporters; and a new law is proclaimed which decrees that no son and

115. See entries 6 and 27.

heir shall be held 'capable of his inheritance at the age of one and twenty, unless he be at that time as mature in obedience, manners and goodness,' and that no wife who has designed her husband's death shall be allowed to marry for ten years after it has taken place. This conception, a very good one of its kind, is carried out with considerable spirit and humour; and much incidental fun is made of a speculative gentleman (Gnotho) who attempts to cut short his wife's period of existence by bribing a clerk to make a trifling change in the register of her birth, and then freely offers 'two to one' on his next matrimonial venture.

Altogether, this comedy makes a most pleasing impression, containing as it does occasional passages of no little tenderness of feeling; while it will hardly cause surprise that no advantage is taken of the subject to suggest the deeper kind of satire for which it might have furnished an occasion, but which would have hardly suited the author's conception of his theme.

[On *Blurt, Master Constable*] The lightness and gaiety of writing in *Blurt, Master-Constable* (printed 1602) cannot render tolerable a play with so vile a plot. Beginning pleasantly and indeed prettily enough, with the sudden passion of a lady for the prisoner brought home from the wars by her lover, it ends offensively with the unfaithfulness of the prisoner, who has escaped and married the lady, and is finally brought back to her by a device which resembles a parody on the plot of *All's Well that Ends Well*. A good deal of humour is however scattered through the piece, and Blurt the Master-Constable, with his attendant Slubber, may be remembered as one of the many counterparts to Dogberry and Verges. The reader may perhaps thank me for rescuing a pretty song from the midst of a mass of ribaldry which he will prefer to avoid:

> 'Love is like a lamb, and love is like a lion;
> Fly from love, he fights, fight, then does he fly on;
> Love is all a fire, and yet is ever freezing;
> Love is much in winning, yet is more in leesing;
> Love is ever sick, and yet is never dying;
> Love is ever true, and yet is ever lying;
> Love does doat in liking, and is mad in loathing;
> Love indeed is anything, yet indeed is nothing.'

[On *The Phoenix*] The comedy of *The Phoenix* (printed 1607) is said to be founded on a Spanish novel (*The Force of Love*); but from whatever source the plot be taken, it is a very ingenious one, and well, though rather lengthily, carried out. Prince Phoenix, being sent on his travels by his aged father to prepare himself for the duties of the throne, prefers to travel at home, and to study in disguise the evils which it will be his province as a sovereign to remove. (We have therefore here a new version of the old Haroun Alraschid device, used in a similar way by Shakspere in his *Measure for Measure*.) He succeeds both in discovering a mass of iniquity, and ultimately in bringing it to justice before the Duke. . . . The whole play is a social satire of some power — especially in the passages directed against the abuse of the law — and in two speeches of the Prince [Law, 1.4 and Matrimony, 2.2] there is true elevation of moral sentiment.

[On *The Witch*] The plot is a tissue, not worth the unravelling, of intrigues, the most important of these being taken, and very much marred in the taking, from the well-known story of the revenge of Rosamond upon Alboin, related in Macchiavelli's *History of Florence*, but probably known to Middleton through Belleforest. The main question of interest with regard to this play is whether the machinery of the witches was borrowed by Middleton from Shakspere, or *vice versâ*.

[On *More Dissemblers Besides Women*] . . . a comedy of intrigue, the plot of which is not infelicitously devised. . . . Thus a satisfactory embroglio results, which is further heightened by the existence of a poor little page, really a girl in disguise, whom the dissolute Lactantio has ruined. The pathos of this latter character is spoilt by some scenes of the grossest indelicacy. A comic character is supplied in Lactantio's servant Dondolo, a successful variation of the Launcelot Gobbo type; while a novelty is introduced in a scene in a gipsy camp, where Dondolo makes some futile attempts to master a language as puzzling to him as it has proved to many other students of philology.

Among Middleton's works this seems to furnish a good example of his versification, which is fluent and pleasing in the dialogue; the numerous lyrics are all trivial.

[On *The Spanish Gypsy*] . . . one might be tempted to ascribe to Rowley's co-operation the marked element of serious purpose which distinguishes this from the generality of Middleton's independently-written plays. . . . This part of the play [Roderigo and Clara] is written with a combination of power and delicacy to which Middleton is in general a stranger; but I would not on a mere conjecture deny to him the credit of scenes which display elements of tragic genius. . . .

The ways of the 'noble gipsies' are depicted with all Middleton's vivacity; and there is much opportunity for humorous scenes. The play within the play is made use of somewhat as in *Hamlet*; but the corregidor's intention to convey a lesson to his guilty son is frustrated by that son himself, who being one of the actors and (for it is an *extempore* play on a given theme) at liberty to say what he likes, says it.

As a whole, this finely-written production is an excellent example of the romantic comedy of the later Elisabethan type.

[On *A Fair Quarrel*] It is not to be denied that this plot furnishes an opportunity for an analysis of character, and for an illustration of a problem of social morality, of a far deeper nature than is usual with so light-hearted a philosopher as Middleton. There is much nobility in the developement of Captain Ager's moral struggle with himself, recalling later attempts of a not dissimilar character, designed to illustrate the distinction — meaningless it would seem to many minds — between moral and merely physical courage. But the flaw in the construction is the ignobility of the hypothesis that a nobly trustful mind would allow itself to entertain doubts on such a charge as that which Captain Ager has in the first instance to meet. The doubts ought by a skilful management of the plot to have been suggested from without; and in such a way as to render excusable on the part of the son a passing hesitation as to the justice of his quarrel. Then would have followed as a crushing confirmation of these doubts the false confession of the mother, and the powerful situation in which the interest of the action centres would have been reached without our sympathy with the hero being impaired. I pass by the painfully offensive bye-plot of the play, as well as the humours, not ill-contrived, of master Chough, a 'Cornish diamond,' and a student in a school of 'roaring' in London — a conception quite worthy of Ben Jonson.

[On *The Changeling*] The unusual strength of the situations in this play, together with comic scenes of an almost equally pronounced kind, account for the great popularity which it enjoyed; it was revived after the Restoration, and the favour with which it was again received is attested by Pepys.[116] The humour of the scenes in the private madhouse will be less acceptable to a modern reader, who is unable to place himself on the standpoint of an age which regarded mental derangement as a subject for fun; but the subject is treated, after Middleton's manner, with more lightness of touch than is shown on a similar occasion by Dekker [in *The Honest Whore*], and the character of Lollio, the mad-doctor's man, is genuinely comic. In the main plot of the piece, on the other hand . . . it is impossible not to recognise a most powerful subject for dramatic treatment, but an offensive developement

116. See entry 33.

is given to its latter part. 'Beatrice-Joana, in order to marry Alsemero, causeth De Flores to murther Alfonso Piracquo, who was a suitor to her. Alsemero marries her, and finding De Flores and her in adultery, kills them both.' The character of De Flores, an ill-favoured villain, hated by Beatrice till he consents to become a murderer on her behalf, is drawn with much force, and has a touch in it of Shakspere's Gloster. But though some of the scenes of this play are beyond a doubt terribly effective, the authors have not worked with sufficient care to reconcile the horrible story with psychological probability, and have needlessly made ghastly additions to a plot the blackness of which required no intensification.

[On *Women Beware Women*] The tragedy . . . may perhaps be taken as an illustration of Middleton's degree of power as a tragic writer, when unassisted by Rowley, and confirm the probability suggested above as to the share attributable to the latter in the joint efforts of these dramatists. . . . Some passages in this tragedy are not devoid of fire, and the scenes in which the Duke's meeting with Bianca is contrived and in which he entertains her at Court, the miserable husband standing by, are written with effective vivacity. But Middleton fails to show himself capable of true tragic dignity; and though his aim is undoubtedly moral, he is unable to furnish any relief of lofty sentiment to the grossness of the situations; while the humorous characters are revoltingly coarse. He lacked, in short, both delicacy of sentiment and sustained earnestness; and this tragedy, though not ineffective, must on the whole be considered an attempt in a direction which Middleton when left to himself was probably incapable of pursuing with real success.

[On *Michaelmas Term*] It is indeed one of the best-constructed and most freshly-written among the numerous Elisabethan comedies of its kind; for the *dramatis personae* are the usual figures of that comedy whose scene lies in the city of London, and whose satire is directed against the every-day follies and vices of the age. . . . The play is written with so much vivacity and, considering the subject, with so little coarseness, that it will be read with great pleasure as a most spirited and healthy satirical sketch of the manners of the times. A very originally-conceived Induction is prefixed to the play. . . .

[On *A Trick to Catch the Old One*] . . . one of Middleton's most vivacious comedies; and from its plot Massinger borrowed a few hints for his famous play of *A New Way to Pay Old Debts*. Though moral justice can certainly not be said to be very symmetrically dealt out to the characters of this piece — for while the usurers are punished, the libertine and his companion

are rewarded — the plot is contrived with considerable ingenuity. . . .
This — in half of its results — more than doubtful plot is carried out in
Middleton's gay, though at times very coarse, manner; and the characters of
the two usurers, their congenial friends and colleagues, and Dampit, a
'trampler' or lawyer of the most disreputable kind, are drawn with
considerable spirit.

[On *The Family of Love*] . . . an ordinary comedy of intrigue; and though
introducing as a comic element some coarse satire on an extravagant
developement of religious enthusiasm, does this in such a way as to lead to
the conclusion that the dramatist knew little or nothing of that which he was
attempting to satirise. Some witty touches are not wanting; but it would be
a mistake to seek here for evidence of anything more than the author's hatred
of a supposed hypocritical cloak for sneaking immorality.

[On *Your Five Gallants*] . . . another comedy of a familiar type.

[On *A Mad World, My Masters*] . . . while written with a full share of
Middleton's usual vivacity and in part very ingenious in construction, [it]
deserves, even more strongly than a play by the same author already noticed
[*A Trick to Catch the Old One*], a reprobation not usually merited by the
Elisabethan comedies, however coarse in their situations or in their language.
The plot is that of the cozening by a young scamp of an old fool his
grandfather; but though a kind of retributive justice is wreaked upon both,
it is hardly equivalent to a punishment in the case of the hero, who is at the
same time the *rascal* of the piece. Could the charge be brought home to the
pre-Restoration drama that, like the Restoration drama, it exhibits any
general tendency towards sympathy with vice, it would be necessary to adopt
a very different tone from that which seems just in criticising its productions.
Now here, after a series of rascally tricks, the only punishment which befalls
Dick Follywit is a marriage which he accepts in very good heart, and which
is further recommended to him by gold, which he says at the conclusion
'makes amends for vice.' It is doubly unfortunate that Middleton should
have so far forgotten himself in this play, as it contains a good deal of
didactic morality in the mouth of a penitent debauchee, who — strangely
enough in such a play — is actually tempted on the stage by a fiend in female
shape.

[On *The Roaring Girl*] In this sketch from real life, at first sight equally
audacious in name and in design, the reader is refreshingly surprised by a
character drawn with an odd combination of realistic vigour, genuine

humour, and very kindly feeling. There are touches in it of that pathetic depth which Dekker could on occasion reveal; but the bright vivacity which gives something like a charm to this strange figure must be owing to Middleton's happier touch. The idea of illustrating by an example boldly taken from real life the fact that virtue may be found in the most unexpected quarters, is both a novel and a healthy one.

[On *The Widow*] . . . there is little which rises above the ordinary level of the popular Elisabethan stage.

[On *A Chaste Maid in Cheapside*] [It] . . . must be passed over as one of the most outrageous examples of the class of comedy to which it belongs. . . . But the offences committed in this play are by no means generally of so venial a character as that of selling meat in Lent. I should have left it unmentioned altogether, were it not that among its comic figures is one of which I know no other example in the Elisabethan drama drawn with the same degree of elaboration [Tim, the Cambridge undergraduate].

[On *Anything for a Quiet Life*] . . . there is little to be commended besides the title. It is one of Middleton's hastiest performances. This is evident from the very form — as to which it is at times difficult to say whether it be verse or prose — though the piece is not devoid of well-written passages. The young stepmother, who cures her husband's follies by apparently obliging him to commit greater to satisfy her whims, fails to arouse our interest, while much in the remainder of the plot is intolerably offensive. This play incidentally proves that Middleton could write very good French.

[On *No Wit, No Help Like a Woman's*] . . . a vivaciously-written comedy of intrigue, made up of two plots, either of which would have sufficed for a play in the earlier days of the English stage. . . . The play, though in passages exceedingly well written, is however rather lengthy; and the author had not sufficient good taste to avoid, or at least to pass quietly over, an exceedingly painful situation wholly unfit for comedy [4.1, in which a marriage appears to be incestuous]. . . .

[On *A Game at Chess*] The literary merits of this dramatic allegory are by no means of a high order, and its political views are, so far as it is possible to judge, of that reckless sort which usually result from an endeavour to suit the current humour of popular sentiment. But while the historical student will not fail to observe with what strength public opinion must have run in the direction of the sentiments of this piece, for its author to have ventured upon producing it, — and for it to have passed the censorship of the Master of the Revels, — neither will literary criticism pass by unheeded so singular a composition. This play, which Ben Jonson is hardly unjust in alluding to as 'poor,'[117] is in fact the solitary work with which the Elisabethan drama fairly attempted to match the political comedies of Aristophanes. No literary species can spring out of the earth in a single day.

[On the pageants]   So far as it is possible to criticise such ephemeral productions as *The Inner-Temple Mask* (produced in 1619) and *The World Tost at Tennis* (attributed to the year 1620), they may be said to exhibit an unusual degree of freshness of invention and vivacity of writing. The best thing in the former is 'the last will and testament of Kersmas' [Christmas], who bequeaths his joys and jollities to his children and kinsmen, humorously named after the most popular games at cards. There is much derision of those restrictions upon unlimited festivity which were doubtless in those days regarded with special disfavour in the Inner Temple Hall. *The World Tost at Tennis* is more ambitious in design; the induction (carried on between the three favourite royal palaces) is pleasing; but the plot of the mask itself, in which the 'world' is passed about like a tennis-ball from one to the other profession, till at last it settles firmly and fairly in the hands of sovereignty, need not be detailed. Its characters are very multifarious, including, besides various allegorical and mythological personages, such old friends as the Devil and the Nine Worthies.

Middleton's rank among our dramatists has been the subject of dispute among the few who have bestowed attention upon this fertile author; but it is quite unnecessary in surveying any period or department of literature to construct tables of precedence. The modesty with which Middleton himself appears to have abstained from any endeavour to assert his claims to fame or eminence of any kind may plead in his favour, and permit us to remain content with the observation, that among the many qualities which constitute a dramatist of the order next to the highest not a few were possessed by him. In the works attributed to him which exhibit the nearest approach to tragic power he had the advantage of William Rowley's co-operation; and it is therefore, to say the least, impossible to allow to Middleton the whole credit of these productions. But he certainly understood the secret of dramatic action, whether serious or comic in the nature of its interest. Upon the whole his plays are strikingly rapid in their movement. It is his usual practice to

117. See entry 22.

combine two plots into a single play; and this he ordinarily effects with much success as a constructor, though he worked too rapidly to attend to minor unevennesses, and though here and there he forgot in his haste fully to carry out the moral lesson which he intended to convey.

What however is to me most striking in Middleton is the absence of effort, which, if combined with a generally true instinct of effect, is a sure sign of genuine artistic power. Something of this may be due to the circumstances of his breeding and training. Apart from the gross indecency which was a characteristic of his times rather than of his class, he writes with the light touch of a well-bred gentleman, and very differently from the ponderous Dekker for instance on the one hand, or the pedantic Marston on the other. He is not in the least desirous of exhibiting his accomplishments as a reader, though he must have been acquainted with various kinds of literature — it is pleasing to note by the way that he was evidently fond of Chaucer. But while he writes with ease, while as a rule he is fluent in his versification and perfectly natural in his prose, he is by no means devoid of force, though it is not his manner to seek effect from mere strength of phrase. From bombast he is upon the whole singularly free.

More than ordinarily successful in romantic comedy, at times very felicitous even here in his choice of subjects, he seems to exhibit his full powers when in contact with his native soil. Upon the whole, Middleton's comedies dealing with the English life of his own age are perhaps the truest dramatic representation of it. He is less intent upon reproducing strong and enduring types of the Jonsonian kind than upon drawing faithful pictures of men and manners which shall bring home in a facile manner the straightforward lessons of morality and virtue which it is in the power of his comic muse to teach. In general therefore it will be less easy to recall particular characters from his dramas, than to remember the admirable effect produced upon the reader by the *ensemble* of such comedies as *Michaelmas Term*, *A Trick to catch the Old One*, or *A Mad World, my Masters*. If it be allowable to regard these plays as fair examples of the comedy of manners which the age enjoyed, and by enjoying acknowledged as true, the value of Middleton's works in our dramatic literature will be apparent. For his whole genius was free from any tendency to exaggeration, while of his moral aim there is no reason whatever to doubt. It may be questioned whether he was cast in a sufficiently strong mould to impress his age with the purpose which animated his satire; but there is no hollowness about the ring of his morality, and no unreality about his method of enforcing it. In brilliancy and in depth of both pathos and humour he falls below many of his fellow-dramatists; but in lightness and sureness of touch it would be difficult — with one exception — to name his superior. His merits, which have never been overrated, accordingly entitle him to a more than passing remembrance.

Adolphus William Ward. *A History of English Dramatic Literature to the Death of Queen Anne.* London: Macmillan, 1875, 2: 67-105.

75. 1882 A Swinburne Sonnet in Tribute

Of all the writers on the Elizabethan and Jacobean drama in the late nineteenth century, Algernon Charles Swinburne may be the most enthusiastic. His interest began early — his cousin Bertram Mitford describes Swinburne entering Eton at the age of twelve with his Bowdler's Shakespeare hugged close[118] — and continued throughout his life. Among his friends were critics William Minto and Edmund Gosse; William Poel, the director who began staging Elizabethan plays in the Elizabethan style; and A. H. Bullen, Middleton's editor.

Although I have not located a publication of the sonnet earlier than 1895, it was written in 1882 and circulated privately: in the 1885 introduction to Middleton's *Works*, Bullen mentions Swinburne's Sonnet IX with pleasure as "the highest tribute that it [Middleton's genius] has yet received" (p. xc). See also entries 82 and 90.

> A WILD moon riding high from cloud to cloud,
>   That sees and sees not, glimmering far beneath,
>   Hell's children revel along the shuddering heath
> With dirge-like mirth and raiment like a shroud:
> A worse fair face than witchcraft's, passion-proud,
>   With brows blood-flecked behind their bridal wreath
>   And lips that bade the assassin's sword find sheath
> Deep in the heart whereto love's heart was vowed:
> A game of close contentious crafts and creeds
>   Played till white England bring black Spain to shame:
> A son's bright sword and brighter soul, whose deeds
>   High conscience lights for mother's love and fame:
> Pure gipsy flowers, and poisonous courtly weeds:
>   Such tokens and such trophies crown thy name.

"Thomas Middleton" [Sonnet IX of *Sonnets on English Dramatic Poets (1590-1650)*]. *The Bibelot* 1 (1895): 174.

118. Jean Overton Fuller, *Swinburne: A Biography*, 23.

76. 1885 William Minto: The Changes of a Decade

When William Minto revised his 1874 analysis of Middleton (see entry 73) for the second edition of *Characteristics of English Poets from Chaucer to Shirley*, he was forty and perhaps more inclined to tragedy than he had been a decade earlier. He also echoes Ward's comparison of Middleton to Shakespeare.

Middleton has not Dekker's lightness of touch and etherial purity of tenderness, but there are qualities in which he comes nearer than any contemporary dramatist to the master mind of the time. There is a certain imperial confidence in his use of words and imagery, a daring originality and impatient force of expression, an easy freedom of humour, wide of range yet thoroughly well in hand, such as we find in the same degree even in that age of giants in no Elizabethan saving only Shakespeare. It was as a comedian that Middleton first made his reputation, about the year 1607, comparatively late in life; and it would seem that he despaired of obtaining recognition for his powers in tragedy, for two of his most striking performances in that kind are interwoven with comic stories and the whole plays named after leading characters in the comic under-plot. Nobody would expect from the title of the "Mayor of Queenborough," the intensity and force that Middleton shows in the tragic scenes of that play. The title seems to require our attention for the humorous antics of the Mayor, Simon the tanner, an imitation of Dekker's Simon Eyre the shoemaker, Mayor of London. And similarly in "The Changeling," which Middleton wrote in conjunction with Rowley, the dramatists seem to modestly intimate that they set store chiefly on the comic portions. Yet there are tragic passages in "The Changeling" unsurpassed for intensity of passion and appalling surprises in the whole range of Elizabethan literature. That these scenes were devised and written by Middleton will hardly be doubted by anybody acquainted with "The Mayor of Queenborough," and his later pure tragedy, "Women Beware Women." This last play is literally open to Jonson's sarcastic note on "Hamlet" — "Here the play of necessity ends, all the actors being killed." The slaughter in "Women Beware Women" extends to every character honoured with a name. Regarded as wholes, Middleton's tragedies fall very far short of the dignity of Shakespeare's. His heroes and heroines are not made of the same noble stuff, and their calamities have not the same grandeur. The characters are all so vile that the pity and terror produced by their death is almost wholly physical. But in the expression of incidental moments of passion, Middleton often rises to a sublime pitch of energy.

It may have been that Middleton, though only six years younger than

Shakespeare, was born too late for tragedy. A complaint is made in "The Roaring Girl," in the composition of which he was conjoined with Dekker. that tragedies had gone out of fashion. "In the time of the great crop doublet," it is said, "your huge bombasted plays quilted with mighty words to lean purpose, were only then in the fashion; and as the doublet fell, neater inventions began to be set up." Under King James the taste was all for "light colour summer stuff, mingled with divers colours."[119] Thus by the time that Middleton came into favour as a playwright, the atmosphere of the theatre was not encouraging to tragic composition. How far this influenced him in the devotion of his versatile powers to comedy, and how much was due to his individual character, it is of course impossible now to determine, for we have nothing but his plays to judge by. He began his literary life, like Marston, as a satirist, writing in the style popular at the end of the sixteenth century; but he achieved no great success in this artificial line of composition. His first triumph as a writer of comedy would seem to have been "A Trick to Catch the Old One." This, along with four others, was licensed in 1607. Chapman's "All Fools," the great exemplar and prototype of the English comedy of "gulling," had taken the town two years before, and Middleton threw himself into the fashion. In this type of comedy he is exceedingly happy, and surpasses his masters in ingenuity of construction, and easy accumulation of mirthful circumstances. The fun begins early, and goes on to the end with accelerating speed. Middleton excels peculiarly in the dramatic irony of making his gulls accessory to their own deception, and putting into their mouths statements that have, to those in the secret, a meaning very much beyond what they intend. "A Mad World, my Masters," licensed in 1608, is one of his happiest efforts in this vein. As bearing on Jonson's description of him as "a base fellow,"[120] it may be remarked that he professes to be more decent than some of his predecessors, and has a gird apparently at Marston or Jonson, as some obscene fellow, who cares not what he writes against others, yet rips up the most nasty vice in his own plays, and presents it to a modest assembly. It is the excellency of a writer, says Middleton, to leave things better than he finds them.[121] According to this principle, in the "Trick to Catch the Old One," and the "Mad World," the courtesans are married and made honest women — the rakes are reclaimed; and though no lesson is weightily inculcated, there is less indecency than in the works of more pretentious moralists.

Middleton's name has of late been revived in connection with the

119. See entry 2.
120. See entry 6.
121. See entry 2.

authorship of "Macbeth." It has been conjectured, on the ground of certain slight coincidences between Middleton's play and the witch scenes, that Middleton had a hand in the composition of "Macbeth."[122] The supposition is about as groundless as any ever made in connection with Shakespeare, which is saying a good deal. Even if either author borrowed the words of the song from the other, that is no evidence of further co-operation. The plays are wholly different in spirit. "The Witch" is by no means one of Middleton's best plays. The plot is both intricate and feeble; and the witches, in spite of Charles Lamb's exquisite comparison of them with Shakespeare's,[123] are, as stage creations, essentially comic and spectacular. With their ribald revelry, their cauldrons, their hideous spells and weird incantations, they are much more calculated to excite laughter than fear as exhibited on the stage, however much fitted to touch the chords of superstitious dread when transported by the imagination to their native wilds. The characters of the play do not treat them with sufficient respect to command the sympathy of the audience for them. Familiarity breeds contempt: if they had been consulted only by the Duchess with a view to the murder of her husband, they might have kept up an appearance of dignity and terror; but when the drunk Almachildes staggers in among them, upsets some of the beldams, and is received by Hecate as a favoured lover, we cease to have much respect for them, even though they do profess to exercise the terrible power of raising jars, jealousies, strifes, and heart-burning disagreements like a thick scarf o'er life. The visit of the fantastical gentleman whom Hecate has thrice enjoyed in incubus, is a very happy inspiration in the same vein as Tam o'Shanter's admiration of the heroine of Alloway Kirk:[124] the scene is a fine opportunity for a comic actor; but it is damaging to the respectability of the dread Hecate.

Characteristics of English Poets from Chaucer to Shirley. 2nd ed. Edinburgh and London: William Blackwood and Sons, 1885, pp. 347-49.

77. 1885 The New Editor, Arthur Henry Bullen, Comments

Middleton was the second writer whose complete works Arthur Henry Bullen chose to edit in his series of Elizabethan dramatists, just after

---

122. William George Clark and William Aldis Wright had so argued in the preface to their edition of *Macbeth*, viii-xii. Frederick Gard Fleay agreed and argued his case before the New Shakspere Society in 1874, provoking a flurry of articles.
123. See entry 55.
124. Tam o'Shanter admired the witch Cutty Sark in Robert Burns's *Tam o'Shanter* (1791).

Christopher Marlowe. By publishing an edition, Bullen both confirmed the regard in which Middleton's plays were coming to be held and stimulated further interest in them, especially since his edition was widely reviewed in England and the United States. These selections are taken from Bullen's introduction.

It should be an editor's aim to cultivate a nice sense of proportion and eschew exaggeration. Uncritical eulogy has the effect of irritating or repelling the reader; and when a poet has stood the test of time for nearly three centuries, his position needs no strengthening by violent displays of editorial zeal. Middleton's most recent critic has not hesitated to affirm that "in daring and happy concentration of imagery, and a certain imperial confidence in the use of words, he of all the dramatists of that time is the disciple that comes nearest to the master."[125] The reader who gives to these volumes the study they deserve will discover that this statement is not made at random, but is the mature judgment of a balanced mind. The comedies of intrigue show ready invention and craftsmanlike skill, though the plots are sometimes thin and the humour often gross; for dignity of moral sentiment the serious scenes of *A Fair Quarrel* have hardly been surpassed; *The Changeling, Women beware Women*, and *The Spanish Gipsy* are among the highest achievements of the English drama.

[On *The Wisdom of Solomon Paraphrased*] As we know of no other writer of the same name, I fear we must hold the dramatist responsible for this intolerable and interminable performance. The fluency of the versification is aggravating to the last degree. Through stanza after stanza and page after page we plod, vainly hoping to find something to reward us, some flash of inspiration; and when we reach the end, we are too dejected to congratulate ourselves on our release. It is extraordinary that a man of Middleton's brilliant ability should have perpetrated so insipid a piece of work. When the dramatists turned their hands to sacred subjects, the result was seldom satisfactory; but few have shown themselves so ill-fitted as Middleton for this class of composition.

[On *Microcynicon*] "Brief, but tedious," will be the censure of most readers, and I dare not question the justice of the finding. Following in the steps of Marston and Hall, Middleton thought it necessary to adopt a rugged rhythm

---

125. The anonymous article on Middleton in the 9th edition of the *Encyclopedia Britannica*. The author may have been William Minto, since similar phraseology appears in the 1885 edition of his *Characteristics of English Poets* (entry 76).

and barbarous phraseology. At the time of publication these "snarling satyres" may have interested a small esoteric circle of readers, who were able to read between the lines and applaud the hits; but the salt has long since lost its savour.

[On *The Mayor of Quinborough*] Many passages are so strikingly fine that I cannot but believe them to have been written when Middleton's genius was in its full maturity. . . . Again and again we are arrested by the bold utterance, the fine dramatic ring of the verse. Yet the play as a whole leaves little impression on the mind, and has the appearance of being an immature production. . . . The plot is repulsive. Vortiger is a monster of iniquity, and his brutality towards his gentle wife, Castiza, is peculiarly disgusting. Roxana is a creature of lust, effrontery, and guile. Middleton's later studies of depraved feminine character are among his highest achievements; but Roxana cannot for a moment compare with Bianca in *Women beware Women* or Beatrice in *The Changeling*. The comic scenes were doubtless effective on the stage; they are somewhat tiresome by the fireside. In Rowley's hands the Mayor would have been a more amusing figure. It is for the detached passages of noble poetry that students will value this tragi-comedy, which is admirably adapted for purposes of quotation.

[On *Blurt, Master Constable*] . . . a sprightly, well-written play, containing some charming poetry.

[On *Father Hubbard's Tales* and *The Black Book*] With a light hand the writer exposes the foibles and vices of the time. He was evidently a great admirer of Nashe — to whom he makes many allusions — and reflects in his own pages something of Nashe's marvellous brilliancy.

[On *The Phoenix*] There is an abundance of amusing intrigue and lively situations. The poetry put into the mouth of Phœnix is of a high order.

[On *Michaelmas Term*] . . . full of excellent fun, and the reader has only himself to blame if he fails to find amusement.

[On *A Trick to Catch the Old One*] It will be seen that in writing this comedy Middleton was more anxious to amuse than to teach a moral lesson. Grave moralists may argue that it is reprehensible for a man to fasten his cast-off mistress on his bride's uncle; nor am I inclined to dispute the reasonableness of the contention. But we must not bring the squint looks of "budge doctors of the stoic fur" to bear on these airy comedies of intrigue.

Middleton could moralise severely enough when the occasion required; but in the present instance his aim was to provide entertainment, and he succeeds admirably. It is impossible not to admire the happy dexterity with which the mirthful situations are multiplied. The interest never flags for a moment, but is heightened at every turn.

[On *The Family of Love*] ... written with Middleton's usual freedom and facility.

[On *A Mad World, My Masters*] The characters of Sir Bounteous Progress, the liberal knight who keeps open house for all comers, and Harebrain, the jealous husband, yoked to a demure light-o'-love, are very ably drawn; and the situations are worked out with the adroit briskness that we admired in *A Trick to Catch the Old One*.

[On *The Roaring Girl*] The conception is strikingly fresh and original. ... The dialogue is conducted with Middleton's usual smartness and rapidity.

[On *The Triumphs of Truth*] Pageants are usually tedious, and *The Triumphs of Truth* is no exception to the rule. The speeches are smoothly written, but the songs are poor.

[On *No Wit, No Help Like a Woman's*] It is one of Middleton's ablest comedies, but it leaves a somewhat unpleasant taste in the mouth.

[On *A Chaste Maid in Cheapside*] The play is exceedingly diverting, but I cannot conscientiously commend it *virginibus puerisque*, for the language and situations occasionally show an audacious disregard for propriety. Lamb quoted the exquisitely droll soliloquy in which Master Allwitt, the contented cuckold, describes the blessedness of his lot. If the reader, disregarding the anathemas of virtuous critics, gives the *Chaste Maid* a hearing, I can promise him plenty of entertainment.

[On *A Fair Quarrel*] It may be said without hesitation that, outside Shakespeare's highest works, there is nothing in the English drama more affecting, nothing nobler, than the colloquy between Captain Ager and his mother. That scene and the duel scene I believe to belong to Middleton. To such a height of moral dignity and artistic excellence Rowley never attained. We may safely assign to Rowley the boisterous comic scenes. Middleton's humour is of a quieter character; he had little liking for noisy horse-play.

[On *The World Tossed at Tennis*] The invention is ingenious, the speeches are finely written, and the songs are smooth. . . . There is one great merit in *The World Tost at Tennis;* it is not tedious, as masques so frequently are. The verse was something more than a peg on which to hang the costumes. By the fireside it can be read with pleasure, and, handsomely mounted, it must have been received on the stage with applause.

[On *The Witch*] . . . [It] has received, owing to its Shakespearean interest, more attention than it deserves on its own merits. It is strangely ill-constructed and is not by any means one of Middleton's finest works, though uncritical writers have absurdly advanced it to the first place.

[On *The Changeling*] Regarded as an artistic whole, *The Changeling* cannot challenge comparison with *The Maid's Tragedy*, *The Broken Heart*, or *The Duchess of Malfi*. It has not the sustained tragic interest of these masterpieces; but there is one scene in *The Changeling* [3.4, in which Beatrice realizes De Flores's intent] which, for appalling depth of passion, is not merely unsurpassed, but, I believe, unequalled outside Shakespeare's greatest tragedies. . . .
 Neither Webster nor Cyril Tourneur nor Ford has given us any single scene so profoundly impressive, so absolutely ineffaceable, so Shakespearean as this colloquy between Beatrice and De Flores. In *A Fair Quarrel* Middleton showed how nobly he could depict moral dignity; but this scene of *The Changeling* testifies beyond dispute that, in dealing with a situation of sheer passion, none of Shakespeare's followers trod so closely in the master's steps.

[On *The Spanish Gypsy*] . . . an admirable example of a well-contrived and well-written romantic comedy. It is at once fantastic and pathetic, rippling with laughter and dashed with tears; a generous, full-blooded play.

[On *Women Beware Women*] It is a pitiful, thrice-pitiful story, worked out with relentless skill to a ghastly catastrophe. The passionate energy and concentrated bitterness of the language is as remarkable as in *The Changeling*.

[On *More Dissemblers Besides Women*] . . . evidently a late work, more elaborate and substantial than the early comedies. . . . The girl-page who accompanies the profligate Lactantio is a pathetic little figure; but it is a pity that Middleton adopted so intolerably gross a device for discovering her condition to the Duchess.

There are critics who station poets in order of merit as a schoolmaster ranges his pupils in the classroom. This process I do not intend to adopt with Middleton. The test of a poet's real power ultimately resolves itself into the question whether he leaves a permanent impression on the mind of a capable reader. A poet may carve cherry-stones with exquisite skill; but mere artistry, though a man might have the very touch of Meleager, soon palls. It becomes more and more a relief to turn from the χελιδονων μουσεια [purple patches] of this refined age to the Elizabethans. Middleton may be charged with extravagance and coarseness. True: but he could make the blood tingle; he could barb his words so that they pierce the heart through and through. If *The Changeling, Women beware Women, The Spanish Gipsy,* and *A Fair Quarrel* do not justify Middleton's claims to be considered a great dramatist, I know not which of Shakespeare's followers is worthy of the title.

"Introduction," *The Works of Thomas Middleton.* Boston: Houghton Mifflin; London: J. C. Nimmo, 1885-86, 1: xi-xciii.

78. 1885, June; 1886, February *The Saturday Review* Praises

The Saturday Review was among the first to respond to Bullen's new Middleton edition. The review appeared in two sections, one of volumes 1-4 and the other of volumes 5-8.

If it could be urged by determined faultfinders against the opening volumes of Mr. Bullen's ambitious venture that a new edition of Marlowe was not very much wanted,.nothing of the same kind can be said of his second "number." For years Middleton has been the most unattainable of all our old dramatists of any mark. His work was never collected in any form, old or new, till Dyce's edition of nearly half a century ago, which edition has not only become very expensive, but is also not to be obtained merely for the ordering by any one who is willing to pay its price. Moreover, even those plays of the author of *Women Beware Women* which were included in the older editions of Dodsley, found, according to the intelligible and blameless rule of the reprints of that work, no place in the last edition. It is true that plays in which he collaborated — *The Honest Whore, The Roaring Girl, The Old Law,* and so forth, have been repeatedly reprinted in the works of his coadjutors. But this, and the occurrence of the same, and others, in the older editions of Dodsley, in Dilke's collection, &c., could not be held to render a fresh edition of his work, as a whole, unnecessary.

Certainly no one who, having previously made acquaintance with him, re-reads these volumes, or who, having a competent knowledge and judgment, reads them for the first time, is likely to say that their rarity is the only or the chief reason for representing them. It so happens, indeed, that neither of Middleton's best plays, which we take to be *The Changeling* and *Women Beware Women*, comes within these four first volumes, and that the two best plays here — *The Roaring Girl* and *The Old Law* — are not wholly Middleton's. But of the other ten not one is wholly worthless, the majority have remarkable merit, and every one stands well out from what may be called the ruck of the Elizabethan drama. The earlier, or what seem to be the earlier, are naturally the weaker, and Middleton's frequent habit of collaboration requires a certain amount of critical divination to be gone through in order to identify his own special characteristics. The first play here given, *Blurt Master Constable*, is a fair, though not more than a fair, specimen of the mixed comedy of romance and manners which ranges from *Twelfth Night* to the lowest dramatic chaff and draff of the time. . . . *The Phoenix* has some beautiful passages, but is spoilt by the extreme improbability which mars so many of these delightful plays. *Michaelmas Term*, having a fantastic, not to say supernatural, element in it, comes off better. It is very noteworthy, by the way, how fond Middleton is of law terms, and, on the well-known argument as to that matter that Shakspeare was Bacon, we can only say that it is quite certain that Middleton was Coke. Then we come to that strange and powerful play *The Mayor of Queenborough*. We remember some thirty years ago coming upon an odd volume of old plays containing this, with *The Fair Quaker of Deal*, *The Belle's Stratagem*, and two or three other strangely-assorted pieces, and being even in our then critical nonage struck by the difference of manner it presented. All the title scenes, as they may be called, are sheer rubbish; as bad as the very worst stuff of the kind to be found in the dregs of Dodsley, or in uncollected dregs more dreggish still, while some of the tragic action is admirable. Of *The Old Law*, as well known from Massinger's works, we say nothing, except to point out once more that Lamb has been quite as unduly hard on Massinger in respect of this piece as Hartley Coleridge was on Dekker with respect to *The Virgin Martyr*. *A Trick to Catch the Old One* is simply one of the best comedies of intrigue of the time. For *The Family of Love* we have less admiration; but the changes of incident and situation in *Your Five Gallants* are excellent. *A Mad World, my Masters* is scarcely inferior to *A Trick to Catch the Old One*. By the way, Mr. Bullen has made a slip here; it is his grandfather's mistress, not his uncle's, that Follywit marries. *The Roaring Girl* we pass over for the same reason as *The Old Law*, and of *A Fair Quarrel* we shall have something to say presently. The last play included in these volumes, *No Wit, no Help like a Woman's*, belongs to the same class as *A Trick to Catch the Old One* and *A Mad World, my Masters*, and is not much below them. Weatherwise's astrological fancies might, indeed, have been more happily managed; but Mrs. Lowater's device and the mixture of hardihood and dexterity with which it is carried out is capital, while the touches of affection for her husband and the knowledge of her wrongs with which the spectator is early furnished prevent his being disgusted at the notion of her making a sham marriage disguised as a man, and carrying off the spoil of the credulous Lady Goldenfleece. In short, all the four volumes are full of pleasant reading. Mr. Bullen has done his part as editor well on the whole, keeping very wisely most of Dyce's editorial apparatus as well as his text. A very little more explanation of words and phrases might be desirable, and we do not quite understand the principle which interprets such universally known terms as "gear" and "hight," while others which are certainly not universally known are left to the reader's erudition or faculty of guessing. We should have liked, too, a short introduction to each play, so that the necessity of referring back in each case to the first volume might have been avoided. Another comment or cavil (if Mr. Bullen likes) that we have to make is that it would have helped the prospects of carrying the whole series through if there had been a little more economy of space. We have before us three or four collections or editions of single authors, the volumes of which are, as nearly as possible, the same size as Mr. Bullen's. One of them averages six plays per volume, another five, and the least economical four. Mr. Bullen has found room for only three, and a collection of the whole Elizabethan drama at three plays a volume menaces the shelves rather seriously. These, however, are "base dunghill censures and mechanical." In a nobler kind we have only to hint to Mr. Bullen that a venture of this kind cannot be satisfactorily carried out in a hurry; while, if we had been guided merely by the pleasure these volumes have given us, we should have had nothing at all but praise for him.

Since we noticed the first half of Mr. Bullen's edition of Middleton last June, he has added considerably to his credit with students of the Elizabethan drama. He has completed his very remarkable privately-printed collection of old plays, giving sixteen pieces practically unknown, and six of them actually unprinted;[126] he has promised, also in the subscription form, the works of Davenport, Nabbes, and William Rowley — minor stars, certainly, but stars by no means deserving to be left in the blackness of darkness in which they are at present involved — and he has now finished his issue of

126. *A Collection of Old English Plays* (1882-85).

by far the most valuable and remarkable of those dramatists whose works have hitherto been difficult to obtain as a whole, the author of *The Changeling* and *Women Beware Women*. For our parts, as we have more than once taken occasion to remark, we hold the man who gives texts, not before easily accessible, in a handsome and convenient form to be ten times worthier as a member of the corporation of letters than the man who is perpetually pottering over questions of authorship, and drawing up rhyme-tests, and tormenting half the country clergymen in England to know whether this poet's great-grandmother married that poet's uncle's father-in-law. [The reviewer suggests Bullen should edit the pseudo-Shakespeare plays.]

The four completing volumes of that poet's work which are before us are not entirely occupied with poetry, or even with drama. The last contains divers specimens of what may be called the pamphlet-journalism of the time — the miscellaneous pieces in verse and prose which formed the ordinary hackwork of Elizabethan and Jacobean men of letters. . . . But in Middleton's special case its interest is so far inferior to that of his drama that it needs little notice. So, too, the masques and entertainments which partly fill the seventh volume, and which Middleton composed in whole or in part as official or semi-official furnisher of such things to the City of London, rather belong to the whole subject of such work than to the subject of his special performance. There remains, however, the whole of two volumes and part of a third containing purely dramatic work, and among it the very best work that Middleton ever did. And this we may proceed to examine.

The play which opens the fifth volume, *A Chaste Maid in Cheapside*, is of the class to which the majority of Middleton's plays belong, the class of citizen-humour comedy. Indeed, not a few of the humours (as Shadwell would have said) are directly repeated from his earlier or in his later work. In language and situations it is one of the least decorous of its author's works, and one particularly disagreeable character of the time — a character which, like other such, has been very remarkably avoided by Shakspeare — the wittol-cuckold who makes a profit of his own and his wife's dishonour, has here his masterpiece in Allwit. The play, like many others of the time (but again *not* like Shakspeare's), surprises the modern reader by the apparent carelessness with which reputable and disreputable characters herd together. The rascality of Allwit and his wife is perfectly well known, as well as its consummation in their shameless ingratitude towards the profligate spendthrift on whom they have lived so long. Yet they figure in the final scene of wedding and other festivities as welcome and honoured guests. The play is full of amusement and very well written, while the fashion in which its plot works out is in marked contrast, as regards neatness of draughtsmanship, with those plays in which Middleton left the comic underplot to Rowley. The piece which follows, *The Widow*, is chiefly remarkable because of the distinguished collaborators, Jonson and Fletcher, who are assigned to Middleton on the title-page. It was, however, never printed till long after the death of all three; the attribution of any share to Jonson and Fletcher seems to have been early disputed, and we quite agree with Mr. Bullen that there is no internal evidence to show any hand but Middleton's. We may add that there is no internal evidence to show Middleton at his best. *Anything for a Quiet Life* brings us back to his characteristic style of comedy when he wrote alone, and is a capital play, despite the scoundrelism of Knavesby, a would-be Allwit with a wife too good for him. Then comes the famous *Witch*, which has supplied some of the most remarkable instances of critical oddity in existence. The intelligent reader who goes calmly through it, and then remembers that other presumably intelligent readers have doubted whether Shakspeare did not imitate it, or whether Middleton had not a hand in *Macbeth*, must wonder not a little. It is perfectly true that the witch part of the play has in itself very great merit. Middleton has taken more pains to work out the full popular conception of the witch character than Shakspeare, who probably did not care to do so. But the play, as a whole, is a mere muddle, as is usual with Middleton (in strange contrast to the workmanlike fashion of his pure comedies) when he tries to mix the styles either with his own pen or by calling in others. In common sense as well as in poetical justice the catastrophe (where the bewitched person is punished and the unworthy lover who has purchased Hecate's aid is rewarded by a most improbable turn of affairs) is all wrong. The lugging in of the story of Rosmunda and the skull is extraordinarily awkward, and the comic or tragi-comic scenes are dull and unnatural. There is some wit in the light-o'-love Francisca, but interest in her is quickly destroyed by her ill nature and shamelessness, and by the introduction of the cowardly and stupid coxcomb on whom, without any apparent reason except that he made her handsome presents, she, a girl of beauty and family who might marry where she pleases, has thrown away her honour.

Very different are three of the four plays (the fourth, *More Dissemblers besides Women*, is a fair specimen of Middleton's ordinary style) which fill vol. vi. The tragic part of *The Changeling* is one of the few things not generally known, and highly praised by the few who do know them, that can disappoint no one who has any taste for literature. Mr. Bullen, contrary to the wont of most editors, but following the more excellent way, confines his praise almost wholly to the single dialogue between Beatrice and De Flores, when the latter, hired by Beatrice to murder her lover that she may marry elsewhere, ruthlessly and successfully demands an undreamt-of guerdon.

But the whole parts of these two characters deserve the very highest praise. Printed (as by a strange chance all Middleton's best plays were) years after his death and in that dead season when the very art and mystery of blank verse had been lost, the text is in very bad condition. But even the obvious text-errors of a bad acting copy cannot spoil the poetry of these scenes, while their dramatic value remains quite unhurt. Beatrice — a specimen of the Southern type of girl as conceived by all our dramatists from Shakspeare downward, prone to violent love and hate, and rapid in her changes of both — is already pledged to Alonso de Piracquo when she sees and falls in love with a new-comer, Alsemero. She muses how to be rid of Alonso, and a certain "honest De Flores," an ill-favoured gentleman of her father's whom she has hitherto treated with special contumely, suggests himself. She tempts him, and he consents, the nature of his reward being, partly by his cunning and her oversight, left unsettled. De Flores murders Alonso, and then comes the great scene so justly praised. But the excellence of the horror does not cease here. Alsemero has the minute jealousy of a Spaniard of his time, and Beatrice has to study how to conceal from him the price she has had to pay. It is managed by the old device, familiar to fabliau-writers of all ages, of substituting her waiting-maid, Diaphanta, on the critical occasion. But the substitute plays her part too zealously, and discovery is feared. Once more De Flores comes to his mistress's rescue, and another murder — that of the luckless Diaphanta — saves Beatrice for the time. But Alonso's brother is already on the track of the murderer, and finally Beatrice is forced to confess. De Flores, stubborn to the last, is confronted with her in private, and stabs her and himself. His part throughout is wonderfully good, being the only following, and that a very independent one, of Iago on the English stage which has any real merit. Single touches, such as the short aside, "Already *my* De Flores!" when the haughty mistress, who has never met him hitherto without a gesture or word of loathing, begins her caresses before tempting him, and the quick dexterity with which he turns Tomaso de Piracquo's suspicious violence, are quite Shakspearian. So are also (whether Shakspeare can or cannot be conceived as choosing the subject) the scene of Beatrice's surrender, and that, the boldest of all, where Beatrice and De Flores wait outside the bridal-chamber planning fresh murder for the tardy Diaphanta. The blending of ferocity and tenderness on the lover's part, and of hatred and enforced admiration for his tremendous "strength" on Beatrice's, has hardly a parallel elsewhere. Even the touches of levity and greed, as well as want of care for her mistress's reputation, which prevent the reader from feeling too much sympathy for Diaphanta herself, are masterly. But, as so frequently happens with Middleton, all the rest of the play is nought. The comic part, which gives the name, is singularly feeble, the minor characters, except the luckless Alonso, who has a certain attractive confidence and guilelessness, are sticks, and the winding up after De Flores's last murder and his suicide is an almost appalling anti-climax.

We have left ourselves little space to speak of the agreeable tragi-comedy of the *Spanish Gipsy* which follows, and of Middleton's masterpiece, as a whole, *Women Beware Women*, which follows that. But Lamb and Hazlitt have dealt with the latter at sufficient length[127] to make it better known than most of its author's work. There is nothing in it which has the tragic grandeur of the Beatrice and De Flores scenes in *The Changeling*, but the play, as a whole, is much superior. Yet the reader hardly feels, as he does at De Flores's last stab, that nothing will do after that, and that he must leave reading for a time in order to cool down. The one play in the seventh volume which demands mention, *A Game at Chess*, is chiefly interesting because of its odd machinery (the characters are all named after the chief pieces), and because of the trouble into which it brought its author, as a violent attack on Spain and on the Church of Rome. It is full of historical references, and from that point of view deserves, perhaps, comment at length. Its satire on current personages and events makes it not unattractive even as literature, and its popularity during the nine days in which it was allowed to be acted before Gondomar procured its suppression was such that the total receipts are said to have amounted to the then enormous sum of fifteen hundred pounds.

In conclusion, we have to note that Mr. Bullen has corrected a slight slip which we pointed out to him in his description of one of the personages in the earlier volumes, and to repeat another suggestion which we made, and which of course he could not adopt in reference to this author. The suggestion (which has since been endorsed by Professor Minto) is that anything in the nature of argument or description or criticism of each play should be prefixed to the several pieces, and not included in the general prefatory notice. It is anything but convenient to have to refer back to vol. i. at the beginning of each new play, and sometimes in the course of reading each. For the rest, the editing of these volumes is satisfactory and their production very handsome, a facsimile being, among other things, given of the curious title-page of *A Game at Chess*.

Anon. "Elizabethan Dramatists." *The Saturday Review*, 27 June 1885, pp. 867-68; "Bullen's Middleton," 27 February 1886, pp. 305-306.

127. See entries 55 and 58.

79. 1885, August *The Academy* Is Impressed

For its review of Bullen's edition, *The Academy* called on one of the foremost names in the field — William Minto.

I must join with a writer in the *Saturday Review* in urging on Mr. Bullen's attention a slight defect in an otherwise excellent and opportune edition of Middleton. Mr. Dyce did much to make this brilliant dramatist easily intelligible to the modern reader, and Mr. Bullen has here supplemented his labours with painstaking and judgment. But one thing is wanting which Mr. Bullen might have supplied — there might have been an argument prefixed to each play, or even a table of the main action of the successive scenes. . . . To get much really dramatic enjoyment out of printed plays requires a special education; and Middleton's plays, being eminently acting plays, with a development suited to the stage and not to the study, are eminently difficult to read. But, with a plan of the scenes to guide him, the general reader might be tempted to make the requisite effort to get full enjoyment of a scene here and there.

It is not, however, mainly for the general reader that a table of the scenes would be an advantage. Few general readers care to visit often the delightful but mazy land of Elizabethan drama; the lovers of these plays are mostly special readers. It is in their interest that we press for this convenience. [Minto goes on to discuss the intricacy of plots in Elizabethan drama.] Of the intricacy of some of Middleton's plays we have a striking illustration in the fact that two such specialists as Mr. Bullen and Prof. Ward are at variance concerning a cardinal incident in the action of "Blurt, Master Constable," the dramatist's first conspicuous success. Was Fontinelle unfaithful to Violetta, or did he only pretend to be? We take it that Mr. Bullen's main motive for defending the constancy of the gay Frenchman was that Mr. Ward had stigmatised the plot as "vile."[128] We should sympathise with Mr. Bullen as against Mr. Ward on this point. The plot is not vile, judged by the Elizabethan standard. It is not viler than scores of other plots that have not been so stigmatised. It is simply an example of Middleton's realism, and he would probably have defended it as Fielding defended similar — but worse — realism in the case of *Tom Jones*. [Minto continues to discuss Fontinelle.] A table of the scenes would make clear any obscurity there is in the plot. The short, but compact, second scene of the third act

128. See entry 74; Bullen responded in his introduction to *The Works of Thomas Middleton*, xxi-xxiii.

shows how the situation in the fifth act came about, though something is left to the imagination. The truth is, that in a bustling comedy like this, with lively banquetting, masquerading, and practical joking to occupy the audience, Middleton would have shown less stage-craft than he proved himself to be master of if he had expressed every turn in the action. It was not a defect that he should send the audience home to wonder how Frisco got out of the dungeon and back for the tricks of the fifth act, or why Fontinelle was rash enough to keep his promise, on his word of honour, to go to Imperia, or to obey his impulse to thank her, or why Hippolito and Camillo taunted Violetta too soon. He took good care that they should not have time to raise such questions while they were in the theatre. He made sure that his scenes should hold the audience. There is no apparent necessity, as Mr. Bullen argues, for the two lovers to find a shelter in Imperia's house; but it was necessary for the dramatist to get all his characters there in the fifth act, and he managed it very cleverly. The rapid brevity with which he indicates the steps is an example of that careless, imperious, force which stood him in good stead in weightier matters of the drama.

It is characteristic of Middleton that he never stuck at improbabilities of behaviour on the part of his personages when the unlikely conduct was necessary to a good situation. He knew human nature, probably, as well as most of his compeers; but "the base fellow," as Jonson called him,[129] would not always take the trouble to write up to his lights. Provided he could run the stream of action through a succession of effective stage scenes, he was not scrupulously particular about fidelity to men as they are. It is this that renders it so difficult to make a conjecture of the slightest value concerning Middleton's full share in the plays that he wrote in conjunction with W. Rowley. [Minto comments on the difficulties of determining authorship.] Middleton's verse is so much superior to Rowley's, his power of expression so much more masterly, that there are many scenes in any play in which the two co-operated that may be assigned without question to the greater dramatist. The great scenes in the "Changeling," for example, must have been written by the author of "The Mayor of Queenborough." There is a distinctive power in them, both of conception and of phrase, that goes beyond any possibility of imitation. So in "A Fair Quarrel" the Hamlet-like soliloquies of Captain Agar, and the dialogue between Agar and his mother, are marked as Middleton's by the diction alone. [Minto argues that Rowley should not be assigned only the comic scenes; Rowley might have had good ideas and then called in better writers like Middleton to execute them.]

Four more volumes are wanted to complete this edition of Middleton.

129. See entry 6.

The issue is doubly justified: first, by the interest and scarcity of the plays, which would have warranted a mere reprint of Dyce, and, second, by the substantial additions Mr. Bullen has made to Dyce's elucidation of the text. We hope he will take in good part the suggestion about a prefatory abstract to each play. One more illustration of its use may be taken from what is in several ways the most interesting play in the present issue, the "Mayor of Queenborough." The leading characters are repulsive, and the action is of bewildering rapidity, but the best scenes in it rank with Middleton's best work. There is nothing more terrifically grand, more tragically horrible, in the whole range of the Elizabethan drama, than the last scene between Vortiger, Horsus, and Rowena. It is a really magnificent conception, worked out with unfaltering power, and shows what Middleton, with all his easy dexterity and deep reserve of confident strength, was capable of when he had a great situation to call forth the full measure of his abilities. But the changes of scene are so frequent, there is such an antiquated air about the subject, such a want of greatness in the general design and the motives of the characters, that few readers seem to have had patience to persevere to the end. In such a case a plan of the scenes would be invaluable, and would make clear besides that, in spite of the straggling appearance of the play, it has really a very even development to the catastrophe, and this, too, although a good deal was evidently added on to Middleton's original after the Restoration, and possibly he had himself an earlier version of the story to reconstruct.

"The Works of Thomas Middleton," The Academy, 22 August 1885, pp. 111-12.

80. 1885, September *The Dial* Is Less So

R. H. Stoddard, the U. S. poet and critic who reviewed Bullen's edition for *The Dial*, was not impressed with Middleton as a dramatist, although he acknowledged Middleton's craft and poetry.

The writings of Middleton possess a greater intellectual value when they are read in connection with the literature which they illustrate than when they are read for themselves alone. He ranks among the body of writers who are loosely classified as Elizabethan Dramatists more because he was contemporaneous with them and worked in their lines than because he was a dramatist. If we read him, it is not as we read Marlowe, who, with all his fustian and bombast, rose at need to the dramatic demands of his subject, as in "Edward the Second" and "Dr. Faustus"; as we read Jonson, who, in spite of the deliberate declamation in which he loved to indulge, was not without tragic and comic power; or as we read Beaumont and Fletcher, who, in the midst of much false writing, were occasionally natural and pathetic. We read him as we read Lyly, and Greene, and Peele, not because he depicts life and character, but because he entertains us by the ingenuity of his action, the movement of his scenes, and the odd sayings that he puts into the mouths of his characters. He is not a dramatist, but a playwright, and a very clever one. The impressions that we derive from Middleton and writers of his class, differ in kind and duration from the impressions that we derive from Shakespeare, Fielding, and Thackeray. It is the difference which separates the world in which we live, move, and have our being, from the world of "The Fairie Queene" and "The Princess," — the world of men and women from the world of poetic shadows. The life of Middleton's plays is not the life that we live, or that anybody ever lived: it is fictitious, unnatural, impossible. We are entertained by it, however, as we are entertained by the personages in a fairy tale or the puppets in a pantomime, though it adds nothing to our permanent intellectual enjoyment.

The little that we know of Middleton does not enlighten us as to his personality, nor does it enable us to understand why he devoted so many years to dramatic writing, for which he had no special aptitude. [Here follows a brief history of Middleton's career.] [His plays] were not written to be published at the expense of the author and read in the closet, but to be purchased by enterprising managers who knew what they wanted, and played to expectant audiences who also knew what they wanted. The audiences that made or marred the fortunes of the old dramatists were not exacting, provided they were sufficiently amused. They went to the Globe, the Blackfriars, or the Curtain, as they went to a wrestling match, a bull baiting, or an execution for high treason. They demanded the horrible in tragedy — clamoring for crimes that could not be expiated, and a succession of catastrophes that strewed the stage with the dead and the dying. What they demanded in comedy we may divine from reading the interludes of Heywood, "Gammer Gurton's Needle," "The Four P's," and other sixteenth century foolery, as we may divine what they demanded in the next century, which was less robustious and more sophisticate, from reading the plays of Middleton, whose predilection as well as his practice was towards the comic in life and character. Like Dekker and Nashe, he was a student of the "humours" of his time. It is not, and could not well be, a nice study, considering the coarse manners and coarser conversation of the time; but it might have been nicer than it was. He lacked the refinement which we feel in Shakespeare, in spite of his indelicate allusions, and he lacked the decorum which is the salvation of comic art. It is a strange life to which he introduces us in "Blurt, Master Constable," "Michaelmas Term," "The Mayor of Queenborough," "A Trick to Catch the Old One," "The Family of Love," "Your Five Gallants," "The Roaring Girl," and "A Mad World," my masters. It is a mad world, indeed, and its inhabitants are worthy of it — haunters of taverns, ordinaries, and stews, addicted to drinking, dicing, and drabbing, spendthrifts and sharpers, cutpurses and catchpoles, bullies and kept women; an Alsatia of animal spirits into which decency never penetrates, and where the name of the Deity is never heard except in imprecations. It does not offend the moral sense, unless it has been emasculated by prudery; at any rate, it need not offend it, for we never for a moment accept it or mistake it for a reality. The life that animates it is not so much immoral as unmoral. It has not abrogated the Ten Commandments; it has simply never heard of them.

Something like this, I imagine, is the impression which the works of Middleton are likely to leave upon the mind that curiously considers them. They have left this impression upon my mind, and it does not lessen the admiration that I feel for Middleton, who was a poet if he was not a moralist. He belonged to a school of poets who sought to interest their countrymen in the fortunes and feelings of mankind. . . . Their poetry may be coarse, but it is never diseased. It differs from ours — and nowhere more than in the dramatic work of Middleton — in its masculinity, its sense, and its contempt of artifice. It is obvious and not recondite, exhaustive and not suggestive, and whatever else it lacks it never lacks expression. We have a larger vocabulary than theirs, but a smaller language.

The length to which this notice has extended prevents me from saying what I intended to say in regard to this edition of Middleton, which leaves nothing to be desired in a classic edition of a favorite Old English Dramatist. [Stoddard concludes by praising Bullen's scholarship.]

Stoddard, R. H. "Thomas Middleton" [Review of Bullen]. *The Dial* 6 (1885): 114-16.

81. 1885, December The *Atlantic Monthly*: An "Unsavory" World

Another American journal found Middleton's plays so much a reflection of the vice-ridden London of his times that his work was of only historical interest. The reviewer opens with a discussion of Marlowe, whose works Bullen had edited just before Middleton's.

On leaving Marlowe and turning to Middleton, the second name in Mr.

Bullen's series, one is perhaps more delightfully impressed by the powerful compulsion with which Shakespeare "worked out the beast and evolved the man" in English drama. If any one thinks that the putting out of Gloster's eyes with hot irons upon the stage is too horrible, let him turn to the old tragedy; and if he thinks Shakespeare is unclean, we commend him to the early plays of Middleton. Vice is the butt of comedy, and burlesque must live with low characters; and perhaps, as men are constituted, it is at least equally effective to make evil ridiculous as to make it terrible. Against certain indecencies the former is the only method open to literature. But not to put too puritanical a point to it, the comedies in these first four volumes, now issued, bring us into very unsavory company. They present a picture of London life, no doubt, as it was lived in certain quarters, and are copious illustrations of the society of the time; but into such quarters and society what need to go? Wit and cleverness there is of a local and temporary kind; or at least it is so closely attached to the town of the time that one cannot get its effect without a sort of expatriation from his own place and putting into abeyance his sense of decency. Moreover, a considerable amount of special information is required to understand the plays; in fact, the contemporary drench is so deep that oblivion can be wrung out of them. It is easy to say that this is of necessity the case with comedy; that the subject is manners, and manners are transitory; and that the aim is to make fun, and fun is for the pit. The point which is aimed at here — and it is one to thank Heaven for — is that Shakespeare rose out of all this, and gave us laughter without fastening upon us the swarm of "wag-tails" and other classes of ill-sounding names, in endless succession, which his fellows transported so plentifully from the London streets; and that he should have done this seems, when we read the comedy of his time, the most marvelous thing about him. In this, too, he was preëminently a free soul.

From what has been written it will be justly inferred that this series is one for scholarly libraries, as is also shown by the fact that only eighty of the whole three hundred and fifty copies, to which the edition is limited, are offered for sale in this country. Scholars will not need to be told what is the value of such a reissue of works which have been published hitherto only in inconvenient editions, now difficult to obtain, and which have never had so careful, well informed, and judicious an editor, whose work is to be highly commended, though occasionally a student may differ from his interpretations, as has sometimes occurred with ourselves. Nor in attempting to illustrate plainly the eternal difference between Shakespeare and his fellows (from which it follows, in our view, that, broadly speaking, the public does not neglect the latter without justice and wisdom) have we meant to obscure a spark of Marlowe's fiery genius, or to slur a syllable of

Middleton's mastery of speech, which, when he puts forth his power, is of the noblest; just as with the remaining members of the series, which is to include Shirley and Beaumont and Fletcher, if not others, we would not even seem to depreciate their charm and force and rightful claim to honorable remembrance, though here and there some sere foliage mingles with and almost hides the leaves that are bright with the living green. To know them well is to know Shakespeare better. The editor has done a service of worth to the great historic body of our literature, and the student who enriches his library with these volumes will have no unimportant fraction of the indispensable wealth which in its fullness makes up a perfect English culture.

Anon. "Shakespeare's Fellows." *Atlantic Monthly* 56 (1885): 853-54.

82. 1886, January Algernon Charles Swinburne Responds

In his late forties, Swinburne was still the *enfant terrible* of English letters when Bullen dedicated *The Works of Thomas Middleton* to him. Swinburne responded with this enthusiastic appraisal of the playwright. To Swinburne, Middleton's tragedies are his claim to renown; Swinburne dismisses the character of Simon that so appealed to seventeenth-century audiences (and suggests Rowley wrote the play's farcical scenes), but the tragic plot of *The Changeling*, Swinburne says, places Middleton second only to Shakespeare.

If it be true, as we are told on high authority, that the greatest glory of England is her literature and the greatest glory of English literature is its poetry, it is not less true that the greatest glory of English poetry lies rather in its dramatic than its epic or its lyric triumphs. The name of Shakespeare is above the names even of Milton and Coleridge and Shelley: and the names of his comrades in art and their immediate successors are above all but the highest names in any other province of our song. There is such an overflowing life, such a superb exuberance of abounding and exulting strength, in the dramatic poetry of the half-century extending from 1590 to 1640, that all other epochs of English literature seem as it were but half awake and half alive by comparison with this generation of giants and of gods. There is more sap in this than in any other branch of the national bay-tree: it has an energy in fertility which reminds us rather of the forest than the garden or the park. It is true that the weeds and briars of the underwood are but too likely to embarrass and offend the feet of the rangers and the gardeners who trim the level flower-plots or preserve the domestic game of enclosed and ordered lowlands in the tamer demesnes of literature. The sun is strong and the wind sharp in the climate which reared the fellows and the followers of Shakespeare. The extreme inequality and roughness of the ground must also be taken into account when we are disposed, as I for one have often been disposed, to wonder beyond measure at the apathetic ignorance of average students in regard of the abundant treasure to be gathered from this widest and most fruitful province in the poetic empire of England. And yet, since Charles Lamb threw open its gates to all comers in the ninth year of the present century,[130] it cannot but seem strange that comparatively so few should have availed themselves of the entry to so rich and royal an estate. The subsequent labours of Mr. Dyce made the rough ways plain and the devious paths straight for all serious and worthy students. And now again Mr. Bullen has taken up a task than which none more arduous and important, none worthier of thanks and praise, can be undertaken by any English scholar. In his beautiful and valuable edition of Marlowe there are but two points to which exception may be taken. It was, I think, a fault of omission to exclude the apocryphal play of *Lust's Dominion* from a place in the appendix: it was, I am certain, a fault of commission to admit instead of it the much bepuffed and very puffy rubbish of the late Mr. Horne. That clever, versatile, and energetic writer never went so far out of his depth, or floundered so pitifully in such perilous waters, as when he ventured to put verses of his own into the mouth of Christopher Marlowe.[131] These errors we must all hope to see rectified in a second issue of the text: and meantime we can but welcome with all possible gratitude and applause the magnificent series of old plays by unknown writers which we owe to the keen research and the fine appreciation of Marlowe's latest editor. Of these I may find some future occasion to speak: my present business is with the admirable poet who has been promoted to the second place in Mr. Bullen's collection of the English dramatists.

The selection of Middleton for so distinguished a place of honour may probably not approve itself to the judgment of all experts in dramatic literature. Charles Lamb, as they will all remember, would have advised the editor 'to begin with the collected plays of Heywood:'[132] which as yet, like the plays of Dekker, of Marston, and of Chapman, remain unedited in any serious or scholarly sense of the term. The existing reprints merely reproduce, without adequate elucidation or correction, the corrupt and chaotic text of the worst early editions: while Middleton has for upwards of half a century enjoyed the privilege denied to men who are usually accounted

130. See entry 55.
131. See entry 63.
132. *Notes, etc., to extracts from the Garrick Plays*, 59.

his equals if not his superiors in poetic if not in dramatic genius. Even for an editor of the ripest learning and the highest ability there is comparatively little to do where Mr. Dyce has been before him in the field. However, we must all give glad and grateful welcome to a new edition of a noble poet who has never yet received his full meed of praise and justice: though our gratitude and our gladness may be quickened and dilated by the proverbial sense of further favours to come.

The first word of modern tribute to the tragic genius of Thomas Middleton was not spoken by Charles Lamb. Four years before the appearance of the priceless volume which established his fame for ever among all true lovers of English poetry by copious excerpts from five of his most characteristic works, Walter Scott, in a note on the fifty-sixth stanza of the second fytte of the metrical romance of *Sir Tristrem*, had given a passing word of recognition to the 'horribly striking' power of 'some passages' in Middleton's masterpiece:[133] which was first reprinted eleven years later, in the fourth volume of Dilke's Old Plays. Lamb, surprisingly enough, has given not a single extract from that noble tragedy: it was reserved for Leigh Hunt, when speaking of its author, to remark that 'there is one character of his (De Flores in *The Changeling*) which, for effect at once tragical, probable, and poetical, surpasses anything I know of in the drama of domestic life.'[134] The praise is not a whit too high: the truth could not have been better said.

The play with which Mr. Bullen, altering the arrangement adopted by Mr. Dyce, opens his edition of Middleton [*Blurt, Master Constable*], is a notable example of the best and the worst qualities which distinguish or disfigure the romantic comedy of the Shakespearean age. The rude and reckless composition, the rough intrusion of savourless farce, the bewildering combinations of incident and the far more bewildering fluctuations of character — all the inconsistences, incongruities, incoherences of the piece are forgotten when the reader remembers and reverts to the passages of exquisite and fascinating beauty which relieve and redeem the utmost errors of negligence and haste. To find anything more delightful, more satisfying in its pure and simple perfection of loveliness, we must turn to the very best examples of Shakespeare's youthful work. Nay, it must be allowed that in one or two of the master's earliest plays — in the *Two Gentlemen of Verona*, for instance — we shall find nothing comparable for charm and sincerity of sweet and passionate fancy with such enchanting verses as these.

133. See entry 53.
134. See entry 68.

O happy persecution, I embrace thee
With an unfettered soul! So sweet a thing
It is to sigh upon the rack of love,
Where each calamity is groaning witness
Of the poor martyr's faith. I never heard
Of any true affection, but 'twas nipt
With care, that, like the caterpillar, eats
The leaves off the spring's sweetest book, the rose.
Love, bred on earth, is often nursed in hell:
By rote it reads woe, ere it learn to spell.

Again: the 'secure tyrant, but unhappy lover,' whose prisoner and rival has thus expressed his triumphant resignation, is counselled by his friend to 'go laugh and lie down,' as not having slept for three nights; but answers, in words even more delicious than his supplanter's;

Alas, how can I? he that truly loves
Burns out the day in idle fantasies;
And when the lamb bleating doth bid good night
Unto the closing day, then tears begin
To keep quick time unto the owl, whose voice
Shrieks like the bellman in the lover's ears:
Love's eye the jewel of sleep, O, seldom wears!
The early lark is wakened from her bed,
Being only by love's plaints disquieted;
And, singing in the morning's ear, she weeps,
Being deep in love, at lovers' broken sleeps:
But say a golden slumber chance to tie
With silken strings the cover of love's eye,
Then dreams, magician-like, mocking present
Pleasures, whose fading leaves more discontent.

Perfect in music, faultless in feeling, exquisite in refined simplicity of expression, this passage is hardly more beautiful and noble than one or two in the play which follows. *The Phœnix* is a quaint and homely compound of satirical realism in social studies with utopian invention in the figure of an ideal prince, himself a compound of Harun al-Rashid and 'Albert the Good,' who wanders through the play as a detective in disguise, and appears in his own person at the close to discharge in full the general and particular claims of justice and philanthropy. The whole work is slight and sketchy, primitive if not puerile in parts, but easy and amusing to read; the confidence reposed by the worthy monarch in noblemen of such unequivocal nomenclature as Lord Proditor, Lussurioso, and Infesto, is one of the signs that we are here still on the debatable borderland between the old Morality and the new Comedy — a province where incarnate vices and virtues are seen figuring and posturing in what can scarcely be called masquerade. But the two fine soliloquies of Phœnix on the corruption of the purity of law (Act i. scene iv.) and the profanation of the sanctity of marriage (Act ii. scene ii.) are somewhat riper and graver in style, with less admixture of rhyme and more variety of cadence, than the lovely verses above quoted. Milton's obligation to the latter passage is less direct than his earlier obligation to a later play of Middleton's, from which he transferred one of the most beautiful as well as most famous images in *Lycidas*: but his early and intimate acquaintance with Middleton had apparently (as Mr. Dyce seems to think) left in the ear of the blind old poet a more or less distinct echo from the noble opening verses of the dramatist's address to 'reverend and honourable matrimony.'

In *Michaelmas Term* the realism of Middleton's comic style is no longer alloyed or flavoured with poetry or fancy. It is an excellent Hogarthian comedy, full of rapid and vivid incident, of pleasant or indignant humour. Its successor, *A Trick to catch the Old One*, is by far the best play Middleton had yet written, and one of the best he ever wrote. The merit of this and his other good comedies does not indeed consist in any new or subtle study of character, any Shakespearean creation or Jonsonian invention of humours or of men: the spendthrifts and the misers, the courtesans and the dotards, are figures borrowed from the common stock of stage tradition: it is the vivid variety of incident and intrigue, the freshness and ease and vigour of the style, the clear straightforward energy and vivacity of the action, that the reader finds most praiseworthy in the best comic work of such ready writers as Middleton and Dekker. The dialogue has sometimes touches of real humour and flashes of genuine wit: but its readable and enjoyable quality is generally independent of these. Very witty writing may be very dreary reading, for want of natural animation and true dramatic movement: and in these qualities at least the rough and ready work of our old dramatists is seldom if ever deficient.

It is, however, but too probable that the reader's enjoyment may be crossed with a dash of exasperation when he finds a writer of real genius so reckless of fame and self-respect as the pressure of want or the weariness of overwork seems but too often and too naturally to have made too many of the great dramatic journeymen whose powers were half wasted or half worn out in the struggle for bare bread. No other excuse than this can be advanced for the demerit of Middleton's next comedy. Had the author wished to show how well and how ill he could write at his worst and at his best, he could have given no fairer proof than by the publication of the two plays issued under his name in the same year 1608. *The Family of Love* is in my judgment unquestionably and incomparably the worst of Middleton's plays: very coarse, very dull, altogether distasteful and ineffectual. As a religious satire it is so utterly pointless as to leave no impression of any definite folly or distinctive knavery in the doctrine or the practice of the particular sect held up by name to ridicule: an obscure body of feather-headed fanatics, concerning whom we can only be certain that they were decent and inoffensive in comparison with the yelling Yahoos whom the scandalous and senseless license of our own day allows to run and roar about the country unmuzzled and unwhipped.

There is much more merit in the broad comedy of *Your Five Gallants*, a curious burlesque study of manners and morals not generally commendable for imitation. The ingenious and humorous invention which supplies a centre for the picture and a pivot for the action is most singularly identical with the device of a modern detective as recorded by the greatest English writer of his day. 'The Butcher's Story,' told to Dickens by the policeman who had played the part of the innocent young butcher, may be profitably compared by lovers of detective humour with the story of Fitsgrave — a 'thrice worthy' gentleman who under the disguise of a young gull fresh from college succeeds in circumventing and unmasking the five associated swindlers of variously villainous professions by whom a fair and amiable heiress is beleaguered and befooled. The play is somewhat crude and hasty in construction, but full of life and fun and grotesque variety of humorous event.

The first of Middleton's plays to attract notice from students of a later generation, *A Mad World, my Masters*, if not quite so thoroughly good a comedy as *A Trick to catch the Old One*, must be allowed to contain the very best comic character ever drawn or sketched by the fertile and flowing pen of its author. The prodigal grandfather, Sir Bounteous Progress, is perhaps the most lifelike figure of a good-humoured and liberal old libertine that ever amused or scandalized a tolerant or intolerant reader. The chief incidents of the action are admirably humorous and ingenious: but the matrimonial part of the catastrophe is something more than repulsive, and the singular intervention of a real live succubus, less terrible in her seductions than her sister of the *Contes Drolatiques*, can hardly seem happy or seasonable to a generation which knows not King James and his Demonology.

Of the two poets occasionally associated with Middleton in the composition of a play, Dekker seems usually to have taken in hand the greater part, and Rowley the lesser part, of the composite poem engendered by their joint efforts. The style of *The Roaring Girl* is full of Dekker's

COMMENTARY 167

peculiar mannerisms: slipshod and straggling metre, incongruous touches or flashes of fanciful or lyrical expression, reckless and awkward inversions, irrational and irrepressible outbreaks of irregular and fitful rhyme. And with all these faults it is more unmistakably the style of a born poet than is the usual style of Middleton. Dekker would have taken a high place among the finest if not among the greatest of English poets if he had but had the sense of form — the instinct of composition. Whether it was modesty, indolence, indifference or incompetence, some drawback or shortcoming there was which so far impaired the quality of his strong and delicate genius that it is impossible for his most ardent and cordial admirer to say or think of his very best work that it really does him justice — that it adequately represents the fullness of his unquestionable powers. And yet it is certain that Lamb was not less right than usual when he said that Dekker 'had poetry enough for anything.'[135] But he had not constructive power enough for the trade of a playwright — the trade in which he spent so many weary years of ill-requited labour. This comedy in which we first find him associated with Middleton is well written and well contrived, and fairly diverting — especially to an idle or an uncritical reader: though even such an one may suspect that the heroine here represented as a virginal virago must have been in fact rather like Dr. Johnson's fair friend Bet Flint; of whom the Great Lexicographer 'used to say that she was generally slut and drunkard; occasionally whore and thief' (Boswell, May 8, 1781). The parallel would have been more nearly complete if Moll Cutpurse 'had written her own Life in verse,' and brought it to Selden or Bishop Hall with a request that he would furnish her with a preface to it. But the seventeenth century was inadequate to so perfect a production of the kind; and we doubt not through the ages one increasing purpose runs, and the thoughts of girls are widened with the process of the suns.

The plays of Middleton are not so properly divisible into tragic and comic as into realistic and romantic — into plays of which the mainspring is essentially prosaic or photographic, and plays of which the mainspring is principally fanciful or poetical. Two only of the former class remain to be mentioned; *Anything for a Quiet Life*, and *A Chaste Maid in Cheapside*. There is very good stuff in the plot or groundwork of the former, but the workmanship is hardly worthy of the material. Mr. Bullen ingeniously and plausibly suggests the partnership of Shirley in this play: but the conception of the character in which he discerns a likeness to the touch of the lesser dramatist is happier and more original than such a comparison would

135. "Characters of Dramatic Writers Contemporary with Shakspeare," *The Works of Charles Lamb*, 2:70.

indicate. The young stepmother whose affectation of selfish levity and grasping craft is really designed to cure her husband of his infatuation, and to reconcile him with the son who regards her as his worst enemy, is a figure equally novel, effective and attractive. The honest shopkeeper and his shrewish wife may remind us again of Dickens by their points of likeness to Mr. and Mrs. Snagsby; though the reformation of the mercer's jealous vixen is brought about by more humorous and less tragical means than the repentance of the law-stationer's 'little woman.' George the apprentice, through whose wit and energy this happy consummation becomes possible, is a very original and amusing example of the young Londoner of the period. But there is more humour, though very little chastity, in the *Chaste Maid*; a play of quite exceptional freedom and audacity, and certainly one of the drollest and liveliest that ever broke the bounds of propriety or shook the sides of merriment.

The opening of *More Dissemblers besides Women* is as full at once of comic and of romantic promise as the upshot of the whole is unsatisfactory — a most lame and impotent conclusion. But some of the dialogue is exquisite; full of flowing music and gentle grace, of ease and softness and fancy and spirit; and the part of a poetic or romantic Joseph Surface, as perfect in the praise of virtue as in the practice of vice, is one of Middleton's really fine and happy inventions. In the style of *The Widow* there is no less fluency and facility: it is throughout identical with that of Middleton's other comedies in metre; a style which has so many points in common with Fletcher's as to make the apocryphal attribution of a share in this comedy to the hand of the greater poet more plausible than many other ascriptions of the kind. I am inclined nevertheless to agree with Mr. Bullen's apparent opinion that the whole credit of this brilliant play may be reasonably assigned to Middleton; and especially with his remark that the only scene in which any resemblance to the manner of Ben Jonson can be traced by the most determined ingenuity of critical research is more like the work of a pupil than like a hasty sketch of the master's. There is no lack of energetic invention and beautiful versification in another comedy of adventure and intrigue, *No Wit, no Help like a Woman's*: the unpleasant or extravagant quality of certain incidents in the story is partially neutralized or modified by the unfailing charm of a style worthy of Fletcher himself in his ripest and sweetest stage of poetic comedy.

But high above all the works yet mentioned there stands and will stand conspicuous while noble emotion and noble verse have honour among English readers the pathetic and heroic play so memorably appreciated by Charles Lamb, *A Fair Quarrel*. It would be the vainest and emptiest impertinence to offer a word in echo of his priceless and imperishable praise.

The delicate nobility of the central conception on which the hero's character depends for its full relief and development should be enough to efface all remembrance of any defect or default in moral taste, any shortcoming on the æsthetic side of ethics, which may be detected in any slighter or hastier example of the poet's invention. A man must be dull and slow of sympathies indeed who cannot respond in spirit to that bitter cry of chivalrous and manful agony at sense of the shadow of a mother's shame: —

> Quench, my spirit,
> And out with honour's flaming lights within thee!
> Be dark and dead to all respects of manhood!
> I never shall have use of valour more.

Middleton has no second hero like Captain Ager: but where is there another so thoroughly noble and lovable among all the characters of all the dramatists of his time but Shakespeare?

The part taken by Rowley in this play is easy for any tiro in criticism to verify. The rough and crude genius of that perverse and powerful writer is not seen here by any means at its best. I cannot as yet lay claim to an exhaustive acquaintance with his works, but judging from what I have read of them I should say that his call was rather towards tragedy than towards comedy; that his mastery of severe and serious emotion was more genuine and more natural than his command of satirical or grotesque realism. The tragedy in which he has grappled with the subject afterwards so differently handled in the first and greatest of Landor's tragedies is to me of far more interest and value than such comedies as that which kindled the enthusiasm of a loyal Londoner in the civic sympathies of Lamb. Disfigured as it is towards the close by indulgence in mere horror and brutality after the fashion of Andronicus or Jeronimo, it has more beauty and power and pathos in its best scenes than a reader of his comedies — as far as I know them — would have expected. There are noticeable points of likeness — apart from the coincidence of subject — between this and Mr. Caldwell Roscoe's noble tragedy of *Violenzia*. But in the underplot of *A Fair Quarrel* Rowley's besetting faults of coarseness and quaintness, stiffness and roughness, are so flagrant and obtrusive that we cannot avoid a feeling of regret and irritation at such untimely and inharmonious evidence of his partnership with a poet of finer if not of sturdier genius. The same sense of discord and inequality will be aroused on comparison of the worse with the better parts of *The Old Law*. The clumsiness and dullness of the farcical interludes can hardly be paralleled in the rudest and hastiest scenes of Middleton's writing: while the sweet and noble dignity of the finer passages have the stamp of his ripest and tenderest genius on every line and in every cadence. But for sheer bewildering incongruity there is no play known to me which can be compared with *The Mayor of Queenborough*. Here again we find a note so dissonant and discordant in the lighter parts of the dramatic concert that we seem at once to recognize the harsher and hoarser instrument of Rowley. The farce is even more extravagantly and preposterously mistimed and misplaced than that which disfigures the play just mentioned: but I thoroughly agree with Mr. Bullen's high estimate of the power displayed and maintained throughout the tragic and poetic part of this drama; to which no previous critic has ever vouchsafed a word of due acknowledgement. The story is ugly and unnatural, but its repulsive effect is transfigured or neutralized by the charm of tender or passionate poetry; and it must be admitted that the hideous villainy of Vortiger and Horsus affords an opening for subsequent scenic effects of striking and genuine tragical interest.

The difference between the genius of Middleton and the genius of Dekker could not be better illustrated than by comparison of their attempts at political and patriotic allegory. The lazy, slovenly, impatient genius of Dekker flashes out by fits and starts on the reader of the play in which he has expressed his English hatred of Spain and Popery, his English pride in the rout of the Armada, and his English gratitude for the part played by Queen Elizabeth in the crowning struggle of the time: but his most cordial admirer can hardly consider *The Whore of Babylon* a shining or satisfactory example of dramatic art. The play which brought Middleton into prison, and earned for the actors a sum so far beyond parallel as to have seemed incredible till the fullest evidence was procured, is one of the most complete and exquisite works of artistic ingenuity and dexterity that ever excited or offended, enraptured or scandalized an audience of friends or enemies: the only work of English poetry which may properly be called Aristophanic. It has the same depth of civic seriousness, the same earnest ardour and devotion to the old cause of the old country, the same solid fervour of enthusiasm and indignation, which animated the third great poet of Athens against the corruption of art by the sophistry of Euripides and the corruption of manhood by the sophistry of Socrates. The delicate skill of the workmanship can only be appreciated by careful and thorough study; but that the infusion of poetic fancy and feeling into the generally comic and satiric style is hardly unworthy of the comparison which I have ventured to challenge, I will take but one brief extract for evidence.

> Upon those lips, the sweet fresh buds of youth,
> The holy dew of prayer lies, like pearl

Dropt from the opening eyelids of the morn
Upon a bashful rose.

Here for once even 'that celestial thief' John Milton has impaired rather than improved the effect of the beautiful phrase borrowed from an earlier and inferior poet. His use of Middleton's exquisite image is not quite so apt — so perfectly picturesque and harmonious — as the use to which it was put by the inventor.

Nothing in the age of Shakespeare is so difficult for an Englishman of our own age to realize as the temper, the intelligence, the serious and refined elevation of an audience which was at once capable of enjoying and applauding the roughest and coarsest kinds of pleasantry, the rudest and crudest scenes of violence, and competent to appreciate the finest and the highest reaches of poetry, the subtlest and the most sustained allusions of ethical or political symbolism. The large and long popularity of an exquisite dramatic or academic allegory such as *Lingua*, which would seem to appeal only to readers of exceptional education, exceptional delicacy of perception, and exceptional quickness of wit, is hardly more remarkable than the popular success of a play requiring such keen constancy of attention, such vivid wakefulness and promptitude of apprehension, as this even more serious than fantastic work of Middleton's. The vulgarity and puerility of all modern attempts at any comparable effect need not be cited to throw into relief the essential finish, the impassioned intelligence, the high spiritual and literary level, of these crowded and brilliant and vehement five acts. Their extreme cleverness, their indefatigable ingenuity, would in any case have been remarkable: but their fullness of active and poetic life gives them an interest far deeper and higher and more permanent than the mere sense of curiosity and wonder.

But if *A Game at Chess* is especially distinguished by its complete and thorough harmony of execution and design, the lack of any such artistic merit in another famous work of Middleton's is such as once more to excite that irritating sense of inequality, irregularity, inconstancy of genius and inconsequence of aim, which too often besets and bewilders the student of our early dramatists. There is poetry enough in *The Witch* to furnish forth a whole generation of poeticules: but the construction or composition of the play, the arrangement and evolution of event, the distinction or development of character, would do less than little credit to a boy of twelve; who at any rate would hardly have thought of patching up so ridiculous a reconciliation between intending murderers and intended victims as here exceeds in absurdity the chaotic combination of accident and error which disposes of inconvenient or superfluous underlings. But though neither Mr. Dyce nor Mr. Bullen has been at all excessive or unjust in his animadversions on these flagrant faults and follies, neither editor has given his author due credit for the excellence of style, of language and versification, which makes this play readable throughout with pleasure, if not always without impatience. Fletcher himself, the acknowledged master of the style here adopted by Middleton, has left no finer example of metrical fluency and melodious ease. The fashion of dialogue and composition is no doubt rather feminine than masculine: Marlowe and Jonson, Webster and Beaumont, Tourneur and Ford, — to cite none but the greatest of authorities in this kind — wrote a firmer if not a freer hand, struck a graver if not a sweeter note of verse: this rapid effluence of easy expression is liable to lapse into conventional efflux of facile improvisation: but such command of it as Middleton's is impossible to any but a genuine and a memorable poet.

As for the supposed obligations of Shakespeare to Middleton or Middleton to Shakespeare, the imaginary relations of *The Witch* to *Macbeth* or *Macbeth* to *The Witch*, I can only say that the investigation of this subject seems to me as profitable as a research into the natural history of snakes in Iceland. That the editors to whom we owe the miserably defaced and villainously garbled text which is all that has reached us of *Macbeth*, not content with the mutilation of the greater poet, had recourse to the interpolation of a few superfluous and incongruous lines or fragments from the lyric portions of the lesser poet's work — that the players who mangled Shakespeare were the pilferers who plundered Middleton — must be obvious to all but those (if any such yet exist anywhere) who are capable of believing the unspeakably impudent assertion of those mendacious malefactors that they have left us a pure and perfect edition of Shakespeare. These passages are all thoroughly in keeping with the general tone of the lesser work: it would be tautology to add that they are no less utterly out of keeping with the general tone of the other. But in their own way nothing can be finer: they have a tragic liveliness in ghastliness, a grotesque animation of horror, which no other poet has ever conceived or conveyed to us. The difference between Michel Angelo and Goya, Tintoretto and Gustave Doré, does not quite efface the right of the minor artists to existence and remembrance.

The tragedy of *Women beware Women*, whether or not it be accepted as the masterpiece of Middleton, is at least an excellent example of the facility and fluency and equable promptitude of style which all students will duly appreciate and applaud in the riper and completer work of this admirable poet. It is full to overflowing of noble eloquence, of inventive resource and suggestive effect, of rhetorical affluence and theatrical ability. The opening or exposition of the play is quite masterly: and the scene in which the forsaken husband is seduced into consolation by the temptress of his wife is worthy of all praise for the straightforward ingenuity and the serious delicacy by which the action is rendered credible and the situation endurable. But I fear that few or none will be found to disagree with my opinion that no such approbation or tolerance can be reasonably extended so as to cover or condone the offences of either the underplot or the upshot of the play. The one is repulsive beyond redemption by elegance of style, the other is preposterous beyond extenuation on the score of logic or poetical justice. Those who object on principle to solution by massacre must object in consistency to the conclusions of *Hamlet* and *King Lear*: nor are the results of Webster's tragic invention more questionable or less inevitable than the results of Shakespeare's: but the dragnet of murder which gathers in the characters at the close of this play is as promiscuous in its sweep as that cast by Cyril Tourneur over the internecine shoal of sharks who are hauled in and ripped open at the close of *The Revenger's Tragedy*. Had Middleton been content with the admirable subject of his main action, he might have given us a simple and unimpeachable masterpiece: and even as it is he has left us a noble and a memorable work. It is true that the irredeemable infamy of the leading characters degrades and deforms the nature of the interest excited: the good and gentle old mother whose affectionate simplicity is so gracefully and attractively painted passes out of the story and drops out of the list of actors just when some redeeming figure is most needed to assuage the dreariness of disgust with which we follow the fortunes of so meanly criminal a crew: and the splendid eloquence of the only other respectable person in the play is not of itself sufficient to make a living figure, rather than a mere mouthpiece for indignant emotion, of so subordinate and inactive a character as the Cardinal. The lower comedy of the play is identical in motive with that which defaces the master-work of Ford: more stupid and offensive it hardly could be. But the high comedy of the scene between Livia and the Widow is as fine as the best work in that kind left us by the best poets and humourists of the Shakespearean age; it is not indeed unworthy of the comparison with Chaucer's which it suggested to the all but impeccable judgment of Charles Lamb.[136]

The lack of moral interest and sympathetic attraction in the characters and the story, which has been noted as the principal defect in the otherwise effective composition of *Women beware Women*, is an objection which cannot be brought against the graceful tragicomedy of *The Spanish Gipsy*. Whatever is best in the tragic or in the romantic part of this play bears the stamp of Middleton's genius alike in the sentiment and the style. 'The code

136. See entry 55.

of modern morals,' to borrow a convenient phrase from Shelley, may hardly incline us to accept as plausible or as possible the repentance and the redemption of so brutal a ruffian as Roderigo: but the vivid beauty of the dialogue is equal to the vivid interest of the situation which makes the first act one of the most striking in any play of the time. The double action has some leading points in common with two of Fletcher's, which have nothing in common with each other: Merione in *The Queen of Corinth* is less interesting than Clara, but the vagabonds of *Beggars' Bush* are more amusing than Rowley's or Middleton's. The play is somewhat deficient in firmness or solidity of construction: it is, if such a phrase be permissible, one of those half-baked or underdone dishes of various and confused ingredients, in which the cook's or the baker's hurry has impaired the excellent materials of wholesome bread and savoury meat. The splendid slovens who served their audience with spiritual work in which the gods had mixed 'so much of earth, so much of heaven, and such impetuous blood' — the generous and headlong purveyors who lavished on their daily provision of dramatic fare such wealth of fine material and such prodigality of superfluous grace — the foremost followers of Marlowe and of Shakespeare were too prone to follow the reckless example of the first rather than the severe example of the second. There is perhaps not one of them — and Middleton assuredly is not one — whom we can reasonably imagine capable of the patience and self-respect which induced Shakespeare to rewrite the triumphantly popular parts of Romeo, of Falstaff, and of Hamlet, with an eye to the literary perfection and permanence of work which in its first light outline had won the crowning suffrage of immediate or spectacular applause.

The rough and ready hand of Rowley may be traced, not indeed in the more high-toned passages, but in many of the most animated scenes of *The Spanish Gipsy*. In the most remarkable of the ten masques or interludes which appear among the collected works of Middleton the two names are again associated. To the freshness, liveliness, and spirited ingenuity of this little allegorical comedy Mr. Bullen has done ample justice in his excellent critical introduction. *The Inner-Temple Masque*, less elaborate than *The World Tost at Tennis*, shows no lack of homely humour and invention: and in the others there is as much waste of fine flowing verse and facile fancy as ever excited the rational regret of a modern reader at the reckless profusion of literary power which the great poets of the time were content to lavish on the decoration or exposition of an ephemeral pageant. Of Middleton's other minor works, apocryphal or genuine, I will only say that his authorship of *Microcynicon* — a dull and crabbed imitation of Marston's worst work as a satirist — seems to me utterly incredible. A lucid and melodious fluency of style is the mark of all his metrical writing: and this stupid piece of obscure and clumsy jargon could have been the work of no man endowed with more faculty of expression than informs or modulates the whine of an average pig. Nor is it rationally conceivable that the Thomas Middleton who soiled some reams of paper with what he was pleased to consider or to call a paraphrase of the *Wisdom of Solomon* can have had anything but a poet's name in common with a poet. This name is not like that of the great writer whose name is attached to *The Transformed Metamorphosis*: there can hardly have been two Cyril Tourneurs in the field, but there may well have been half a dozen Thomas Middletons. And Tourneur's abortive attempt at allegoric discourse is but a preposterous freak of prolonged eccentricity: this paraphrase is simply a tideless sea of limitless and inexhaustible drivel. There are three reasons — two of them considerable, but the third conclusive — for assigning to Middleton the two satirical tracts in the style of Nash, or rather of Dekker, which appeared in the same year with his initials subscribed to their prefatory addresses. Mr. Dyce thought they were written by the poet whose ready verse and realistic humour are both well represented in their text: Mr. Bullen agrees with Mr. Dyce in thinking that they are the work of Middleton. And Mr. Carew Hazlitt thinks that they are not.[137]

No such absolute and final evidence as this can be adduced in favour or disfavour of the theory which would saddle the reputation of Middleton with the authorship of a dull and disjointed comedy, the work (it has hitherto been supposed) of the German substitute for Shakespeare. Middleton has no doubt left us more crude and shapeless plays than *The Puritan*; none, in my opinion, — excepting always his very worst authentic example of farce or satire, *The Family of Love* — so heavy and so empty and so feeble. If it must be assigned to any author of higher rank than the new Shakspere, I would suggest that it is much more like Rowley's than like Middleton's worst work. Of the best qualities which distinguish either of these writers as poet or as humourist, it has not the shadow or the glimmer of a vestige.

In the last and the greatest work which bears their united names — a work which should suffice to make either name immortal if immortality were other than an accidental attribute of genius — the very highest capacity of either poet is seen at its very best. There is more of mere poetry, more splendour of style and vehemence of verbal inspiration, in the work of other poets then writing for the stage: the two masterpieces of Webster are higher in tone at their highest, more imaginative and more fascinating in their expression of terrible or of piteous wrath: there are more superb harmonies,

---

137. See the Dyce and Bullen editions; William Carew Hazlitt's statements are unknown. Ward said none of the non-dramatic works ascribed to Middleton was "demonstrably his" (*History of English Dramatic Literature*, 2: 67).

more glorious raptures of ardent and eloquent music, in the sometimes unsurpassed and unsurpassable poetic passion of Cyril Tourneur. But even Webster's men seem but splendid sketches, as Tourneur's seem but shadowy or fiery outlines, beside the perfect and living figure of De Flores. The man is so horribly human, so fearfully and wonderfully natural, in his single-hearted brutality of devotion, his absolute absorption of soul and body by one consuming force of passionately cynical desire, that we must go to Shakespeare for an equally original and an equally unquestionable revelation of indubitable truth. And in no play by Beaumont and Fletcher is the concord between the two partners more singularly complete in unity of spirit and of style than throughout the tragic part of this play. The underplot from which it most unluckily and absurdly derives its title is very stupid, rather coarse, and almost vulgar: but the two great parts of Beatrice and De Flores are equally consistent, coherent and sustained, in the scenes obviously written by Middleton and in the scenes obviously written by Rowley. The subordinate part taken by Middleton in Dekker's play of *The Honest Whore* is difficult to discern from the context or to verify by inner evidence: though some likeness to his realistic or photographic method may be admitted as perceptible in the admirable picture of Bellafront's morning reception at the opening of the second act of the first part. But here we may assert with fair confidence that the first and the last scenes of the play bear the indisputable sign-manual of William Rowley. His vigorous and vivid genius, his somewhat hard and curt directness of style and manner, his clear and trenchant power of straightforward presentation or exposition, may be traced in every line as plainly as the hand of Middleton must be recognized in the main part of the tragic action intervening. To Rowley therefore must be assigned the very high credit of introducing and of dismissing with adequate and even triumphant effect the strangely original tragic figure which owes its fullest and finest development to the genius of Middleton. To both poets alike must unqualified and equal praise be given for the subtle simplicity of skill with which they make us appreciate the fatal and foreordained affinity between the ill-favoured, rough-mannered, broken-down gentleman, and the headstrong unscrupulous unobservant girl whose very abhorrence of him serves only to fling her down from her high station of haughty beauty into the very clutch of his ravenous and pitiless passion. Her cry of horror and astonishment at first perception of the price to be paid for a service she had thought to purchase with mere money is so wonderfully real in its artless and ingenuous sincerity that Shakespeare himself could hardly have bettered it:

Why, 'tis impossible thou canst be so wicked,

And shelter such a cunning cruelty,
To make his death the murderer of my honour!

That note of incredulous amazement that the man whom she has just instigated to the commission of murder 'can be so wicked' as to have served her ends for any end of his own beyond the pay of a professional assassin is a touch worthy of the greatest dramatist that ever lived. The perfect simplicity of expression is as notable as the perfect innocence of her surprise; the candid astonishment of a nature absolutely incapable of seeing more than one thing or holding more than one thought at a time. That she, the first criminal, should be honestly shocked as well as physically horrified by revelation of the real motive which impelled her accomplice into crime, gives a lurid streak of tragic humour to the lifelike interest of the scene; as the pure infusion of spontaneous poetry throughout redeems the whole work from the charge of vulgar subservience to a vulgar taste for the presentation or the contemplation of criminal horror. Instances of this happy and natural nobility of instinct abound in the casual expressions which give grace and animation always, but never any touch of rhetorical transgression or florid superfluity, to the brief and trenchant swordplay of the tragic dialogue.

That sigh would fain have utterance: take pity on 't,
And lend it a free word; 'las, how it labours
For liberty! I hear the murmur yet
Beat at your bosom.

The wording of this passage is sufficient to attest the presence and approve the quality of a poet: the manner and the moment of its introduction would be enough to show the instinctive and inborn insight of a natural dramatist. As much may be said of the few words which give us a ghastly glimpse of supernatural terror:—

Ha! what art thou that tak'st away the light
Betwixt that star and me? I dread thee not:
'Twas but a mist of conscience.

But the real power and genius of the work cannot be shown by extracts — not even by such extracts as these. His friend and colleague Dekker shows to better advantage by the process of selection: hardly one of his plays leaves so strong and sweet an impression of its general and complete excellence as of separate scenes or passages of tender and delicate imagination or emotion beyond the reach of Middleton: but the tragic unity and completeness of conception which distinguish this masterpiece will be sought in vain among the less firm and solid figures of his less serious and profound invention. Had *The Changeling* not been preserved, we should not have known Middleton: as it is, we are more than justified in asserting that a critic who denies him a high place among the poets of England must be not merely ignorant of the qualities which involve a right or confer a claim to this position, but incapable of curing his ignorance by any process of study. The rough and rapid work which absorbed too much of this poet's time and toil seems almost incongruous with the impression made by the noble and thoughtful face, so full of gentle dignity and earnest composure, in which we recognise the graver and loftier genius of a man worthy to hold his own beside all but the greatest of his age. And that age was the age of Shakespeare.

"Thomas Middleton." *The Nineteenth Century* 19 (1886): 138-53.

83. 1886, May *The Athenæum*: **"Plenarily Inspired"**

The Athenæum's anonymous reviewer finds Middleton's ruder era an advantage: unlike modern, tame playwrights, the Renaissance dramatists had daring and spirit. The reviewer hopes that, even though *The Changeling*'s "passion" renders it "unsuited to modern tastes," it might one day be played again, "before a select audience."

It is not altogether easy to fix the position of Middleton in the hierarchy of the Elizabethan dramatists. In what rank he is placed necessarily depends upon the system of classification. Assigning Shakspeare a class to himself, and confining the second class to those who came nearest him, Marlowe, Webster, Beaumont and Fletcher, and Jonson, it is yet difficult to say whether the merits of Middleton do not entitle him to a place in it. In some respects he is thoroughly representative of his epoch. At his best he is on a level with any of the later Elizabethan dramatists except Shakspeare, at his worst he sinks no lower than sink Heywood and Decker, Shirley, Massinger, and Chapman. His work has, moreover, all the characteristics of the age. It is daring, imaginative, quaintly written, plenarily inspired. It shows a kind of realism in search of which modern literature is groping often in wrong places, and it has a scorn of the possibilities of bathos that is heroic. In lighter and more facile comedies Middleton shows himself a species of dramatic pamphleteer, taking upon himself in plays, like Nash and Decker in pamphlets, to depict the seamy side of the life of the town, and to scourge the backs of thieves, pimps, panders, and others of the like kidney. Nowhere in Elizabethan literature, indeed, is there to be seen a collection of rogues and vagabonds such as he puts upon the stage. In the imaginative drama Middleton holds his own. His delight is to deal with gipsies and vagrants, to depict the young heir cozening his uncle, or the liver by his wits fleecing the gentleman. Lesage himself is not happier than is Middleton in depicting the tricks by which innocence is wheedled or the manner in which the knave is developed from the dupe. High as is the work in 'The Changeling,' in 'A Fair Quarrel,' and in 'Women beware Women,' it is rather in such pieces as 'A Trick to Catch the Old One' that Middleton moves most at his ease.

To analyze the entire contents of Mr. Bullen's eight volumes is out of the question. The plays, fortunately, with one or two exceptions, range themselves easily under two heads, and a selection from these leaves no aspect of Middleton's talent unshown. The two plays in which Middleton reaches his highest point are 'Women beware Women' and 'The Changeling,' though some others run them near. So far as regards construction, and, with some allowance for the taste of the day, execution also, 'Women beware Women' may stand side by side with any non-Shakspearean work of the epoch. It is deficient, like many of Middleton's plays, in tenderness, a quality in which both Heywood and Decker are his superiors. Its plot is, however, powerful, its characters are drawn to the life, its dialogue is rich in poetry, and the whole has a grim irony that lifts it into the highest regions of the drama. The opening scenes are singularly romantic. Bianca, a Venetian beauty, has left a home in which she enjoyed every luxury to share the fortunes of Leantio, a young Florentine factor, whom she has espoused and with whom she lives in bonds of happiest union. Compelled by business occupations to quit his home, Leantio leaves his wife in the charge of his mother, whom he bids to keep his treasure carefully guarded from view. Bianca is, however, seen by the duke, who falls in love with her, and who employs as a procuress Livia, a clever and an unscrupulous lady of his court. The corruption of the heroine, when once she is unsuspectingly brought alone into the presence of the duke, is easily accomplished, a few threats, flatteries, and promises achieving the task. Upon his return, Leantio finds her shameless and hardened, weary of the squalour around her, and determined to return to her royal lover. From her behaviour in the presence of the duke and from the honours squandered upon himself he learns the truth. Up to this point the workmanship is all of the best. Leantio is not, however, the direct executant of his own vengeance. He lapses into a dishonouring connexion with Livia, the executant of the duke's wishes and the agent in his own shame, and loses his life at the hands of her brother, whom such a connexion offends, and who has been warned of its existence by the duke, acting on the suggestion of Bianca. The *dénoûment* of the play, which involves a general slaughter and is not more grim than fantastic, is, as in some other plays of the epoch, brought about during the representation of a masque.

The opening scenes are delicious. The means used to bring about the seduction of the heroine belong to the highest order of comedy, and the change in the nature of Bianca which follows her surrender to the duke is admirably conceived. If the termination is scarcely satisfactory, it is in keeping with the taste of an age which drew largely from the Italian. The workmanship at least resembles that in the best plays of Webster. In spite of a corrupt text, many passages of exquisite poetry may be selected. The following short extract has been given by Lamb[138] — when did he overlook a passage of the kind? — but has not received the recognition it merits. Few passages in the drama are, in their way, more characteristic of the epoch than is this: —

> Prithee forgive me,
> I did but chide in jest; the best loves use it
> Sometimes, it sets an edge upon affection:
> When we invite our best friends to a feast,
> 'Tis not all sweetmeats that we set before them;
> There's somewhat sharp and salt, both to whet appetite
> And make 'em taste their wine well; so, methinks,
> After a friendly, sharp, and savoury chiding,
> A kiss tastes wondrous well, and full o' the grape.

Less sustained in workmanship than 'Women beware Women,' 'The Changeling' touches a higher point. Following the lead of Dyce and Mr. Bullen, we unhesitatingly ascribe to Middleton the serious parts of this play, which was written in conjunction with William Rowley. A portion of its intrigue is one of the most stupendous things in the drama. Affianced to one man and in love with another, Beatrice-Joanna turns about her to see how she shall divest herself of her troublesome suitor. In her extremity she appeals to De Flores, an ill-favoured and bankrupt dependent upon her father's court, who has long pestered her with attentions which were only saved from being loathsome by being preposterous. Eagerly De Flores accepts her commission, and her importunate suitor and affianced husband is treacherously slain. A few smiles and a good store of ducats will, she

138. *Specimens of English Dramatic Poets*, 156.

supposes, free her from all responsibility for the deed. Slowly and amazedly she learns her mistake. Her possession is the only payment that will be accepted as recompense for a crime undertaken by De Flores solely with the purpose of reducing her to his level. It is difficult to find in the entire range of the drama anything greater than the treatment of these scenes. Speech after speech of De Flores displays an insight into the human heart which no writer whatever, from Shakspeare to Balzac, needs disown. It is natural to compare De Flores with Iago, and the comparison has been made. In more than one respect, however, De Flores is the more striking character. His motives are the more human, since the prize is to him worth the forfeit. It is as though he should, with Helena,

> love a bright particular star
> And think to wed it;

and then see a means not, indeed, of climbing up to it, but of dragging it down to him. His scheme succeeds. There is no help for it; the heroine may flutter her wings, but she is in the clutch of the falcon. Misery, shame, and death follow in the fated course. De Flores is prepared for all. He has emptied the cup of pleasure, and pays the forfeit with a smile. An exhibition of passion so fine as this is rare in literature. It is greatly to be regretted that the subject is so unsuited to modern tastes, no modification of it that would fit it for the stage is conceivable. De Flores was a great character of Betterton. If ever again a tragedian in whom the emotional overpowers the intellectual should appear, the play should be given before a select audience.

Equally impossible is it to quote from a play such as this the successive passages in which this admirably conceived and stupendous character is exhibited, and to indicate the plays in which Middleton comes nearest this mark. The same volume which contains these two works contains also 'The Spanish Gipsey' and 'More Dissemblers besides Women.' Both these plays are entitled to rank high among the dramas of the day. Commencing with a scene of ravishment which is at once romantic and pathetic, and is probably conceivable nowhere else than in Spain, the story of 'The Spanish Gipsey' skilfully avoids a tragic termination and ends happily. It is, as Mr. Bullen says, "a full-blooded play," and is delightful reading. 'More Dissemblers besides Women' is a good comedy, coarse in parts, like much of Middleton's work, but ingenious in treatment and containing some agreeable scenes and some pleasing language.

Among the comedies of manners 'A Trick to Catch the Old One' may be accepted as representative. Witgood, a young gallant who, in consequence of his dissipated ways, has reduced himself to sorest straits, determines to obtain from his uncle, to whom his property is mortgaged, means enough to make a new start in the world. He introduces accordingly a courtesan as a rich widow whom he is about to espouse. With the most mercenary motives the uncle consents to aid his nephew, and the plot then presents the quarrel between two usurers who, seeking to injure each other, are jointly bled and befooled for the benefit of youth. No more tolerant of age than subsequent writers of comedy, Molière included, is Middleton. The old man is a hunks and a churl, and youth and improvidence are rulers of the world. Lucre and other characters of the same kind are, in fact, precursors of Harpagon, and the world is for Witgood and Host as it is for Cléante and Mariane. For Frosine, meanwhile, or for Mascarille a score of prototypes are supplied. 'The Game of Chess' is chiefly interesting for the historical allusions with which it abounds, and for the bitterness of its satire upon Gondomar (the Black Knight), Antonio de Dominis (the Fat Bishop), and others of the party of Spain. Mr. Bullen has shown much ingenuity in fitting to historical personages the characters in this play, and the introductory matter to it is of great value.

The main interest in 'The Witch' has hitherto centred in the dispute as to whether this play or 'Macbeth' was the earlier. It is ridiculous, however, though one or two ripe scholars propound the heresy, to believe that Shakspeare was the later in the field. Concerning the production of 'The Witch' nothing definite is known. The piece, as students of the drama are aware, was first printed by Isaac Reed in 1770 [1778] from a MS. then in the possession of Major Pearson, and now preserved in the Malone Collection at Oxford. Mr. Bullen's speculations as to its date are, to say the least, plausible, and he is fully justified in stating "that there is not a tittle of evidence, whether internal or external," to support the view that Shakspeare was indebted to Middleton.

With the masques and with the miscellaneous writings of Middleton there is no temptation to deal. The former, written, for the most part, perfunctorily, are inferior to those of Middleton's greatest contemporaries; the latter have slight interest. Against the poem called 'The Wisdom of Solomon Paraphrased' Mr. Bullen issues a preliminary caution. At the close the following note, wrung from the tortured editor, stands in the full dignity of print, without a single omission or asterisk: "I have read at various times much indifferent verse and much execrable verse, but I can conscientiously state that 'The Wisdom of Solomon Paraphrased' is the most damnable piece of flatness that has ever fallen in my way. Silius Italicus is bracing after it." It is easy to conceive the relief that the writing of this note must have afforded.

Concerning the value of the edition two opinions will not be held.

Middleton, accessible only in the costly edition of Dyce, demanded attention, and a reprint of his works in the handsome volumes Mr. Nimmo has taught us to expect is a real boon to students of the Elizabethan drama. More carefully and competently edited volumes are scarcely to be hoped for. A good base was, of course, supplied in the edition of Dyce. To the value of this, however, Mr. Bullen has greatly added. To the knowledge and acumen indispensable to a high-class editor Mr. Bullen adds a justness of taste and a clearness of insight that are less common than they should be with the tasters of our literary food. His introduction to the various plays combines sound criticism with penetrative insight. In the course of many hundred emendations of a text exceptionally and regrettably corrupt, Mr. Bullen, of course, challenges discussion. So few are, however, the cases in which we are at issue with him, it is scarcely worth while, by mentioning them, to impart to recognition a flavour of controversy. More than one alteration, moreover, which in reading failed to commend itself, has, upon returning to it, seemed capable of defence. The appearance of Mr. Bullen's Beaumont and Fletcher will be eagerly anticipated, though this is to be preceded by Marston.

Anon. "Drama." *The Athenæum*, 8 May 1886, pp. 625-627.

84. 1886, August *The Spectator* Has Criticism and Praise

Like *The Dial*'s reviewer, *The Spectator*'s critic praises the "masculinity" of the early dramatists and contrasts their vigor with the weakness of contemporary literature. The critic emphasizes unity of action as an evaluative criterion and argues that Middleton, like Shakespeare, distanced himself from his characters, presented them without presenting himself, a critical position that would be renewed in the early twentieth century when scholars examined Middleton's irony and detachment.

The glories of the Elizabethan drama have been the theme of much eloquent writing in the present century; yet, with the exception of Shakespeare, and perhaps Marlowe, its great masters are still, we fear, practically unknown to the ordinary student of our literature. The truth is, the legitimate drama has been, at least for a time, all but completely superseded by the modern novel, the only species, indeed, of imaginative literature which can be said to have any extensive popularity, for most even of our greatest poets are little more than names to the average Englishman of to-day. When the rage for novels and the spurious modern drama, which does not claim to be literature at all, shall have subsided, and a more masculine taste shall again prevail, the great satellites of Shakespeare whom our forefathers honoured may once more take their proper place in the popular estimation.

Owing chiefly to the great scarcity, and consequent expensiveness of copies of previous editions of his works, Middleton has been hitherto more neglected, even by the professed student of our older literature, than any of his fellow-playwrights or immediate predecessors of equal rank, though *The Witch*, still erroneously regarded by many as his masterpiece, has always enjoyed a certain notoriety from its partial affinity to *Macbeth*. Mr. Nimmo has therefore done a real service to would-be readers of Middleton, by his recent reprint of the great dramatist's complete works in eight handsome volumes. They are admirably got up in every respect, and their price, all things considered, is as moderate as it could well be. Mr. Bullen furnishes an excellent introduction, and in his notes, every obscure or obsolete phrase or allusion in the plays is so fully yet concisely explained, as to render all of them easily intelligible, so far, at least, as language is concerned, to any reader of average capacity and patience.

The plays of Middleton are among the most extreme examples we have of the romantic, as distinguished from the classic drama. In none of them do we find, as in the latter, the severe and steady development of a single plot and a few great characters. On the contrary, there are some, especially among the earlier comedies, which can scarcely be said to have any plot at all; and the number of characters in almost every play may well prove a source of bewilderment to the superficial or unpractised reader. Even of those plays which are least inartistic in point of construction, it must be owned that their unity and consistency are seriously impaired by underplots which are always uninteresting and generally disgusting. When the interest of the reader has been awakened in the beginning of a play by the critical situations of its leading characters, it is always weakened, and sometimes hopelessly destroyed, by the sudden and unwelcome introduction of subordinate characters who have little or no concern in the main plot, and seldom compensate for their intrusion by being even diverting. The most perfect of Middleton's works is *The Changeling*, its main plot being skilfully managed throughout, which is seldom the case with his other plays; yet even here the reader's pleasure is considerably abated by the gross and tedious underplot from one of whose characters the title of the drama is most injudiciously taken. The "winding-up" of this play is, however, thoroughly satisfactory, which is more than can be said of most of the others; the conclusion of such a masterpiece as *Women, beware Women*, for instance, being as "lame and impotent" as that of almost any drama of the period. No doubt, much of the incongruity which we find in Middleton's plays may be referred to his co-operation in their production with other and inferior dramatists. This co-operation has been praised by Lamb as a generous characteristic of the age; but in Middleton's case it can hardly be said to have been attended with happy results. For, if it gave variety to his plays, it was certainly fatal to their unity and consistency.

The blank verse employed by Middleton in his plays is apparently as much a protest against the "sequestration of pauses" (so general in the blank verse of some of his predecessors) as Mrs. Browning alleged Milton's to be. Yet, unlike the latter, its variety of harmony or modulation is by no means in keeping with its variety of pause. Though nearly always fluent and graceful, it has little subtlety of music, and its best notes appear to us rather sweet than sublime. Of the severer and statelier melodies of Marlowe, Webster, and Tourneur, we shall find scarcely any example in the blank verse of Middleton, which seems, indeed, for the most part, to have been composed with as much ease as the slipshod prose of many of our modern novelists. Middleton, however, who was more of a "realist" than most of his fellows, and who, in writing blank verse at all, was probably actuated less by his own choice than by the requirements of his age, may have thought the kind of verse he wrote the best vehicle that could be employed for realistic purposes next to prose, from which it is sometimes, indeed, difficult to distinguish it. His rapid and fluent versification is often delightful, and may afford even greater pleasure to some minds than the more majestic measures of the mightiest masters of harmony. As for the substance of his verse, we find many poetical, fine, and just thoughts, felicitously expressed, scattered throughout his numerous plays, but hardly any that are equally distinguished by their profundity or their applicability to our daily life. In this respect he must, we think, be pronounced decidedly inferior to such dramatists as Webster, Tourneur, and even Beaumont and Fletcher. If any of our readers should be disposed to think this judgment partial or unjust, we would ask them to compare the two speeches — the one for, and the other against marriage — of Leantio in the third act of *Women, beware Women*, and which are certainly among the happiest and weightiest utterances in all Middleton's plays, with these two lines in Webster's *Vittoria Corombona:* —

> "We cease to grieve, cease to be fortune's slaves,
> Nay, cease to die, by dying!"

That the latter are incomparably superior in terseness and profundity, very few, we believe, will be inclined to dispute. Unlike other dramatists of that age, Middleton was not a born lyrist. Among all the lyrics interspersed throughout his dramas, we shall not find one which has that witchery of music and felicity of phrase which distinguish the best of those of Webster and Fletcher, no less than they do all that Shakespeare ever wrote. The highest qualities of Middleton's most successful lyrics are their *abandon* and their contagious exuberance of animal spirits. *The Witch*, poor as a play, furnishes many characteristic examples of this kind, as well as some of Middleton's choicest blank verse.

Middleton's dialogues are always dramatic and lively, and the number and variety of his characters are amazing. His delineations are mostly successful, and many of them are masterly. As a comic dramatist, he may challenge comparison with any except Shakespeare and Jonson; while in the versatility of his genius, he more nearly approaches the former than any other of the "Elizabethans," except perhaps Beaumont and Fletcher. He has written one scene at least — the last of the third act of *The Changeling* — which entitles him to rank, as a tragic dramatist, nearly on a level with Marlowe, Webster, and Ford, and perhaps above the authors of *The Revenger's Tragedy* and *The Duke of Milan*. His gift of humour was unshared by any of these great masters of tragedy. Middleton appears to have stood as completely aloof from his own creations as Shakespeare is popularly believed to have stood from his. Unless we identify him with the reckless and unprincipled gallants who figure in so many of his comedies — in which case Jonson's description of him as a "base fellow"[139] would be intelligible enough — his absorption of himself in his characters must be thought as complete as that of Shakespeare in his. Like the latter, too, and Scott, and unlike such writers as Massinger and Tourneur, he is never angry with his vicious characters. Nothing can be more striking than the contrast between the calm and good-humoured, not to say cold-blooded, manner in which Middleton depicts the manifold vices and excesses of his period, and the *sæva indignatio* against them, the misanthropy, cynicism, and life-weariness which characterise every utterance of Vindici in *The Revenger's Tragedy*, — that great and awful figure on which Tourneur has evidently impressed so much of his own striking personality. What struck horror into the mind of Tourneur seems only to have been food for mirth and pleasantry to Middleton. His estimate of women, judging from his plays, was certainly not a high one. The best are amiable, and nothing more, and the remainder are represented as being either prone to evil from the first, or very easily seduced into the paths of sin. Perhaps the most shrewd and intelligent of all his female characters is the Livia of *Women, beware Women*, and she is certainly not distinguished by the purity of her morals or her strict regard for

139. See entry 6.

truth. The Clara of the delightful romantic drama of *The Spanish Gipsy* is perhaps, on the whole, the most pleasing, interesting, and pathetic of all Middleton's heroines. Yet even she, in gladly consenting to marry her ruffianly ravisher, Roderigo, on his somewhat suspicious pledge of amendment in his future conduct, sinks far below the typical heroine of fiction of what is usually regarded as a far less heroic and more prosaic age than that in which Middleton wrote. We refer, of course, to Richardson's Clarissa Harlowe, who prefers death to marriage with a much more brilliant and captivating betrayer than Roderigo.

The Changeling undoubtedly ranks first in importance among the works of Middleton. Without it we should have had no revelation of his highest power, for it is on this play that his reputation as a tragic dramatist mainly rests. The outline of the principal plot is as follows: — Alsemero, who is thus described by his nearest friend in the opening of the tragedy, —

> "Lover I'm sure you're none; the stoic was
> Found in you long ago; your mother nor
> Best friends who have set snares of beauty, ay
> And choice ones too, could never trap you that way," —

chances to see Beatrice-Joanna, the daughter of the Governor of the castle of Alicant, in a temple, and at once falls hopelessly in love with her. She is contracted to Alonzo de Piracquo, to whom she is at first attached; but after making the acquaintance of Alsemero, her affection is diverted to the latter. Her nuptials with Alonzo being now, however, fully arranged, she sees no other mode of escape than by employing De Flores, a needy attendant on her father, to murder him. Though she hates De Flores for his ill-favoured countenance, rough address, and importunity, and has perpetually flouted him, she has the most implicit reliance on his fidelity to her interests, and appears to think that a gift of money and jewels, and "speaking him fair" in the future, will be accepted by him as ample recompense for the deed. After the murder, De Flores brings to her the dead man's finger, with a ring on it that Beatrice had given to him for a token, and assures her that "Piracquo is no more." Beatrice is so little suspicious of the issue, that she replies, —

> "My joys start at mine eyes; our sweet'st delights
> Are evermore born weeping."

When De Flores expresses himself offended even by the offer of all her wealth, and declares that nothing less than the sacrifice of her honour to him will satisfy him, her horror and astonishment are extreme. It is in this great scene that Middleton's genius touches the highest point it ever reached. In depth and concentration of passion, in realistic force, and in rapid and fiery dialogue, it is equal to anything out of Shakespeare. The fierce and inexorable purpose of De Flores is expressed in words which have the vehemence and precision of Webster and Tourneur's most memorable utterances: —

> "Can you weep fate from its determined purpose?
> So soon may you weep me."

This scene would be impressive enough even if detached from the remainder of the play, but its electric and startling power can only be fully felt by those who read what precedes it. Yet it must be owned that there is no element of pathos in it, for it is impossible to feel any pity for Beatrice. While, therefore, Middleton may be allowed to be equal to Marlowe, Webster, and Ford in the delineation of strong passions, he must be pronounced inferior to them in that blending of pathos with power which we find in the last act of *Faustus*, the scene of the murder of the King in *Edward II.*, and the most tragic portions of *The Duchess of Malfi* and *The Broken Heart*. Beatrice is, of course, compelled to yield to De Flores. She, however, afterwards marries Alsemero, and various devices are employed by her and her accomplice to conceal her loss of honour from her husband. The suspicions of the latter being at length fully roused, she confesses all, and her husband shuts her in a closet and sends for De Flores. On his arrival, he is apprised of Beatrice's confession, and requests to be put in the closet with her, which is conceded. Alsemero then sends for the friends and relatives of the culprits. De Flores, in the presence of all, kills Beatrice in the closet, and then stabs himself. The cynical triumph of his last words is admirably in keeping with his character in the other portions of the play.

Of Middleton's poems there is no need to say much. His satirical pieces are almost as scabrous as those of Donne, and are much more pointless and heavy. His *Wisdom of Solomon Paraphrased*, and shorter poems scattered throughout his unimportant prose works, are wholly unworthy of the author of *The Changeling* and *The Spanish Gipsy*. They have, however, the same ease and fluency of versification which we find in Middleton's comedies, and we see no good reason for denying them a place, as some have done, among the veritable productions of the dramatist. If they do not soar above mediocrity, neither do many of the blank-verse passages in the earlier plays.

Anon. "The Works of Thomas Middleton." *The Spectator* 59 (1886): 1119-1121.

COMMENTARY 189

85. 1886, December Ambrosia in an "Earthern Vessel"

The *Overland Monthly*'s reviewer, like most Victorian writers, makes morality a primary criterion for judgment: Middleton may be a genius, but his works are too coarse for youth — and sometimes for adults.

These are dainty volumes, whose elegant, cream-tinted paper, clear type, and luxurious margins, speedily engage the attention of the book-lover. The name of Thomas Middleton, Gent., of whom the *vera effigies* greets us at the opening, is included in the list of those who are called the great dramatists of the Elizabethan age, whose works are found upon the shelves of all true lovers and students of dramatic literature. It would seem an act of presumption after the reputation of an author has survived the passage of almost three centuries to appear to question his longer immortality. As a bit of literary history many a name has come to us from beyond the beginning of the Christian era, but the works of the author have passed to that Nirvana to which they doubtless belong; and it must be true, that while the fame of most writers is but ephemeral, there will come an end at last, to the publication and reading even of those works that have continued for two or three centuries, a merely library existence, leaving to survive only such as are of the generation of those few great souls that were born to live forever.

The works of Middleton were, as far as ascertained, edited in 1840, by Alexander Dyce, one of the ablest of literary editors, in an edition of five volumes. It was apparently because that edition was out of print, that the able editor of this edition says that "the need of a new edition was keenly felt," and so, as we are informed upon an early page in a publisher's notice, "three hundred and fifty copies of this edition have been printed and the type distributed. *No more will be published.*" The italics are the publisher's. It would scarcely appear that the want of a new edition was keenly felt by a very large portion of the reading, or even the studious public. We do not know but that the italicised sentence may be worldly and everlasting truth.

Middleton was the sole author of fifteen dramas, the joint author with Phillip Massinger and William Rowley of three, with Thomas Dekker of one, with Ben. Jonson and John Fletcher of one, and with William Rowley of two. The literary partnerships of Middleton with dramatists who have achieved as great names as these, indicate the high esteem in which he was held by contemporaries, and justify the expectancy with which his name commenced the voyage to posterity.

The distinction and fame of the mere dramatist is among his contemporaries, and is transient. The times and the manners change; the topics of interest in which are found merely dramatic situations are but short-lived; and the play, whether comedy or tragedy, which is simply a drama, is equally as short-lived, and its fame but as the perfume of to-day's garland. The people who come to the playhouse in the next century find the language antiquated, the manners out of fashion, the wit musty and ill-flavored. The number of plays that for mere dramatic interest hold the stage to-day, that have come to us from another century, is limited almost to the fingers of one's hand. There is a quality, however, that determines the lasting literary existence of anything written for the stage. That quality is poetry, the finer way of uttering beautiful ideas. The infusion of its spirit embalms the otherwise perishable drama, and the fullness of that embalming determines the measure of its immortality.

Thomas Middleton was born about 1570, and died in 1627. One of his name was admitted a member of Gray's Inn in 1593, and it is claimed that it was he who was afterwards the dramatist. Very little is absolutely known of this author, except that he was the author of the works now re-published; that in 1620 he was appointed to the office of City Chronologer of London, to which, upon his death, Ben. Jonson succeeded; and that he was imprisoned in 1624 for personating His Majesty, the King of Spain, Gondomar, the Spanish Ambassador, and others in the comedy of "The Game of Chess," and for inserting therein passages found to be "offensive and scandalous." A copy of that play, preserved in the Dyce Library at South Kensington, has the following manuscript notes:

[See entry 22 for the notes and poem].

So great a boon as liberty was seldom acquired for the consideration of so small a jest.

Middleton's first literary work was in 1597. "The wisdom of Solomon Paraphrased," an effusion of some seven hundred stanzas, in the whole length of which one finds only an aggravating facility of versification without freshness or sparkle, and only a barren waste of words. When one tastes the quality of the comedies of this and other writers of that time, he is not slow in coming to the conclusion that sacred writing is not exactly the kind of production one could reasonably expect from the author. In 1597 he wrote "Microcynicon, Six Snarling Satyres," that likewise seem to carry with them no excuse for republication at this time. In 1604 he published two tracts, "Father Hubbard's Tale, or the Ant and the Nightingale," and "The Black Book," which are chiefly interesting to students of the social life of the sixteenth century, the former depicting a prodigal driven to the life of the sharpers who have fleeced him, and the latter making us familiar with the lowest parts of London, "Turnbull street and Birchin Lane, the haunts of drabs and thieves."

In the beginning of the seventeenth century he appeared as a writer of plays, producing comedies and tragi-comedies. "Blurt, Master Constable," was the earliest of his printed plays, having been published in 1602. Its plot is not very savory and it contains little that is quotable, though in it is the following love-song, the most musical product of his pen:

> Love is like a lamb, and love is like a lion,
> Fly from love, he fights, fights then does he fly on;
> Love is all in fire and yet is ever freezing;
> Love is much in winning, yet is more in leesing;
> Love is ever sick, and yet is never dying;
> Love is ever true and yet is ever lying;
> Love does doat in liking, and is mad in loathing;
> Love indeed is everything, yet indeed is nothing.

Of his comedies the greatest merit is claimed for "A Trick to Catch the Old One" and "A Chaste Maid in Cheapside." If we are right in believing there is any standard of purity to which a book should attain before it could be commended as reading matter for any people, or take its place in literature, it seems to us that that standard is too high for any discussion of such works as these. The plot of the former takes the reader among persons noted chiefly for their vices — a young rake and his male and female companions, of the same characterless sort, at work upon a finally successful scheme to get money to cancel the debts of former profligate living. The trick is gross, and while the action of the play is rapid and some of the scenes not without considerable humor, it is of the kind that one cannot retell in polite society. The editor of these volumes stands well to his work, as if, engaged upon a not very savory task, he felt in honor bound to defend the author. He admits that "in writing this comedy Middleton was more anxious to amuse than teach a moral lesson," bids for withholding of censure upon these "airy comedies of intrigue," and asserts the success of the author in what he undertook. "It is impossible," he adds, "not to admire the happy dexterity with which the mirthful situations are multipled." And yet, with all the relish of audiences of the present day for amusement and the entertainment that exists in "mirthful situations," there is no manager so bold as to venture to produce this "excellent old play;" and what discriminating faculty we have fails in its attempt to make quotation from its pages by which the play could commend itself to the admiration or entertainment of our readers. Perhaps the best that can be said of it is, that this play furnishes the plot to the much more admirable and still extant play of "A New Way to Pay Old Debts," by Phillip Massinger, a contemporary of Middleton. "A Chaste Maid in Cheapside" is spoken of by the editor as extant. "The play," he says, "is exceedingly diverting, but I cannot conscientiously commend it *virginibus puerisque*, for the language and situations occasionally show an audacious disregard for propriety." When Middleton quits for a while the task of being simply amusing, and becomes serious, he sometimes assumes a tone of tender sentiment. In this mood he utters in this play the following pretty lyric strain:

> "Weep, eyes, break heart!
> My love and I must part.
> And fates true love do soonest sever;
> O, I shall see thee never, never, never!
> O, happy is the maid whose life takes end
> Ere it knows parent's frown or loss of friend!
> Weep, eyes, break heart!
> My love and I must part."

To Middleton and William Rowley are to be credited the authorship of "A Fair Quarrel" but the credit of all that is seriously worth attention in the play plainly belongs to Middleton.[140] Lightness and airiness and rollicking humor seem to be the characteristics of Rowley's ability, and these in admirable measure seem not present herein. "In 'A Fair Quarrel,'" says the editor, "Middleton showed how nobly he could depict moral dignity." But the modern reader advances amazed through the scenes that depict the real cause of this so-called "Fair Quarrel," conscious that his moral sense and delicacy of feeling are therein wantonly wounded, and though there comes at length evidence of self-respect, and a personal integrity too late awakened, the finer sense holds it all but as a moral spasm, in which, like an interpolation of some foreign intelligence, appears a tone of dignity out of all keeping with the tone or with any suggestion of all the rest of the play. And then the drama proceeds by the devious paths of a weak and impossible plot, with characters beneath contempt and a *dénouement* lame and impotent, wherein morality and dignity seem to have faded into forgetfulness.

The play which seems to have made the name of Middleton most widely known is the tragi-comedy called "The Witch." It was printed by Isaac Reed in 1770 [1778], and in Steven's note to Reed's edition of Shakespere, to this play is given the credit of the origin of the scenes of the witches in Macbeth.

140. Emendations: *William* for *Witliam* and the dropping of a semi-colon after *worth*.

Malone at first accepted the theory of Shakespere's indebtedness to Middleton, but afterwards rejected it;[141] and later critics, doubting its truth, come generally to think that the refrain, common to both,

"Black spirits, and white, red spirits and gray,
Mingle, mingle, mingle, you that mingle may."

came from a much earlier day, from the common songs of the people. There is a certain resemblance between two scenes in each play, in which the witches appear, attributable to the certain amount of concession to the common idea of witches. Those of Middleton have more of worldly tissue in them, having earthly habitations and alliances and offspring, while those of Shakspere are virtueless hags, coming in thunder and lightning, having no earthly ties nor relations. The first assembly of the witches, and the incantation scene in both plays, bear strong resemblance to each other, but in no other particular do the plays have the slightest similarity. This common aspect came undoubtedly from the writers upon witchcraft who were popular at that day, and who pretended to a knowledge of the characteristics of spirits, witches, urchins, elves, hags, satyrs, pans, faunes, sylvans, centaurs, tritons, dwarfs, giants, nymphes, and the like. The first assembly of the witches, and the
In Act. V., Sc. 1 is a single song, characteristic of the time, written with some lyric facility:

In a maiden-time profest,
Then we say that life is best;
Testing once the married life,
Then we only praise the wife;
There's but one state more to try,
Which makes women laugh or cry —
Widow, widow: of these three
The middle's best, and that give me.

One may search all the rest of the play and be rewarded with scarcely a sentence or line that shows genius, poetry or originality. If it be true that Middleton was the master of Shakspere in the single instance of "The Witch," the gift was returned or taken back with interest by Middleton, who, in many instances in several of his plays, presents the same ideas in phrases too near those of Shakspere, to be satisfactorily explained as a mere coincidence.

141. See entry 48.

If Middleton has any claim to immortality as an author, it must come from something greatly superior to any comedy he has written, or anything within the limits of "The Witch." As compared with other so-called great dramatists of his time, excepting always Shakspere, he is to be credited with facility of language and considerable humor, and in his serious plays with great moral dignity, an imagination largely superior to his fellow playwrights, and with an occasional exhibition of tenderness and sweetness in some of his lyrics.

The maturity of his genius is seen in the tragedy "Women beware Women," of which he was the sole author, and in the tragedy of "The Changeling," and the romantic comedy of "The Spanish Gipsey," both written jointly with Mr. Rowley.

In "Women beware Women," founded upon the story of Bianca Capello; Leantio, a young factor of Florence, elopes with Bianca, a Venetian beauty.

> "A creature
> Able to draw a state from serious business,
> And make it their best piece to do her service.

and brings her to the poorer residence of his mother.

> From Venice, her consent and I have brought her,
> From parents great in wealth, more now in rage;
> But let storms spend their furies; now we've got
> A shelter o'er our quiet, innocent loves,
> We are contented; little sh' as brought me;
> View but her face, you may see all her dowry,
> Save that which lies lock'd up in hidden virtues,
> Like jewels kept in cabinets.

His mother fears the change from wealth to the narrow fortunes of her house.

> What I can bid you welcome to is mean,
> But make it all your own; we're full of wants,
> And cannot welcome worth.

But Bianca, full of young affection for her husband, is happy in his love and accepts his fortune willingly.

> I'll call this place the place of my birth now,

> And rightly too, for here my love was born,
> And that's the birthday of a woman's joys.

Leantio must go away on the morrow, and is jealous of what may happen in his absence.

> Should we show thieves our wealth, 'twould make 'em bolder:
> Temptation is a devil will not stick
> To fasten upon a saint.

He goes reluctantly, while she lovingly bids him put off his leave until another day, but he fears one day's delay in her sweet company may beget still another day's delay, for

> Love that's wanton must be rul'd awhile
> By that that's careful, or all goes to ruin;
> As fitting is a government in love
> As in a kingdom.

He departs, and leaves standing at the window his mother and his wife in tears. They do not go from the window before there passes a procession of celebration, headed by the Lord Cardinal and the Duke, his brother. Her eye is quick at detecting the glances of the latter, and she asks,

> Did not the Duke look up? methought he saw us
> *Moth.* That's every one's conceit that sees a duke.
> If he look steadfastly, he looks straight at them,
> When he perhaps, good careful gentleman,
> Never minds any, but the look he casts
> Is at his own intentions, and his object
> Only the public good.
> *Bian.* Most likely so.

From that moment the Duke had an object besides "the public good," and to effect it he employs Livia, a court lady of abandoned character to ensnare Bianca for him, and with final success. Her mother finds a change in her after their visit to court.

> She was but one day abroad, but ever since
> She's grown so cutted, there is no speaking to her;

> Whether the sight of great cheer at my lady's
> And such mean fare at home, work discontent in her,
> I know not; but I'm sure she's strangely alter'd.
> I'll ne'er keep daughter-in-law i' th' house with me
> Again if I had an hundred.

Leantio returns after five days, full of high hope and joyful anticipation in meeting his bride. And the author here rises to the farther heights of poetry in his expression of tenderness and affection, and in the noble tribute which he makes Leantio pay to honorable marriage, ending with the sweetest utterances of longing for his intercepted joy.

> How near am I now to a happiness
> That earth exceeds not! not another like it;
> [3.1.82-109, with some lines dropped].

Alas! the welcome was but a word of greeting, and no caress attending. Even while they converse, a messenger from the duke invites her and the mother, and they do not resist, but leave Leantio in amazement.

> O thou the ripe time of man's misery, wedlock,
> When all his thoughts like overladen trees,
> Crack with the fruits they bear in cares, in jealousies!

Amid his bitter musings the messenger returns and summons him to the Duke. He soon finds himself at a banquet where the Duke presides, attended by Bianca. His first glance tells him where the heart of his wife resides. The Duke appoints him to the captaincy of the fort at Rouans, but the honor bestowed takes not away the dishonor already cast upon him. The Duke pledges Bianca, the entertainment proceeds, but Leantio tastes only the bitter food of reflection, and his only utterances are asides, that tell how deep his wounds, till at last the banqueters depart, leaving only himself in the presence of Livia, who was the hostess, and who plies him unheeding her, but soliloquising his dear remembrances of Bianca.

> Cans't thou forget
> The dear pains my love took? how it has watch'd
> Whole nights together, in all weathers, for thee,
> Yet stood in heart more merry than the tempest
> That sung about mine ears, — like dangerous flatterers,

That can set all their mischiefs to sweet tunes, —
And then receiv'd thee, from thy father's window,
Into these arms at midnight; when we embraced
As if we had been statues only made for't,
To show art's life, so silent were our comforts,
And kiss'd as if our lips had grown together?

Livia pretends to offer consolation to him, telling him,

You miss'd your fortunes when you met her, sir.
Young gentlemen that only love for beauty,
They love not wisely; such a marriage rather
Proves the destruction of affection.

And when he is not touched by her words and is left alone, he breaks
forth overwhelmed by the wretchedness of his state in the loss of Bianca:

She's gone forever, utterly; there is
As much redemption of a soul from hell,
As a fair woman's body from this palace.
Why should my love last longer than her truth?
What is there good in women to be lov'd,
When only that which makes her so has left her?
I cannot love her now but I must like
Her sin and my own shame too, and be guilty
Of law's breach with her, and mine own abusing;
All which were monstrous; then my safest course
For health of mind and body, is to turn
My heart and hate her, most extremely hate her.

An instance of the superior imaginative power of Middleton is found in
Act. IV. Sec. 1, where the Cardinal reproaches this duke for his course of
life, and the example set by a great man.

Every sin thou committ'st shows like a flame
Upon a mountain, 'tis seen far about,
And with a big wind made of popular breath,
The sparkles fly through cities, here one takes,
Another catches there, and in a short time
Wastes all to cinders; but remember still,

What burnt the valleys first came from the hill:
Every offence draws his particular pain,
But 'tis example proves the great man's bane.

There is nothing else finer in the whole play, unless it be the reply,
strangely put into the mouth of Bianca, which is made to the Cardinal's
further reproaches, even after the duke has tried to cure the evil wrought, by
a subsequent marriage.

Sir, I have read you over all this while
In silence, and I find great knowledge in you
[4.3.47-69].

There is no cheer in all the play. The way out to the consummation of
the plot is dark and the catastrophe melancholy, and as pitiful as that of
Hamlet.

Two other plays, "The Changeling," and "The Spanish Gipsey," demand
the attention of the student who would enjoy all the finer expressions of
Middleton's genius. Although William Rowley was joint author in these, it
is generally conceded by critics that he wrote only the underplot of the
former, and the purely gipsey scenes of the latter, and that to Middleton
alone is due the credit for the greater scenes. "The Changeling" is a dark-
colored tragedy, the story of Beatrice, a daughter of the governor of the
castle of Alicant, who, upon the eve of her marriage to Alonzo de
Piracquo,[142] sees and falls deeply in love with Alsemero. Desperate at the
impending loss of her new love, she engages De Flores to make way with her
affianced husband. The scene which follows the murder, between Beatrice
and De Flores, wherein he refuses her gold, and claiming that she is partner
in his guilt, demands as his compensation the surrender of herself to him, is
one of the most startling and strongly drawn pictures of deep passion in
dramatic literature, scarcely surpassed by any dramatist save Shakspere. His
demand she does not at first understand; and, finding him not satisfied with
the proffered gold, she offers to double the sum and demands his departure.

Beat.   For my fear's sake,
I prithee, make away with all speed possible;
And if thou be'st so modest not to name
The sum that will content thee, paper blushes not;
Send thy demand in writing, it shall follow thee;

142. Emended from *Pivacquo*.

But prithee, take thy flight.
D. F. You must fly too then.
Beat. I?
D. F. I'll not stir a foot else.
Beat. What's your meaning?
D. F. Why, are not you as guilty? in, I'm sure
As deep as I; and we should stick together.
Come, your fears counsel you but ill: my absence
Would draw suspect upon you instantly.
There were no rescue for you.

Beginning to suspect the meaning of his demand, she cries,

Beat. O, I never shall!
[3.4.102-127, with lines omitted].

He will not listen to her claim of the distance her birth has made between them, and he bids her

"Fly not to your birth, but settle you
In what the act has made you; you're no more now.
You must forget your parentage to me;
You are the deed's creature; by that name
You lost your first condition, and I challenge you,
As peace and innocency has turned you out,
And made you one with me."

He threatens that he will blast the hopes and joys of marriage, and confess all, rating his life at nothing.

De F. She that in life and love refuses me,
In death and shame my partner she shall be.
Beat. [kneeling] "Stay, hear me once for all;
I make thee master
Of all the wealth I have in gold and jewels;
Let me go poor unto my bed with honour,
And I am rich in all things!"

He will hear to no pleading, and raising her bids her

"Come, rise and shroud thy blushes in my bosom;

Silence is one of pleasure's best receipts;
Thy peace is wrought forever in this yielding."

Though with far less cunning, the character of De Flores may worthily compete with that of Iago for pre-eminence in complete depravity.

This play was first produced about 1621, and was revived at the Restoration. In Pepy[s]'s diary under date of 23d February, 1660-61, we find the following entry:

[See entry 33.]

The "Spanish Gipsey" is a romantic comedy altogether different in tone and color from the play last named. It has its serious aspects, but it seems more natural and human, and offers a story that in itself is attractive and pleasing. It furnishes many lines of pure poetic imagery, and several songs that display the height of the author's lyric quality.

One cannot penetrate very far into the heart of the dramatic literature of the early part of the seventeenth century, without finding that the tone of society has greatly changed in our day, and he must speedily conclude that the works of Middleton, like those of his contemporaries, are almost wholly for the student, and him alone; that if one would read them in peace he had better take them, not only to his own closet, but to the innermost recess thereof, lest in a moment of absorption, which the interest of the work may induce, he may feel a blush rising, if perchance a silent intruder glances over his shoulder. Society, happily we think, forbids allusion in the presence of virtue to the commoner assaults of vice, and scarcely tolerates chastity to be sneered at, and its opposite boisterously laughed over and connived at; but in the early days of unwashed civilization, when fingers at their tables did the service of forks at ours, and the manners of society were on the same indecorous level, the plays of the day took the tone of society, and the themes of the street and the conversation of the court are doubtless clearly reflected in the volumes of the dramatists. Considering these things, it seems strange rather that there is so little than that there is so much coarseness in Shakspere, and not at all strange that in the lesser dramatists like Middleton there should be so much.

As Landor says of the other writers of the time

"They stood around
The throne of Shakspere, sturdy but unclean."[143]

143. "To the Author of *Festus*, On the Classick and Romantick," *The Complete Works of Walter Savage Landor*, p. 165, ll. 60-61.

While we should commend the plays of Middleton to the student of dramatic literature for the frequent display of great poetic genius, a lofty imagination, pictures of deepest passion, and at times passages of the highest moral dignity, we should greatly hesitate to put any volume of these works, or even any one play into the hands of youth, whose minds and hearts are easily hurt by coarseness of allusion and by indelicacy of expression. It may be that we should not decline ambrosia though offered in an earthern vessel, but we want it certain that the vessel, though roughly made, yet shall not give its earthy taste to the heavenly food, but give it up clear and pure and uncolored as the water from an earthly spring.

Anon. *"The Works of Thomas Middleton." Overland Monthly* 8 (1886): 652-60.

86. 1887 George Saintsbury Speaks

George Saintsbury, critic, journalist, and literary historian, produced an enormous body of work between his first publication in 1875 and his death in 1933. When Bullen's edition of Middleton appeared in 1885, Saintsbury was *The Saturday Review*'s assistant editor; thus he knew its reviews (entry 78) and may have written them. As a critic, he was interested in what he called *transport*, the ability of a work to absorb and involve a reader. This selection is from Saintsbury's 1887 *History of Elizabethan Literature*.

It has not been usual to put Thomas Middleton in the front rank among the dramatists immediately second to Shakespere; but I have myself no hesitation in doing so. If he is not such a poet as Webster, he is even a better, and certainly a more versatile, dramatist; and if his plays are inferior as plays to those of Fletcher and Massinger, he has a mastery of the very highest tragedy, which neither of them could attain. Except the best scenes of *The White Devil*, and *The Duchess of Malfi*, there is nothing out of Shakespere that can match the best scenes of *The Changeling;* while Middleton had a comic faculty, in which, to all appearance, Webster was entirely lacking. A little more is known about Middleton than about most of his fellows. He was the son of a gentleman, and was pretty certainly born in London about 1570. . . . [Here Saintsbury describes Middleton's life, commenting only briefly on *The Wisdom of Solomon Paraphrased*, "which makes even that admirable book unreadable," and *Microcynicon*, "one of the worst and feeblest exercises in the school — never a very strong one — of Hall and Marston."]

Middleton's acknowledged, or at least accepted, habit of collaboration in most of the work usually attributed to him, and the strong suspicion, if not more than suspicion, that he collaborated in other plays, afford endless opportunity for the exercise of a certain kind of criticism. By employing another kind we can discern quite sufficiently a strong individuality in the work that is certainly, in part or in whole, his; and we need not go farther. He seems to have had three different kinds of dramatic aptitude, in all of which he excelled. The larger number of his plays consist of examples of the rattling comedy of intrigue and manners, often openly representing London life as it was, sometimes transplanting what is an evident picture of home manners to some foreign scene apparently for no other object than to make it more attractive to the spectators. To any one at all acquainted with the Elizabethan drama their very titles speak them. These titles are *Blurt Master Constable, Michaelmas Term, A Trick to Catch the Old One, The Family of Love* (a sharp satire on the Puritans), *A Mad World, my Masters*; *No Wit no Help Like a Woman's, A Chaste Maid in Cheapside, Anything for a Quiet Life, More Dissemblers besides Women*. As with all the humour-comedies of the time, the incidents are not unfrequently very improbable, and the action is conducted with such intricacy and want of clearly indicated lines, that it is sometimes very difficult to follow. At the same time, Middleton has a faculty almost peculiar to himself of carrying, it might almost be said of hustling, the reader or spectator along, so that he has no time to stop and consider defects. His characters are extremely human and lively, his dialogue seldom lags, his catastrophes, if not his plots, are often ingenious, and he is never heavy. The moral atmosphere of his plays is not very re-fined, — by which I do not at all mean merely that he indulges in loose situations and loose language. All the dramatists from Shakespere downwards do that; and Middleton is neither better nor worse than the average. But in striking contrast to Shakespere and to others, Middleton has no kind of poetical morality in the sense in which the term poetical justice is better known. He is not too careful that the rogues shall not have the best of it; he makes his most virtuous and his vilest characters hobnob together very contentedly; and he is, in short, though never brutal, like the post-Restoration school, never very delicate. The style, however, of these works of his did not easily admit of such delicacy, except in the infusion of a strong romantic element such as that which Shakespere almost always infuses. Middleton has hardly done it more than once — in the charming comedy of *The Spanish Gipsy*, — and the result there is so agreeable that the reader only wishes he had done it oftener.

Usually, however, when his thoughts took a turn of less levity than in these careless humorous studies of contemporary life, he devoted himself not to the higher comedy, but to tragedy of a very serious class, and when he did this an odd phenomenon generally manifested itself. In Middleton's idea of tragedy, as in that of most of the playwrights, and probably all the playgoers of his day, a comic underplot was a necessity; and, as we have seen, he was himself undoubtedly able enough to furnish such a plot. But either because he disliked mixing his tragic and comic veins, or for some unknown reason, he seems usually to have called in on such occasions the aid of Rowley, a vigorous writer of farce, who had sometimes been joined with him even in his comic work. Now, not only was Rowley little more than a farce writer, but he seems to have been either unable to make, or quite careless of making, his farce connect itself in any tolerable fashion with the tragedy of which it formed a nominal part. The result is seen in its most perfect imperfection in the two plays of *The Mayor of Queenborough* and *The Changeling*, both named from their comic features, and yet containing tragic scenes, the first of a very high order, the second of an order only overtopped by Shakespere at his best. The humours of the cobbler Mayor of Queenborough in the one case, of the lunatic asylum and the courting of its keeper's wife in the other, are such very mean things that they can scarcely be criticised. But the desperate love of Vortiger for Rowena in *The Mayor*, and the villainous plots against his chaste wife, Castiza, are real tragedy. Even these, however, fall far below the terrible loves, if loves they are to be called, of Beatrice-Joanna, the heroine of *The Changeling*, and her servant, instrument, and murderer, De Flores. The plot of the tragic part of this play is intricate and not wholly savoury. It is sufficient to say that Beatrice having enticed De Flores to murder a lover whom she does not love, that so she may marry a lover whom she does love, is suddenly met by the murderer's demand of her honour as the price of his services. She submits, and afterwards has to purchase fresh aid of murder from him by a continuance of her favours that she may escape detection by her husband. Thus, roughly described, the theme may look like the undigested horrors of *Lust's Dominion*, of *The Insatiate Countess*, and of *The Revenger's Tragedy*. It is, however, poles asunder from them. The girl, with her southern recklessness of anything but her immediate desires, and her southern indifference to deceit of the very man she loves, is sufficiently remarkable, as she stands out of the canvas. But De Flores, — the broken gentleman, reduced to the position of a mere dependant, the libertine whose want of personal comeliness increases his mistress's contempt for him, the murderer double and treble dyed, as audacious as he is treacherous, and as cool and ready as he is fiery in passion, — is a study worthy to be classed at once with Iago, and inferior only to Iago in their class. The several touches with which these two characters and their situations are brought out are as Shakesperian as their conception, and the whole of that part of the play in which they figure is one of the most wonderful triumphs of English or of any drama. Even the change of manners

and a bold word or two here and there, may not prevent me from giving the
latter part of the central scene: —

> *Beat.* "Why, 'tis impossible thou canst be so wicked,
>   Or shelter such a cunning cruelty,
>   To make his death the murderer of my honour!
>   [3.4.121-71].

Two other remarkable plays of Middleton's fall with some differences
under the same second division of his works. These are *The Witch* and
Women Beware Women. Except for the inevitable and rather interesting
comparison with *Macbeth*, *The Witch* is hardly interesting. It consists of
three different sets of scenes most inartistically blended, — an awkward and
ineffective variation on the story of Alboin, Rosmunda and the skull for a
serious main plot, some clumsy and rather unsavoury comic or tragi-comic
interludes, and the witch scenes. The two first are very nearly worthless; the
third is intrinsically, though far below *Macbeth*, interesting enough and
indirectly more interesting because of the questions which have been started,
as to the indebtedness of the two poets to each other. The best opinion seems
to be that Shakespere most certainly did not copy Middleton, nor (a strange
fancy of some) did he collaborate with Middleton, and that the most probable
thing is that both borrowed their names, and some details from Reginald
Scot's *Discovery of Witchcraft*. *Women Beware Women* on the other hand
is one of Middleton's finest works, inferior only to *The Changeling* in parts,
and far superior to it as a whole. The temptation of Bianca, the newly-
married wife, by the duke's instrument, a cunning and shameless woman, is
the title-theme, and in .this part again Middleton's Shakesperian
verisimilitude and certainty of touch appears. The end of the play is
something marred by a slaughter more wholesale even than that of *Hamlet*,
and by no means so well justified. Lastly, *A Fair Quarrel* must be
mentioned, because of the very high praise which it has received from Lamb
and others. This praise has been directed chiefly to the situation of the
quarrel between Captain Ager and his friend, turning on a question (the point
of family honour), finely but perhaps a little tediously argued. The comic
scenes, however, which are probably Rowley's, are in his best vein of
bustling swagger.

I have said that Middleton, as it seems to me, has not been fully
estimated. It is fortunately impossible to say the same of Webster, and the
reasons of the difference are instructive. Middleton's great fault is that he
never took trouble enough about his work. A little trouble would have made
The Changeling or *Women Beware Women*, or even *The Spanish Gipsy*,

worthy to rank with all but Shakespere's very masterpieces. Webster also was a collaborator, apparently an industrious one; but he never seems to have taken his work lightly. He had, moreover, that incommunicable gift of the highest poetry in scattered phrases which, as far as we can see, Middleton had not.

A History of Elizabethan Literature. London and New York: Macmillan, 1887, pp. 266-73.

87. 1894 The *Dictionary of National Biography*

While not quite as eulogistic as some of the recent commentary, Charles Harold Herford's article on Middleton reveals the extent to which Middleton's reputation had risen by the end of the century. The article was reprinted in subsequent editions of the *DNB*. Herford opens with a brief biography.

Within the next few years, however, he had discovered a more congenial path, the comedy of contemporary manners, and to this species the abounding energy, vivacity, and invention of his early maturity were devoted. His prose tracts of 1603-4, 'The Black Book' and 'Father Hubburd's Tales,' are vivid and richly coloured satirical sketches of London life, in the manner of Nashe and Dekker. The publication of not less than six plays of his in 1607-8 shows with what success he worked this vein on the stage. These plays contain, however, much poor and hasty work, as well as a good deal of scattered excellence, and it is likely that Middleton abused his facile powers under the stimulus of popularity. The remainder of his extant plays appeared (so far as their dates are known) at longer intervals, and they include his most powerful work.

. . . Unlike his successor, Jonson, Middleton evidently gave high satisfaction in his function of 'city chronologer,' and his pageants were admired by his city patrons. He seems also to have been popular with the playgoing public both before and after the civil wars. None of his pieces is known to have failed on the stage. But before the revolution he had fallen, in common with all but one or two of his dramatic contemporaries, into a neglect from which he has been among the last to recover. This is partly due to his striking inequality. A facile and inventive writer, he could turn out an abundance of sufficiently effective work with little effort; but he had little sustained inspiration; he is very great only in single scenes. He is rather prone to repeat motives (e.g. the 'Mayor of Quinborough,' 'A Mad World,' and the 'Spanish Gipsy,' all contain variations of the play within the play); in his earlier plays the same stock types incessantly reappear, and many of them are not only gross but dull. Yet even here he habitually shows keen observation of the London world he knew, and of which he is, on the whole, the most veracious painter, avoiding both the airy extravagance of Dekker and the laborious allusiveness of Jonson. His later plays show more concentrated as well as more versatile power. His habitual occupation with depraved types becomes an artistic method; he creates characters which fascinate without making the smallest appeal to sympathy, tragedy which harrows without rousing either pity or terror, and language which disdains charm, but penetrates by remorseless veracity and by touches of strange and sudden power. While, however, his greatest triumphs are in the region of moral pathology, he could on occasion represent with great force and brilliance fresh and noble types of character, such as Captain Ager . . . Pretiosa . . . Phœnix . . . and the 'Roaring Girl'. . . .

[Herford follows with a list of works; excerpts appear below.]

[*The Old Law*] The play, granting the farcical extravagance of its motive, is highly effective.

[*The Mayor of Quinborough*] A romantic drama, crude in structure and treatment, but finely written.

[*Blurt, Master Constable*] The plot, which contains effective elements, is not quite clearly worked out. Lazarillo is a portrait in Jonson's elaborate manner; Blurt has traces of Dogberry; but the imitation is nowhere close.

[*The Phoenix*] A felicitous conception, allied both to the Jonsonian humour comedy (a virtuous critic or censor contemplating a corrupt world) and to 'Measure for Measure' (the censor being a prince in disguise), but where Jonson paints follies Middleton paints crimes.

[*Michaelmas Term*] A lively and effective comedy of city intrigue.

[*A Trick to Catch the Old One*] A highly ingenious and well-constructed plot, the strongest of Middleton's comedies of intrigue.

[*The Family of Love*] . . . a comedy of intrigue of the usual kind.

[*Your Five Gallants*] A hasty and loosely constructed comedy of intrigue.

[*The Roaring Girl*] Middleton, who was strong in moral pathology, has idealised her character in an unexpected and remarkable way. . . .

[*A Fair Quarrel*] The main plot is without a parallel in Middleton's plays for intensity of moral passion. But it is easier to assign it to Middleton, a man of refined sensibility who chose to deal with gross materials, than to Rowley's coarse though gifted nature.

[*The Changeling*] The extraordinary strength of one scene (iii. 4) has given this play a reputation which as a whole it hardly deserves. This scene, however, shows in the highest degree Middleton's power of producing intense dramatic effects without the aid of sympathetic characters.

[*The Spanish Gypsy*] . . . one of Middleton's most attractive plays.

[*A Game at Chess*] The piece does not stand high in strictly dramatic qualities: the action is thin, and to a modern reader in parts obscure, but it is written with great satiric brilliance, and abounds with telling dialogue.

[*A Chaste Maid in Cheapside*] No other play of his is so rich in humour extracted from situations of unvaried, but by no means insidious, grossness.

[*No Wit, No Help Like a Woman's*] It is ingeniously contrived, with a romantic plot of classical rather than Elizabethan type.

[*Women Beware Women*] This is no doubt the most powerful single play of Middleton's. The main plot is worked out with great mastery, the leading characters are most vividly drawn, and, unattractive as they all are, strikingly illustrate what Middleton could achieve by sheer dramatic force.

[*The Witch*] The play, which is gross without being effective, derives its whole interest from certain points of contact with 'Macbeth.'

[*Anything for a Quiet Life*] A not very striking play of intrigue.

[*The World Tossed at Tennis*] By far the most elaborate and striking of Middleton's masques. Like Jonson's later masques it shows a marked approximation to the drama.

C[harles] H[arold] H[erford]. "Middleton, Thomas." *DNB*. Edited by Sidney Lee. Vol. 37. London: Smith, Elder, 1894, pp. 357-63.

88. 1894 Middleton Approved

Edmund Gosse was a poet, Cambridge lecturer, and critic who introduced the English public to Ibsen and the new realism through reviews and translations, including a translation of Ibsen's *The Master-Builder* done with William Archer a year before *The Jacobean Poets* appeared. It seems odd, then, that in *The Jacobean Poets* he should be disturbed by what he terms the "disagreeable" story of *Women Beware Women*. An original subscriber to the Elizabethan Stage Society and a proponent of the Jacobeans, he spoke Swinburne's prologue when the Society produced Middleton and Rowley's *The Spanish Gypsy* in 1898.

One of the latest to attract attention of all the Jacobean dramatists was Thomas Middleton, to whom, however, recent criticism assigns an ever-increasing prominence. Neither Hazlitt nor Charles Lamb, although the latter did Middleton the signal service of copious quotations, was nearly so much struck by his powers as our latest critics have been. The reason, probably, was to be found in Middleton's extreme inequality, or rather, perhaps, in the persistence with which he combined with men of talent far inferior to his own. He seems to have had no ambition, and his best plays were all posthumously published. He attracted very little notice in his own lifetime; to Ben Jonson he was nothing but "a base fellow."[144] His style was irregular and careless; but no one even in that age had a more indubitable gift of saying those "brave sublunary things" which stir the pulse. A very odd tradition of criticism was, that Middleton's genius was essentially un-romantic. This came possibly from the exclusive study of his somewhat boisterous comedies, but more probably arose from his direct and penetrating diction, which was singularly remote from the pompous and bombastic tradition of Elizabethan tragedy.
[Here he summarizes Middleton's career.] The strength of Middleton lies, not in his rather gross and careless comedies, but in his romantic dramas, his singularly imaginative tragedies and tragi-comedies. Lamb, although he seems scarcely to have appreciated Middleton, speaks with extreme felicity of his "exquisiteness of moral sensibility, making one to gush out tears of delight."[145] There is, unfortunately, too much of Middleton in existence; a single volume might be selected which would give readers an exceedingly high impression of his genius. He had no lyrical gift, and his verse, although it is enlivened by a singularly brilliant and unexpected

144. See entry 6.
145. See entry 55.

diction, is not in itself of any great beauty. There is no better example of Middleton's work, to which a student can be recommended, than the serious part of *The Changeling*. Mr. Bullen has spoken of the great scene between De Flores and Beatrice as "unequalled outside Shakespeare's greatest tragedies,"[146] and the praise can hardly be held excessive. The plot of *The Changeling*, which turns on the stratagem of a girl who, being in love with one man, and affianced to a second, turns to a third to extricate her from her difficulty, is in the highest degree curious and novel. But when De Flores has been persuaded to murder Alonzo, Beatrice is no nearer to Alsemero; for De Flores and his insolent conditions stand in her way. At length she has to confess Alonzo's murder to her lover, and the play ends, crudely, in a cluster of deaths. But nothing in Jacobean drama is finer than the desperate flutterings of Beatrice, or the monstrous determination of De Flores.

Another great play of Middleton's is *The Spanish Gipsy*, but this is of a far less gloomy type, although it opens with menacing gravity. The air lightens as the plot develops, and we assist at length at the denoûment of a graceful and peaceful comedy, drawn on the combined lines of two stories from Cervantes. Some writers have considered that the finest of Middleton's plays is the tragedy of *Women beware Women*, but to admit this would be to excuse too much what we may call the ethical tastelessness of the age. The story of *Women beware Women* is so excessively disagreeable, and the play closes in a manner so odious, that the reader's sympathy is hopelessly alienated. This radical fault may perhaps disturb, but can scarcely destroy our appreciation of the beauty and invention of the style. The scene between Livia and the widow may be by Middleton or by Rowley; the polish and elasticity of the verse may probably induce us to conjecture the former. We have yet to mention, in analyzing Middleton's masterpieces, the passages which he contributed to *A Fair Quarrel*. The duel scene in which Captain Agar fights with his friend the colonel to avenge his mother's honour is the best-known existing page of Middleton, for Charles Lamb drew especial attention to it in his *Specimens*. That it is Middleton's can scarcely be questioned; all competent critics will agree with Mr. Bullen when he says, "to such a height of moral dignity and artistic excellence Rowley never attained."[147]

The early comedies of Middleton are curiously incoherent in form; scarcely one but contains passages of high romantic beauty. Later on, his comic talent became more assured and less fitful, but the plays lose the Elizabethan flavour of romance; passages of pure poetry become rarer and

146. See entry 77.
147. See entry 77.

rarer in them. It is very difficult to obtain any satisfaction out of such incongruous work as, for instance, *More Dissemblers besides Women*. On the other hand, *A Game of Chess*, which gained for Middleton more money and notoriety than all of his other works put together, is a patriotic comedy of real delicacy and distinction, and of all Middleton's non-tragic plays is probably the one which may be studied with most satisfaction by the modern reader. Popular as political scandal made this play, it is yet almost incredible that the receipts at its performance amounted to fifteen hundred pounds, but if half of this is true, it must have thrown a flush of real success over the close of Middleton's laborious life.

The following speech of Isabella, in the tragedy *Women beware Women*, may serve as an example of the style of Middleton —

> Marry a fool!
> Can there be greater misery to a woman
> That means to keep her days true to her husband,
> [1.2.162-86].

It is exceedingly difficult to disengage Middleton from his obscurer coadjutor William Rowley, who was probably about fifteen years Middleton's junior. . . . So far, however, as we are able to form an opinion, we are apt to consider that the influence of Rowley upon Middleton was an unwholesome one. Middleton was strangely compacted of gold and clay, of the highest gifts and of the lowest subterfuges of the playwright. In Rowley, all that was not clay was iron, and it is difficult to believe that he sympathized with or encouraged his friend's ethereal eccentricities. That Rowley had a hand in the underplot of several of Middleton's noblest productions does not alter our conviction that his own sentiments were rather brutal and squalid, and that he cared for little but to pander to the sensational instincts of the groundlings. The mutual attitude of these friends has been compared to that of Beaumont and Fletcher, but it is hard to think of Middleton in any other light than as a poet unequally yoked with one whose temper was essentially prosaic.

Edmund Gosse. *The Jacobean Poets*. New York: Charles Scribner's Sons, 1894, pp. 123-31.

89. 1895 A Note from an American

Felix E. Schelling, professor at the University of Pennsylvania, was one of the first U.S. academics to gain credibility in England as a critic of English Renaissance literature. His *Book of Elizabethan Lyrics* is an anthology of extracts, with brief notes and discussions. Quoted here is his biographical note on Middleton.

> *Thomas Middleton*, a man of good birth and education, was sometime a student of Grey's Inn, a productive and highly successful playwright and writer of pageants, and, from 1620 to his death, chronologer of the city of London. Few of the lyrics of Middleton are altogether satisfactory; in all his work, like Massinger and some others, Middleton seems to inhabit that dangerous limbo that lies between the realms of the highest genius and the ordinary levels of a work-a-day world; making, it is true, an occasional flight into the former, but more usually contentedly trudging along the highways of the latter.

Felix E. Schelling. *A Book of Elizabethan Lyrics.* Boston: Ginn, 1895, p. 264.

90. 1898 *The Spanish Gypsy* with a Swinburne Prologue

On April 5, 1898, the Elizabethan Stage Society under William Poel revived *The Spanish Gypsy* at St. George's Hall, the first and only time a Middleton play was produced in the nineteenth century. *The Spanish Gypsy* was a logical choice, since recent critics had praised it as one of Middleton's best and lightest, and ethically most acceptable, plays.

This production notice appeared in *The Academy* and included Swinburne's prologue, which is more effusive than was his sonnet (entry 75).

> THE Elizabethan Stage Society's representation of Middleton's *Spanish Gipsy*, on Tuesday night, was prefaced by the delivery of a resonant prologue, written for the occasion by Mr. Swinburne. The poet's mouthpiece was Mr. Gosse. He came on the stage accompanied by a blue-coat boy, who carried a lantern. Mr. Gosse wore the costume of to-day, but the blue-coat dates, of course, from Edward the Sixth, and was no anachronism. The boy held the lantern so that the light shone upon the paper, and Mr. Gosse then read the poem, which we print in full:
>
> > "The wind that brings us from the springtide south
> > Strange music as from love's or life's own mouth
> > Blew hither, when the blast of battle ceased
> > That swept back southward Spanish prince and priest,

A sound more sweet than April's flower-sweet rain,
And bade bright England smile on pardoned Spain.
The land that cast out Philip and his God
Grew gladly subject where Cervantes trod.
Even he whose name above all names on earth
Crowns England queen by grace of Shakespeare's birth
Might scarce have scorned to smile in God's wise down
And gild with praise from heaven an earthlier crown.
And he whose hand bade live down lengthening years
Quixote, a name lit up with smiles and tears,
Gave the glad watchword of the gipsies' life,
Where fear took hope and grief took joy to wife.
Times change, and fame is fitful as the sea:
But sunset bids not darkness always be,
And still some light from Shakespeare and the sun
Burns back the cloud that masks not Middleton.
With strong, swift strokes of love and wrath he drew
Shakespearean London's loud and lusty crew:
No plainer might the likeness rise and stand
When Hogarth took his living world in hand.
No surer than his fire-fledged shafts could hit,
Winged with as forceful and as faithful wit:
No truer a tragic depth and heat of heart
Glowed through the painter's than the poet's art.
He lit and hung in heaven the wan fierce moon
Whose glance kept time with witchcraft's air-struck tune:
He watched the doors where loveless love let in
The pageant hailed and crowned by death and sin:
He bared the souls where love, twin-born with hate,
Made wide the way for passion-fostered fate.
All English-hearted, all his heart arose
To scourge with scorn his England's cowering foes:
And Rome and Spain, who bade their scorner be
Their prisoner, left his heart as England's free.
Now give we all we may of all his due
To one long since thus tried and found thus true."

Anon. "Notes and News." *The Academy*, 9 April 1898, pp. 397-98.

91. 1898 *The Spanish Gypsy* Panned

Not everyone agreed with critics who would elevate Middleton to a status next to Shakespeare. This *Athenæum* reviewer finds little to praise in *The Spanish Gypsy.*

The play chosen by the Elizabethan Stage Society for its latest and, in some respects, most interesting experiment is thoroughly characteristic of Middleton. What Rowley's share is in this work or in others in which his name is associated with that of Middleton remains doubtful. Prof. Ward fancies that his is the stronger hand not only in his collaboration with Middleton, but in that with Heywood.[148] We are disposed to attribute to Rowley the comic rather than the dramatic scenes. Both suppositions are, in fact, gratuitous. Middleton's chief deficiency is in construction. Absolutely just is what Hazlitt affirms, that a play of Middleton is like

"the rough draught of a tragedy with a number of fine things thrown in and the best made use of first; but it tends to no fixed goal, and the interest decreases instead of increasing as we read on, for want of previous arrangement and an eye to the whole."[149]

Hazlitt then proceeds, after the fashion customary in dealing with the minor dramatists of the Tudor epoch, to say many fine and unmerited things concerning Middleton's excellences. These, in 'The Spanish Gipsy,' are notably absent, while, on the other hand, the treatment of the two *novelas* of Cervantes which he has sought to weld together in the play is inadequate, and even inept. The opening scenes are, in their way, full of promise. Brutal as it is, the rape of Clara by Don Roderigo has a certain strength, and the manner in which the betrothed of the heroine is converted into one of her abductors holds out promise of a strong romantic drama, or, indeed, of a tragi-comedy. A flash of manliness or of picturesque and passionate utterance raises the piece now and then from the grovelling level of the comic scenes. It consists, however, ordinarily of a line or two, rarely more; there are few graces of imagination or poetry, and the work, if it stood alone, would scarcely justify us in assigning its authors a position in the third rank of the Tudor dramatists. In the scene in which Clara, her ruin accomplished, remonstrates with Roderigo there is some plaintiveness, the effect of which

---

148. *A History of English Dramatic Literature to the Death of Queen Anne*, 2: 127.
149. See entry 58.

is impaired by her assailant's monosyllabic interjections of "Husht!" "Pish!" "Umh!" There is one line expressive of indignation almost adequate to the offence, and there is at the end of the scene a touch of not too convincing pathos. At the close of the third act, again, when Clara has discovered that the violator is the son of the Corregidor, who sympathizes with her and disowns his son, she still speaks as though the end should be tragic: —

> Sins are heard farthest when they cry in blood.

After this it is with something like a shock that we find the heroine, on a hint that Roderigo may marry her, speak of being the happiest woman, say, when he calls her wronged, —

> I was, but now am
> Righted in noble satisfaction,

and declare, —

> My care
> Shall live about me to deserve your love.

Yet the offence thus readily condoned went in brutality far beyond that of Tarquin. Fernando de Azevida, the Corregidor, is, on the whole, the worthiest character in the piece, and to him are assigned the best lines. The scene in which he kneels to Clara and her parents, craving their pardon, has sureness of touch not elsewhere to be found, and the close of his speech is fine: —

> I do not plead for pity to a villain:
> O, let him die as he hath lived, dishonourably,
> Basely, and cursedly! I plead for pity
> To my till now untainted blood and honour:
> Teach me how I may now be just and cruel,
> For henceforth I am childless.

In the comic scenes founded on the 'Gitanilla,' the character of Pretiosa, otherwise Costanza, is pleasantly sketched, but it is not filled out. What is said of her is pleasing enough, and there is an attempt to assign her a certain measure of archness. It comes to little. The songs introduced are quaint, but show nothing of the imagination or the lyrical power of those in 'The Witch.' Soto, a clown, seems to be an attempt to rival or imitate Shakspeare — we

are perpetually conscious in Middleton of an effort of the kind, but it comes
to nothing. As regards the interpretation and accessories, the best thing was
the music, though one or two parts were agreeably sustained.   Mr.
Swinburne's admirable prologue was well spoken by Mr. Edmund Gosse.

Anon. "The Week." *The Athenæum*, 9 April 1898, pp. 479-80.

92. 1898 William Archer Continues the Attack

William Archer was a leader of the Ibsen movement, as were fellow-
critics George Bernard Shaw and Edmund Gosse. As a reviewer, Archer was
bright and thoughtful, but often abrasive, and hard on Poel, a talented
director working with amateur actors and making enormous strides toward
restoring original texts and staging plays in a more Elizabethan style. *The
Changeling* was the source for one of Archer's three original plays, *Beatriz
Juana*, published in 1927, but he has little good to say of *The Spanish Gypsy*
in his review of the Elizabethan Stage Society's production.

Among the many heroic qualities of the Elizabethan Stage Society, that
which I chiefly admire is its magnanimity in continuing to invite me to its
performances. For, though I have always been friendly to its aims and
efforts, my friendship has been of that candid quality which it needs some
greatness of soul to appreciate. I have sometimes been well-nigh driven to
the abhorrent conclusion that the Elizabethans did not read my criticisms, so
completely did they abstain from either resenting or profiting by them. They
held the even tenor of their way with a lofty indifference, a serene obduracy,
that was eminently and admirably British. "Theirs not to make reply, theirs
not to reason why" — they simply strode onwards from stupidity to
stupidity, from countersense to countersense, indomitable and imperturbable.
At last, however, through one chink or another, a glimmer of common-sense
seems to have lightened the darkness of their counsels. The performance of
The Spanish Gipsy at St. George's Hall actually made some approach to
realising the purpose of the Society and justifying its existence. The purpose
of the Society is to present the less-known plays of the Elizabethan period
after the manner, and under the scenic conditions, which obtained at that
period, as nearly as we can reconstruct or conjecture them. This simple and
laudable aim the Society has hitherto done its best to obscure, by excessive
curtailments and wanton rearrangements of text, by slow and languid
recitation, by meaningless eccentricities of stage-management, by using the
upper stage where the poet clearly did not intend it to be used, and neglecting

to use it where he did — in short, by making every effort (or so it seemed) to show how things were *not* done in the sixteenth and early seventeenth centuries. With *The Spanish Gipsy* they have turned over a new leaf — or rather they began to turn it, and then lost heart and let it slip back again. Up to the close of the fourth act, they played the scenes in the order in which they were written, with considerable, but not stultifying, curtailments, with a spirit and self-abandonment most creditable in amateurs, and at a fairly rapid, though steadily diminishing, pace. So far good; but in the last scene of the fourth act, Mr. Poel seems suddenly to have repented him of his docility, and from that point onwards he made an incomprehensible and purposeless jumble of the concluding scenes. The last act, as it stands in the text, is tolerably clear and perfectly playable. Mr. Poel, by "slightly rearranging it," made it utterly meaningless and unspeakably tedious. But it would be ungrateful to dwell on this brief relapse. I prefer to emphasize the fact that the first four acts were treated in reasonable consonance with common-sense and with the principles of the Society. The carrying-in of Clara in bed was, I believe, an archæological error. There is no doubt that actors and pieces of furniture could be "discovered" by the withdrawing of "traverses" or cross-curtains, and that this is what was done when the stage-direction says (for example), "Enter Desdemona in her bed." In this very play the use of traverses is indicated where, at the end of Act III. the stage-direction runs "Exeunt all except Clara, on whom the scene shuts." I assume that this stage-direction is found in the early copies, since there could be no reason for a modern editor to add it; and if the traverses could be "shut on" Clara, it is plain that they could, and should, be opened on her as well. This was the only notable eccentricity of stage-management. In the interests of mere humanity, I would suggest to Mr. Poel that he should allow us a few minutes' breathing-space in the course of a five-act play. That the entr'acte was not quite unknown to the Elizabethans is proved by a stage direction in *The Changeling*, another play by Middleton and Rowley, where we read at the beginning of the third act *"In the act-time*, De Flores hides a naked rapier behind a door." If not after each act, at any rate at some convenient point midway in the play, Mr. Poel might vouchsafe us an "act-time" of five minutes.

As to the play, which Mr. Swinburne calls a "graceful tragicomedy," and Professor A. W. Ward an "excellent example of the romantic comedy of the later Elizabethan type,"[150] I can only say that I envy those critics who can find the slightest grace or vitality in that part of the plot from which it takes its title. The only real merit of the play, it seems to me, lies in the portion

150. See entries 82 and 74.

borrowed from *La Fuerza de la Sangre*, and especially in the picturesque opening scenes. Anything more frigidly conventional than the "gipsy" intrigue, and the antics of Sancho and Soto, it would be hard to conceive. One fine scene, indeed, belongs to this part of the play — the disclosure of Alvarez to Louis in Act V. scene 2. For the rest, the gipsy-story is not only uninteresting but incredibly ill-told, so that I am quite sure those of the St. George's Hall audience who had not read the text beforehand, are to this moment asking themselves in vain what it was all about. The play, in short, has all the inequality of *The Changeling*, though in a somewhat different fashion. The childish part is not quite so childish in *The Spanish Gipsy* as in *The Changeling*, but it bulks much more largely in proportion to the rest; while, on the other hand, the story of Roderigo and Clara is not to be compared for tragic intensity with the story of De Flores and Beatrice-Joanna. It is rather odd, by the bye, that Mr. Poel should have chosen to make his excisions mainly in the blank-verse passages of the play, while the comic scenes, which can never have been good and are now as dead as Nebuchadnezzar, were gone through with relentless fidelity.

"*The Spanish Gipsy.*" Reprinted in his *Study and Stage: A Year-Book of Criticism*. London: Grant Richards, 1899, pp. 234-37.

93. 1898 An Austrian Psychological Analysis

R. Fischer believed that English scholars had underrated Middleton and his London comedies. Appropriately for a critic writing in Freud's Vienna, Fischer in this article approaches Middleton theoretically and psychologically.

Playwright Thomas Middleton is a step-child of literary history. During his lifetime, the first quarter of the seventeenth century, he fared visibly better. As a beginner he enjoyed the professional support of excellent collaborators. His later work enabled him to hold an important literary position, and he did not lack recognition by the general public. He wrote extensively, utilizing a variety of topics and plots, and was encouraged by stage successes until his death. Even after his death, his name continued to evoke interest in his work and spell success for his plays. At the time of the Restoration, after the re-opening of the theaters, several of his dramas — and not even his best ones — were republished and reprinted. But then he disappeared.

Only recently has he been unearthed by scholars. Interest, however, has been restricted to a circle of literary specialists, and that circle has been tightly drawn; only specialists in the Jacobean period have concerned themselves with him. His modern audience therefore has been small. And even they have not treated him well; for in their largely one-sided appraisals of him, they have not regarded him as an original literary figure, but rather in the light of other masters, as an imitator. Middleton thus has been of secondary concern to literary historians instead of primary concern to admirers of artistic talent.

Thereby an injustice has been done him. Middleton was admittedly no shining star in the theatrical heavens of his time. He was not a greatly original and creative genius. He was, however, a most interesting literary artist, if one follows his inner development, and among his many dramas he has produced several masterpieces. That these have not been accorded the recognition they deserve can be attributed to their genre: down-to-earth, realistic London comedies. Oddly enough this genre generally has met with a cool reception on the part of modern English literary historians — and until now it has usually been the English who have concerned themselves with Middleton. By their failure to fully appreciate one of the most significant and deserving literary talents of their nation, English scholars have deprived Middleton of his rightful place in English literary history as a writer of true-to-life comedies that portray in intimate detail the life and culture of the common man in the London of his time.

[Fischer says he plans to do justice to Middleton and explains that little is known about Middleton's life.] Our author was a true child of London: he was born in London and grew up there in comfortable circumstances.

Later he received a university education. As a young man in London again, he no doubt participated in the merry theatrical activities of his city in spite of his juristic aspirations. For it was not by himself that he first appeared on the theatrical scene, but with celebrated authors of the day. With them he collaborated on several plays, as was the custom then. So it was in the year 1602. Only about six years younger than Shakespeare, Middleton entered the world of drama twelve years later than he, at the age of thirty-two. This is important, because it sheds light on several aspects of his career. It explains, for example, the lack of inner youthfulness in early works that have the outer shortcomings that often beset a beginner. It explains the artist's rapid development and perfection in technique. It explains finally the quick discovery of his individual talent, which matured in modern realistic comedy, a genre that presupposes an experienced knowledge of human nature in the author as a person.

[Fischer says too little is known of Middleton's life for scholars to see a relationship between his fate as a human being and his development as a writer. For the latter, he says, one looks to the plays, and begins with what is known of their chronology and what can be supposed on the basis of similarities in content.] This in turn enables one to complete the chronological table: the seven dramas that cannot be assigned from external evidence can now be joined, with almost full assurance, to their categories. Middleton, of course, is a genuine artist, one who creates only from artistic impulses and in accordance with specific phases of his artistic temperament. Variation in the absolute worth of the pieces — as measured by our subjective evaluation — may occur, a worse piece may follow a better one, but only within the same genre. For it would be highly improbable that a writer like Middleton, who has developed almost in accordance with theoretical principles, could be guilty of sporadically reverting from a genre he has attained to one that is already conquered and passé for him.

[Fischer explains how scholars can examine the contradictions between a play and the requirements of the genre or of the underlying ideas and thus investigate "the author's unconscious creative work." He argues that a writer like Middleton, with a talent for comedy, will be able to create harmony between the medium and the impression on the reader only in that genre.] By deliberately imitating, he will be able to make the medium and ideas of other genres his own to a certain degree, though never fully. He will — with the goal of the moment before his eyes — still more or less consciously cast a sidelong glance toward his area of talent. If he progresses in his development — as Middleton does — from a distant starting-point instinctively toward that area of talent, he will try to create work which is inwardly foreign to him, but in all likelihood he will choose the wrong medium for it. Then he will bring his work closer to his genre. This is how Middleton solves the problem. A slave to tradition, he begins with tragedy, which is foreign to him. Having grappled with this genre, he turns out dramatic plays. From there it is only a short step to moral plays and dramas of manner, which in turn lead to his real domain: modern realistic comedy.

The comedies are the height of Middleton's artistic achievement. Yet he does not remain long at the pinnacle he has achieved. He routinely applies his talent at the expense of the underlying idea. He creates ever more effortlessly in the medium, developing the works ever more fully. They acquire, in a sense, a life of their own, without regard to the ideal purpose of the genre. They change the effect of the genre, and a new genre results, as it were, unconsciously, sub rosa. His realistic comedy gains in realism and loses in comedy. The author portrays more of life than he can artistically assimilate within the framework of the piece. The idea is hard-pressed by the material, and the comedy of manners is the result. Since as the concept of comedy fades, the comic artistic standards are lowered, it stands to reason that the realism progressively expands to include a larger slice of life, to the extent that not only the funny aspects of life, but also — if for no other reason than variety — the more serious aspects are presented. And thus the comedy of manners develops organically, commensurate with the deterioration of the author's comic artistic ability, and changes to serious drama. It can be distinguished from similar genres at other times in his career by its lack of moralizing. Its overriding purpose is illustration. With that, Middleton faces artistic bankruptcy, which he candidly and cheerfully displays in a piece that parodies his former works [The Witch], and the author comes to the end of his life as a creative artist. What follows testifies to new artistic life, but it is a second-hand life, an imitation. Middleton comes under the influence of the dramatic fashion of the day in the new romantic dramas of Massinger, and again he makes a significant contribution to drama — his individual talent manifests itself in shining fashion in the comic subplots. Overall, however, this very last period of his work is of only secondary interest. [Fischer then discusses how each play fits his theory.]

R. Fischer. "Thomas Middleton: Eine literarhistorische Skizze." Festschrift zum VIII: Allgemeinen deutschen Neuphilologentage in Wien, Pfingsten, 1898. Ed. by Jakob Schipper. Vienna: W. Braumüller, 1898, pp. 107-141. Trans. by Guenter G. Schmalz.

Works Cited

Abbott, Claude Colleer. *The Life and Letters of George Darley, Poet and Critic.* London: Humphrey Milford, Oxford University Press, 1928.

Anon [C. W. Dilke?]. "Art. VII. *The Witch, The Changeling, Women Beware of Women.*" *Retrospective Review* 8 (1823): 125-45.

Anon. "Bullen's Middleton." *The Saturday Review*, 27 February 1886, pp. 305-306.

Anon. "Drama." *The Athenæum*, 8 May 1886, pp. 625-27.

Anon. "Elizabethan Dramatists." *The Saturday Review*, 27 June 1885, pp. 867-68.

Anon. "Middleton's *Game at Chess.*" *The Theatre: A Weekly Critical Review* 1, no. 16 (15 May 1877): 202.

Anon. "Notes and News." *The Academy*, 9 April 1898, pp. 397-98.

Anon. "Reader Spotlight." *Folger News*, Spring 1990, p. 4.

Anon. "Shakespeare's Fellows." *Atlantic Monthly* 56 (1885): 851-54.

Anon. "The Week." *The Athenæum*, 9 April 1898, pp. 479-80.

Anon. "*The Works of Thomas Middleton.*" *The Gentleman's Magazine* 14 (1840): 563-87.

Anon. "*The Works of Thomas Middleton.*" *Overland Monthly* 8 (1886): 652-60.

Anon. "The Works of Thomas Middleton." *The Spectator* 59 (1886): 1119-21.

Archer, William. "*The Spanish Gipsy.*" 1898. Reprint. *Study and Stage: A Year-Book of Criticism.* London: Grant Richards, 1899, pp. 234-37.

B[agnall?], W[illiam?]. "The *Authors* Friend to the Reader," commendatory verses to Philip Massinger's *The Bond-Man.* London: Edw. Allde, for John Harison and Edward Blackmore, 1624, sig. A4r.

[Baker, David Erskine.] *The Companion to the Play-House: Or, An Historical Account of All the Dramatic Writers (and Their Works) That Have Appeared in Great Britain and Ireland, from the Commencement of Our Theatrical Exhibitions, Down to the Present Year 1764.* 2 vols. London: for T. Becket, et al., 1764.

Baker, David Erskine, Isaac Reed, and Stephen Jones. *Biographia Dramatica; or, A Companion to the Playhouse.* 3 vols. London: Longman, Hurst, et al., 1812.

Balch, Marston Stevens. "The Dramatic Legacy of Thomas Middleton: A Study of the Uses of His Plays from 1627 to 1800." Ph.D. dissertation, Harvard University, 1930.

Bald, R[obert] C[ecil], ed. *A Game at Chesse.* Cambridge: the University Press, 1929.

————. "Middleton's Civic Employments." *Modern Philology* 31 (1933): 65-78.

Bawcutt, N. W. "The Revival of Elizabethan Drama and the Crisis of Romantic Drama." *Literature of the Romantic Period, 1750-1850.* Ed. R. T. Davies and B. G. Beatty. New York: Barnes and Noble, 1976, pp. 96-113.

Bentley, Gerald Eades. *The Jacobean and Caroline Stage.* Vol. 4. Oxford: Clarendon, 1956.

————. "John Cotgrave's English Treasury of Wit and Language and the Elizabethan Drama." *Studies in Philology* 40 (1943): 186-203.

Bergeron, David M[oore]. "Middleton's Moral Landscape: *A Chaste Maid in Cheapside* and *The Triumphs of Truth.*" *"Accompaninge the Players" : Essays Celebrating Thomas Middleton, 1580-1980.* AMS Studies in the Renaissance, 8. Ed. Kenneth Friedenreich. New York: AMS Press, 1983, pp. 133-46.

Braunmuller, A. R. "'To the Globe I Rowed': John Holles Sees *A Game at Chess.*" *English Literary Renaissance* 20 (1990): 340-56.

Brittin, Norman A[ylsworth]. *Thomas Middleton.* Twayne's English Author Series, 139. New York: Twayne, 1972.

Brome, Richard. *The Northern Lasse, A Comœdie.* London: by Aug. Mathewes, to be sold by Nicholas Vavasour, 1632.

Bullen, A[rthur] H[enry], ed. *A Collection of Old English Plays.* London: Wyman and Sons, 1882-85.

————. "Introduction." *The Works of Thomas Middleton.* Boston: Houghton Mifflin; London: J. C. Nimmo, 1885-86, 1: xi-xciii.

Bullough, Geoffrey. "*The Game at Chesse*: How It Struck a Contemporary." *Modern Language Review* 49 (1954): 156-63.

Busino, Horatio. "Relation of Horatio Busino." *Calendar of State Papers and Manuscripts, Relating to English Affairs, Existing in the Archives and Collections of Venice. And in the Other Libraries of Northern Italy.* Vol. 15, *1617-1619.* Ed. Allen B. Hinds. London: for His Majesty's Stationery Office, by Anthony Brothers, 1909, no. 103A, pp. 58-63.

Campbell, Thomas. *Specimens of the British Poets; With Biographical and Critical Notices, and an Essay on English Poetry.* London: John Murray, 1819.

[Capell, Edward.] *The School of Shakespeare: Or, Authentic Extracts from Divers English Books, That . . . Contribute to a Due Understanding of His Writings, or Give Light to the History of His Life, or to the Dramatic History of His Time.* Vol. 3 of *Notes and Various Readings to Shakespeare.* London: by Henry Hughs, for the Author, [1779].

Chamberlain, John. *The Letters of John Chamberlain.* Ed. Norman Egbert McClure. Philadelphia: The American Philosophical Society, 1939.

Chapman, George. Dedicatory Epistle to his translation of *Homer's* Odysses. London: by Rich. Field for Nathaniell Butter, c. 1615, sig. A3r-A6r.

[Chetwood, William Rufus.] *The British Theatre. Containing the Lives of the English Dramatic Poets.* Dublin: for Peter Wilson, 1750.

Chetwood, W[illiam] R[ufus], ed. *A Select Collection of Old Plays*. Dublin: by the Editor, 1750.

Cibber, [Theophilus]. *The Lives of the Poets of Great Britain and Ireland, to the Time of Dean Swift*. Vol. 1. London: for R. Griffiths, 1753.

Clark, W[illiam] G[eorge], and W[illiam] A[ldis] Wright. Preface to *Macbeth*. Clarendon Press Series, English Classics. Oxford: Clarendon, 1869, pp. viii-xii.

Cogswell, Thomas. "Thomas Middleton and the Court, 1624: *A Game at Chess* in Context." *Huntington Library Quarterly* 47 (1984): 273-88.

[Coleridge, Samuel Taylor?] "Art. III. *Specimens of English Dramatic Poets*." *Annual Review and History of Literature* 7 (1808): 562-70.

Collier, J[ohn] Payne. *The History of English Dramatic Poetry to the Time of Shakespeare: And Annals of the Stage to the Restoration*. Vol. 1. London: John Murray, 1831.

_____, ed. *A Select Collection of Old Plays*. 12 vols. London: Septimus Prowett, 1825-27. [3rd. ed. of Dodsley's *Select Collection of Old Plays*, see Dodsley below.]

Core, Susan, and George Core. "London Theater-Going." *Hudson Review* 41 (1989): 608-611.

Cotgrave, John. *The English Treasury of Wit and Language, Collected Out of the Most, and Best of Our English Drammatick Poems; Methodically Digested into Common Places for Generall Use*. London: for Humphrey Moseley, 1655.

Craik, Geo[rge] L[illie]. *Sketches of the History of Literature and Learning in England*. Vol. 3, *From the Accession of Elizabeth to the Revolution of 1688*. London: Charles Knight, 1845.

D'Avenant, William. *The Works of Sir William Davenant Knight*. Vol. 2. London: by T. N. for Henry Herringman, 1673.

Dawson, Giles E. "John Payne Collier's Great Forgery." *Studies in Bibliography* 24 (1971): 1-26.

Dibdin, [Charles]. *A Complete History of the English Stage*. Vol. 3. London: for the Author, [1800].

[Dilke, Charles Wentworth, ed.] *Old English Plays*. 6 vols. London: Whittingham and Rowland for John Martin, 1814-15.

Dobrée, Bonamy. *English Literature in the Early Eighteenth Century, 1700-1740*. Oxford: Clarendon, 1959.

Dodsley, Robert, ed. *A Select Collection of Old Plays*. 12 vols. London: R. Dodsley, 1744.

_____. *A Select Collection of Old Plays*. 2nd ed., rev. and aug. by Isaac Reed. 12 vols. London: J. Dodsley, 1780.

Downes, John. *Roscius Anglicanus, or an Historical Review of the Stage*. London: H. Playford, 1708.

Drake, Nathan. *Shakspeare and His Times*. Vol. 2. London: for T. Cadell and W. Davies, 1817.

Dyce, Alexander. "Some Account of Middleton and His Works." *The Works of Thomas Middleton*. Vol. 1. London: Edward Lumley, 1840: ix-lvii.

[Eliot, Thomas Stearns.] "Thomas Middleton." *Times Literary Supplement* (London), 30 June 1927, pp. 445-46.

Ellis, Havelock. "Preface." *Thomas Middleton.* The Mermaid Series. Vol. 2. London: Vizetelly, 1890, vii-xiii.

Epperly, Elizabeth R. *Anthony Trollope's Notes on the Old Drama.* ELS Monograph Series, 42. Victoria: University of Victoria, 1988.

Evelyn, John. *The Diary of John Evelyn.* Ed. E. S. de Beer. Oxford: Clarendon, 1955.

Finkelpearl, Philip J. "'The Comedians' Liberty': Censorship of the Jacobean Stage Reconsidered." *English Literary Renaissance* 16 (1986): 123-38.

Fischer, R. "Thomas Middleton: Eine literarhistorische Skizze." *Festschrift zum VIII: Allgemeinen deutschen Neuphilologentage in Wien, Pfingsten, 1898.* Ed. Jacob Schipper. Vienna: W. Braunmüller, 1898, pp. 107-141.

Fleay, F[rederick] G[ard]. "On *Macbeth.*" In *Shakespeare Manual.* London: Macmillan, 1876, pp. 245-61.

_____. "On Two Plays of Shakspere's, the Versions of Which as We Have Them Are the Results of Alterations by Other Hands: Part 1, *Macbeth.*" *Transactions of the New Shakspere Society* 2 (1874): 339-57.

Fletcher, John. *Rule a Wife and Have a Wife.* Oxford: Leonard Lichfield, 1640.

Fuller, Jean Overton. *Swinburne: A Biography.* New York: Schocken, 1971.

Furness, Horace Howard, ed. *"The Witch."* In *Macbeth.* New Variorum Edition, Vol. 2. Philadelphia: J. B. Lippincott, 1873, pp. 388-405.

Furnivall, [Frederick James], and [J. W.] Hales. "Discussion on Mr. Fleay's *Macbeth* and *Julius Caesar* Paper, *June* 26, 1874." *Transactions of the New Shakspere Society* 2 (1874): 498-509.

Gayton, Edmund. *Pleasant Notes upon Don Quixot.* London: William Hunt, 1654.

[Genest, John.] *Some Account of the English Stage, from the Restoration in 1660 to 1830.* Vols. 6 and 10. Bath: H. E. Carrington, 1832.

Gifford, William, ed. *The Works of Ben Jonson.* New ed. London: Routledge, Warne, and Routledge, 1860.

_____, ed. *The Plays of Philip Massinger.* Vol. 1. London: G. and W. Nicoll, *et al.,* 1805.

Gilchrist, Octavius. *A Letter to William Gifford, Esq. on the Late Edition of Ford's Plays.* London: for John Murray, 1811.

Gilliland, Thomas. *The Dramatic Mirror.* Vol. 1. London: for C. Chapple by B. McMillan, 1808.

Gosse, Edmund. *The Jacobean Poets.* New York: Charles Scribner's Sons, 1894.

Greg, Walter Wilson. *A List of Masques, Pageants, &c. Supplementary to* A List of English Plays. London: for the Bibliographical Society by Blades, East and Blades, 1902.

_____. "Theatrical Repertories of 1662." *Gentleman's Magazine* 301 (1906): 69-72.

Hallam, Henry. *Introduction to the Literature of Europe in the Fifteenth, Sixteenth, and Seventeenth Centuries.* Vol. 3. London: John Murray, 1839.

Hales, J. W. "On the Porter in *Macbeth.*" *Transactions of the New Shakspere Society* 2 (1874): 255-69.

Harvey, Geoffrey. "Trollope's Debt to the Renaissance Drama." *Yearbook of English Studies* 9 (1979): 256-69.

Hayley, William. *Memoirs of the Life and Writings of William Hayley, Esq.* Ed. John Johnson. Vol. 1. London: for Henry Colburn, *et al.*, 1823.

_____. *Plays of Three Acts; Written for a Private Theatre.* London: for T. Cadell, 1784.

Hayward, Thomas, ed. *The British Muse, or, a Collection of Thoughts Moral, Natural, and Sublime, of Our English Poets; Who Flourished in the Sixteenth and Seventeenth Centuries.* 3 vols. London: F. Cogan and J. Nourse, 1738.

Hazlitt, William. *The Complete Works of William Hazlitt.* Ed. P. P. Howe. Vol. 6. 1931. Reprint. New York: AMS Press, 1967.

_____. *Lectures Chiefly on the Dramatic Literature of the Age of Elizabeth. Delivered at the Surry Institution.* London: Stodart and Steuart, 1820.

Heinemann, Margot. *Puritanism and Theatre: Thomas Middleton and Opposition Drama Under the Early Stuarts.* Cambridge and London: Cambridge University Press, 1980.

Hemminge, William. *William Hemminge's Elegy on Randolph's Finger, Containing the Well-Known Lines "On the Time-Poets."* Ed. G. C. Moore Smith. Oxford: Basil Blackwell, Shakespeare Head Press, 1923.

Herbert, Henry. *The Dramatic Records of Sir Henry Herbert, Master of the Revels, 1623-1673.* Ed. Joseph Quincy Adams. New Haven: Yale University Press, 1917.

H[erford], C[harles] H[arold]. "Middleton, Thomas." *The Dictionary of National Biography.* Ed. by Sidney Lee. Vol. 37. London: Smith, Elder, 1894, pp. 357-63.

[Herringman, Henry.] Publisher's Epistle. *The Mayor of Quinborough: A Comedy. As It Hath Been Often Acted with Much Applause at Black-Fryars, By His Majesties Servants.* London: for Henry Herringman, 1661, sig. A2^r.

Heywood, Thomas. *The Hierarchie of the Blessed Angells. Their Names, Orders and Offices. The Fall of Lucifer with His Angells.* London: by Adam Islip, 1635.

Horne, R[ichard] H[enry]. *The Death of Marlowe: A Tragedy.* London: Saunders and Otley, 1837.

Howes, Edmund. *The Annales, or Generall Chronicle of England, Begun First by Maister John Stow, and After Him Continued and Augmented with Matters Forreyne, and Domestique, Anncient and Moderne, unto the Ende of This Present Yeere, 1614.* London: Thomas Adams, 1615.

Hunt, Leigh. *Imagination and Fancy; Or Selections from the British Poets.* London: Smith, Elder, 1844.

J[acob], G[iles]. *The Poetical Register: Or, The Lives and Characters of the English Dramatick Poets.* London: for E. Curll, 1719.

Johnson, Edgar. *Sir Walter Scott: The Great Unknown.* 2 vols. New York: Macmillan, 1970.

Jonson, Ben. *Conversations with William Drummond of Hawthornden.* In *Ben Jonson.* Vol. 1. Ed. C. H. Herford and Percy Simpson. Oxford: Clarendon, 1925.

_____. *The Staple of Newes.* In *Ben Jonson.* Vol. 6. Ed. C. H. Herford, Percy Simpson, and Evelyn Simpson. Oxford: Clarendon, 1938.

K., H. A. "Middleton's *Game at Chess.*" *Westminster Papers,* 2 April 1877, pp. 227-28.

K., T. H. "Notices of the Lives and Writings of Our Early Dramatists: Thomas Middleton." *Dramatic Magazine* 2 (May 1830): 107-113.

Kingsley, Charles. "Plays and Puritans." *North British Review* 49 (1856). Reprint. *Plays and Puritans, and Other Historical Essays.* London: Macmillan, 1873, pp. 3-79.

Lamb, Charles. *Notes, etc., to Extracts from the Garrick Plays.* 1827; reprinted in *Lamb's Criticism: A Selection from the Literary Criticism of Charles Lamb.* Ed. E. M. W. Tillyard. Cambridge University Press, 1923. Reprint. Westport, Conn.: Greenwood Press, 1970.

_____. *Specimens of English Dramatic Poets, Who Lived About the Time of Shakspeare.* London: for Longman, Hurst, Rees, and Orme, 1808.

_____. *The Works of Charles Lamb.* Vol. 2. London: C. and J. Ollier, 1818.

Lancashire, Anne. "*The Witch*: Stage Flop or Political Mistake?" "*Accompaninge the Players*" : *Essays Celebrating Thomas Middleton, 1580-1980.* AMS Studies in the Renaissance, 8. Ed. Kenneth Friedenreich. New York: AMS Press, 1983, pp. 161-81.

Landor, Walter Savage. "To the Author of *Festus*, On the Classick and Romantick." *The Complete Works of Walter Savage Landor.* Vol. 15, *Poems.* Ed. by Stephen Wheeler. Reprint. New York: Barnes and Noble; London: Methuen, 1969, p. 165.

Langbaine, Gerard. *An Account of the English Dramatick Poets.* Oxford: by L. L. for G. West and H. Clements, 1691.

_____. *The Lives and Characters of the English Dramatick Poets.* Rev. by Charles Gilden. London: for The. Leigh, 1699.

_____. *Momus Triumphans; or, The Plagiaries of the English Stage.* London: for Nicholas Cox, 1688.

Limon, Jerzy. *Dangerous Matter: English Drama and Politics in 1623/24.* Cambridge: Cambridge University Press, 1986.

London, Corporation of. *Analytical Index to the Series of Records Known as the Remembrancia. Preserved Among the Archives of the City of London. A. D. 1579-1664.* London: E. J. Francis, 1878.

Lowell, J[ames] R[ussell]. "The Plays of Thomas Middleton." *The Pioneer* 1 (1843): 32-39.

Malcolmson, Cristina. "'As Tame as the Ladies': Politics and Gender in *The Changeling.*" *English Literary Renaissance* 20 (1990): 320-39.

Malone, Edmond. *The Life of William Shakspeare, by the Late Edmond Malone: And an Essay on the Phraseology and Metre of the Poet and his Contemporaries, by James Boswell.* Privately Printed, 1821.

_____. *Supplement to the Edition of Shakespeare's Plays Published in 1778 by Samuel Johnson and George Steevens*. 2 vols. London: for C. Bathurst, *et al.*, 1780.

Medwin, Thomas. *Journal of the Conversations of Lord Byron: Noted During a Residence with His Lordship at Pisa, in the Years 1821 and 1822*. London: for Henry Colburn, 1824.

_____. *The Life of Percy Bysshe Shelley*. Introd. by H. Buxton Forman. London: Humphrey Milford, Oxford University Press, 1913.

[Merivale, Herman?]. "Art. VIII. *Introduction to the Literature of Europe in the Fifteenth, Sixteenth, and Seventeenth Centuries.*" *Edinburgh Review* 72 (Oct. 1840): 194-226.

Middleton, Thomas. *The Famelie of Love. Acted by the Children of His Majesties Revells*. London: for John Helmes, 1608.

_____. *The Inner-Temple Masque. Or Masque of Heroes. Presented (as an Entertainement for Many Worthy Ladies:) By Gentlemen of the Same Ancient, and Noble House*. London: for John Browne, 1619.

_____. *The Roaring Girle. Or Moll Cut-Purse. As It Hath Lately Beene Acted on the Fortune-Stage by the Prince His Players*. London: for Thomas Archer, 1611.

_____. *The Widdow. A Comedie. As It Was Acted at the Private House in Black-Fryers, with Great Applause, by His Late Majesties Servants* [attributed to Ben Jonson, John Fletcher, and Thomas Middleton]. London: for Humphrey Moseley, 1652.

_____. *The Witch*. Ed. W. W. Greg and F. P. Wilson. The Malone Society Reprints. N. pl.: Oxford University Press, 1948 (1950).

Minto, William. *Characteristics of English Poets from Chaucer to Shirley*. Edinburgh and London: W. Blackwood and Sons, 1874.

_____. *Characteristics of English Poets from Chaucer to Shirley*. 2nd ed. Edinburgh and London: William Blackwood and Sons, 1885.

[Minto, William?] "Middleton, Thomas." *Encyclopedia Britannica*. 9th ed. Vol. 16. Edinburgh: Adam and Charles Black, 1878, pp. 282-83.

Minto, W[illiam]. "*The Works of Thomas Middleton.*" *The Academy*, 22 August 1885, pp. 111-12.

Moseley, Humphrey. "To the Reader." *Two New Playes. Viz*. More Dissemblers Besides Women. Women Beware Women. London: for Humphrey Moseley, 1657, sig. A3r-v.

Newcome, Henry. Commonplace Book. Folger MS. V. a. 232.

Nicholson, Brinsley. "On the Dates of *A Chaste Maid in Cheapside, Northward Ho*, and *The Northern Lass.*" *Notes & Queries* 47 (19 April 1873): 317-19.

Nicoll, Allardyce. *A History of Early Eighteenth Century Drama, 1700-1750*. Cambridge: the University Press, 1925.

_____. *A History of English Drama, 1660-1900*. Vols. 1-4. Cambridge: the University Press, 1952-59.

_____. *A History of Late Eighteenth Century Drama, 1750-1800*. Cambridge: the University Press, 1927.

_____. *A History of Restoration Drama, 1660-1700*. Cambridge: the University Press, 1923.

Old English Drama, The. Vol. 3. London: T. White, 1830.

Pepys, Samuel. *The Diary of Samuel Pepys*. Ed. Robert Latham and William Matthews. 11 vols. Berkeley: University of California Press, 1970-83.

Phialas, Peter G. "An Unpublished Letter About *A Game at Chess*." *Modern Language Notes* 69 (1954): 398-99.

Phillips, Edward. *Theatrum Poetarum, or a Compleat Collection of the Poets, Especially the Most Eminent, of All Ages*. London: for Charles Smith, 1675.

Richards, Nath[anael]. "Upon the Tragedy of My Familiar Acquaintance, *Tho. Middleton*." *Two New Playes. Viz*. More Dissemblers Besides Women. Women Beware Women. London: for Humphrey Moseley, 1657, sig. A4ʳ.

Roberts, Marilyn. "A Preliminary Check-List of Productions of Thomas Middleton's Plays." *Research Opportunities in Renaissance Drama* 28 (1985): 37-61.

Rose, Mary Beth. *The Expense of Spirit: Love and Sexuality in English Renaissance Drama*. Ithaca and London: Cornell University Press, 1988.

S., J. "The Printer and Stationer to the Gentle READER." *A Mad World My Masters: A Comedy. As It Hath Bin Often Acted at the Private House in Salisbury Court, by Her Majesties Servants*. London: for J. S. and are to be sold by James Becket, 1640, sigs. A3ʳ-A4ʳ.

Saintsbury, George. *A History of Elizabethan Literature*. London and New York: Macmillan, 1887.

Schelling, Felix E. *A Book of Elizabethan Lyrics*. Boston: Ginn, 1895.

Schulz, Otto. *Über den Blankvers in den Dramen Thomas Middletons*. Halle: C. A. Kaemmerer, 1892.

[Scott, Walter, ed.] *The Ancient British Drama*. 3 vols. London: for William Miller by James Moyes, 1810.

_____, ed. *Sir Tristrem; A Metrical Romance of the Thirteenth Century*. Edinburgh: James Ballantyne, for Archibald Constable and Longman and Rees, 1804.

Shepherd, Simon. *Amazons and Warrior Women: Varieties of Feminism in Seventeenth-Century Drama*. New York: St. Martin's Press, 1981.

Spalding, Thomas Alfred. "On the Witch-Scenes in *Macbeth* (An Attempt to Rebut Some of the Arguments Put Forward by the Rev. F. G. Fleay in a Paper Read Before This Society on June 26th, 1874)." *Transactions of the New Shakspere Society* 5 (1877-79): 27-40.

Spalding, William. *The History of English Literature*. Edinburgh: Oliver and Boyd, 1853.

Steen, Sara Jayne. "The Response to Middleton: His Own Time to Eliot." *Research Opportunities in Renaissance Drama*, 28 (1985): 63-71.

_____. *Thomas Middleton: A Reference Guide*. A Reference Guide to Literature, ed. James Harner. Boston: G. K. Hall, 1984.

Steevens, George, ed. *The Plays of William Shakespeare . . . To Which Are Added Notes by Samuel Johnson and George Steevens*. 2nd ed., rev. and aug. 10 vols. London: for C. Bathurst, *et al.*, 1778.

Stoddard, R[ichard] H[enry]. "Thomas Middleton." *The Dial* 6 (1885): 114-16.

Swinburne, Algernon Charles. "Thomas Middleton" [Sonnet IX of *Sonnets on English Dramatic Poets (1590-1650)*]. *The Bibelot* 1 (1895): 174.

_____. "Thomas Middleton." *The Nineteenth Century* 19 (1886): 138-53.

[Talfourd, T. N. ?] "Art. X. Lectures on the Dramatic Literature of the Age of Elizabeth." *Edinburgh Review* 34 (Nov. 1820): 438-49.

Taylor, Gary. *Reinventing Shakespeare: A Cultural History, from the Restoration to the Present.* New York: Weidenfeld & Nicolson, 1989.

Taylor, John. *The Praise of Hemp-Seed. With the Voyage of Mr Roger Bird and the Writer Hereof, in a Boat of Brown-Paper, from London to Quinborough in Kent.* London: for H. Gosson, 1620.

Taylor, Thomas, F[rederick] J[ames] Furnivall, and [?] Marshall. "Discussion on Fifth Paper, Porter in *Macbeth*, May 22, 1874." *Transactions of the New Shakspere Society* 2 (1874): 270-84.

Trollope, Anthony. *An Autobiography.* Ed. by Frederick Page. London: Oxford University Press, 1950.

_____. Ms. Notes in his set of *The Works of Thomas Middleton*, edited by Alexander Dyce. Folger Shakespeare Library, PR 2711 .D8 As. Col.

Valaresso, Alvise. Dispatch to the Doge and Senate. *Calendar of State Papers and Manuscripts, Relating to English Affairs, Existing in the Archives and Collections of Venice, and in Other Libraries of Northern Italy.* Vol. 18, *1623-25.* Ed. Allen B. Hinds. London: by His Majesty's Stationery Office, 1912, no. 557: 423-26.

Virgil. *The Whole XII. Bookes of the AEneidos . . . Newly Set Forth, by Thomas Twyne, Gentleman.* London: Wyllyam How for Abraham Veale, 1573.

Wagner, Bernard M. "New Allusions to *A Game at Chesse*." *PMLA* 44 (1929): 827-34.

Ward, Adolphus William. *A History of English Dramatic Literature to the Death of Queen Anne.* London: Macmillan, 1875.

Wasserman, Earl Reeves. "The Scholarly Origin of the Elizabethan Revival." *Journal of English Literary History* 6 (1937): 213-43.

Watson, William. "Some Literary Idolatries." Reprint. *Excursions in Criticism: Being Some Prose Recreations of a Rhymer.* London: Elkin Mathews and John Lane; New York: Macmillan, 1893, pp. 1-22.

Weisinger, Herbert. "The Seventeenth-Century Reputation of the Elizabethans." *Modern Language Quarterly* 6 (1945): 13-21.

Whincop, Thomas. *Scanderbeg: Or, Love and Liberty. A Tragedy. To Which Are Added a List of All the Dramatic Authors, with Some Account of Their Lives; And of All the Dramatic Pieces Ever Published in the English Language, to the Year 1747.* London: for W. Reeve, 1747.

Whipple, E[dwin] P[ercy]. "Minor Elizabethan Dramatists." *Atlantic Monthly* 20 (1867): 692-703.

_____. "Minor Elizabethan Dramatists." *The Literature of the Age of Elizabeth.* Boston: Fields, Osgood, 1869, pp. 119-56.

Williams, Robert D. "Antiquarian Interest in Elizabethan Drama Before Lamb." *PMLA* 53 (1938): 434-44.

Wilson, Edward M., and Olga Turner. "The Spanish Protest Against *A Game at Chesse.*" *Modern Language Review* 44 (1949): 476-82.

Winstanley, William. *The Lives of the Most Famous English Poets, or the Honour of Parnassus.* London: for Samuel Manship, 1687. Reprint. Gainesville, Florida: Scholars' Facsimiles and Reprints, 1963.

Witts Recreations. Selected from the Finest Fancies of Modern Muses. With a Thousand Outlandish Proverbs. London: for Humph. Blunden, 1640.

Woodbridge, Linda. *Women and the English Renaissance: Literature and the Nature of Womankind, 1540-1620.* Urbana and Chicago: University of Illinois Press, 1986.

Wright, James. *Country Conversations: Being an Account of Some Discourses That Happen'd in a Visit to the Country Last Summer, on Divers Subjects.* London: for Henry Bonwicke, 1694.

_____. *Historia Histrionica: An Historical Account of the English Stage.* London: by G. Croom for William Haws, 1699.

Yachnin, Paul. "*A Game at Chess*: Thomas Middleton's 'Praise of Folly'." *Modern Language Quarterly* 48 (1987): 107-123.

Index

AMS Studies in the Renaissance: No. 31

ISSN: 0195-8011

Other Titles in This Series:

1. Hilton Landry, ed. *New Essays on Shakespeare's Sonnets.* 1976.
2. J. W. Williamson. *The Myth of the Conqueror: Prince Henry Stuart, a Study of 17th Century Personation.* 1978.
3. Philip C. McGuire and David A. Samuelson, eds. *Shakespeare: The Theatrical Dimensions.* 1979.
4. Paul Ramsey. *The Fickle Glass: A Study of Shakespeare's Sonnets.* 1979.
6. Raymond C. Shady and G.B. Shand, eds. *Play-Texts in Old Spelling: Papers from the Glendon Conference.* 1984.
7. Mark Taylor. *Shakespeare's Darker Purpose: A Question of Incest.* 1982.
8. Kenneth Friedenreich, ed. *"Accompaninge the players."* *Essays Celebrating Thomas Middleton. 1580-1980.* 1983.
9. Sarah P. Sutherland. *Masques in Jacobean Tragedy.* 1983.
10. Margaret Loftus Ranald, *Shakespeare and His Social Context: Essays in Osmotic Knowledge and Literary Interpretation.* 1987.
11. Clifford Leech, *Christopher Marlowe: Poet for the Stage,* Ed. Anne Lancashire. 1986.
12. Clifford Davidson, C.J. Gianakaris, and John H. Stroupe, eds. *Drama in the Renaissance: Comparative and Critical Essays.* 1986.
13. Georgianna Ziegler, ed. *Shakespeare Study Today: The Horace Howard Furness Memorial Lectures.* 1986.
14. Kenneth Friedenreich, Roma Gill, and Constance B. Kuriyama, eds. *"A Poet and a filthy Play-maker." New Essays on Christopher Marlowe.* 1988.
15. W.R. Streitberger, *Edmond Tyllney, Master of the Revels and Censor of Plays.* 1986.
17. Donald K. Anderson, Jr., ed. *"Concord in Discord": The Plays of John Ford, 1586-1986.* 1987.
18. Thomas P. Roche, Jr., *Petrarch and the English Sonnet Sequences.* 1989.
19. Herbert Berry, *Shakespeare's Playhouses,* illus. by C. Walter Hodges. 1987.
20. Nancy Klein Maguire, ed. *Renaissance Tragicomedy: Explorations in Genre and Politics.* 1987.
21. Clifford Chalmers Huffman, *Elizabethan Impressions: John Wolfe and His Press.* 1988.
22. Clifford Davidson, *The Guild Chapel Wall Paintings at Stratford-upon-Avon.* 1988.
23. James M. Gibson. *The Philadelphia Shakespeare Story: Horace Howard Furness and the Variorum Shakespeare.* 1990.
26. John Hazel Smith. *Shakespeare's* Othello: *A Bibliography.* 1988.
27. Alan R. Young, ed. *His Majesty's Royal Ship: A Critical Edition of Thomas Heywood's "A True Description" (1637).* 1990.
28. M.J.B. Allen, D. Baker-Smith, and A.F. Kinney, eds. *Sir Philip Sidney's Achievements.* 1990.
30. Paul Bertram and Bernice W. Kliman, eds. *The Three-Text Hamlet: Parallel Texts of the First and Second Quartos and First Folio.* 1991.